The
Auschwitz
Kommandant

The
Auschwitz
Kommandant

A Daughter's Search
for the Father
She Never Knew

BARBARA U. CHERISH

The
History
Press

First published 2009

The History Press
The Mill, Brimscombe Port
Stroud, Gloucestershire, GL5 2QG
www.thehistorypress.co.uk

British Library Cataloguing in Publication Data.
A catalogue record for this book is available from the British Library.

ISBN 978 0 7524 4900 5

Typesetting and origination by The History Press
Printed in Great Britain

Dedicated especially

in loving memory to

my father, Arthur Wilhelm Liebehenschel

and my mother, Gertrud Baum Liebehenschel,

with love and gratitude for the gift of life

from one of 'The Other Children.'

'History is in the mind of the teller,

Truth is in the telling ...'

Anonymous

Contents

Foreword

Growing up without a father is a burden. If the memory of a father is reduced to a single photograph a child is forced to hide, even deny, this is too much for them to carry. The photograph that Barbara Cherish has kept closely guarded since childhood shows a seemingly cultivated man with a mild gaze, wearing the uniform of the SS. A relic of a time supposedly past, but yet still carefully concealed, it depicts Arthur Liebehenschel, appointed by the National Socialist regime, made commander at Auschwitz during the winter of 1943–44, transferred to Majdanek, and executed in Poland in January 1948 as a war criminal.

Out of grief, yet with shame, and with a longing that never faded but hurt more each year, Barbara follows the trail of her missing father. Years of searching through archives and talks with members of the family and contemporaries allowed her to discover important, so far unknown facts, and to listen to the opinions of others, as well as her father's own words, his letters and diaries, his official correspondence, his hearings and statutory declarations.

Thus we are confronted with a human tragedy that forces us to think carefully before forming a judgement. The simple categories of good and evil do not necessarily fit when we consider Arthur Liebehenschel, just as they may not always apply to the many others who chose to believe in National Socialism initially, but yet still remained faithful and obedient, once the regime no longer hid its criminal intentions. It is always possible that her father questioned the system. He may have suffered more and more, but yet still followed orders with the inevitable consequence of being found guilty. Did he have a choice? Is there a time at which the father of a family could have turned to follow his conscience rather than his desire to provide security? The tribunal in Krakow pronounced their judgement. His daughter does not presume to do so again. We readers should be open to Barbara Cherish's nuances, and show appreciation for her life experiences, her courage, her frankness, her love.

Melissa Müller is the author of *Until the Final Hour: Hitler's Secretary tells her Life* and *Anne Frank: the Biography*.

Preface

Soon you will be at an age where one looks at
everything through clear and different eyes.
Do this and judge in peace and fairness for yourself,
when in a distant time you are moved toward that direction …

*from a letter written by my father, Arthur Liebehenschel,
as he awaited trial on charges of war crimes in Dachau, 1945*

Last night I dreamed of Papa again … can't really say 'again' as I only remember one other dream of him.

He looked like he does in the favorite photograph I have of him. Early forties, handsome, with smooth black hair wearing his uniform. But in my dream he was thinner, his stature seemed smaller and his gentle and somewhat humble appearance was enveloped in an aura of defeat. I felt his loneliness.

He had been released from prison, found 'not guilty', and had been searching to find me and my sister Brigitte. We were at some kind of small airport making reservations to go home. He talked with us in a quiet manner but it seemed to me he didn't know that I was his daughter. Through our conversation he was beginning to realize who I was. I pulled him over to the side and asked if he knew who I was and if he liked who I had grown up to be? He answered yes, and that he felt very drawn to me and he thought I was pretty. Then he affectionately embraced me. We joked and he was even laughing – not serious as he appears in all of his photos.

Brigitte and I convinced him to come home with us and he picked up his small worn duffel bag, which was the extent of his belongings. I kept thinking to myself, 'I finally found him but I must be dreaming!' … only to awaken and find that I was.

The Photograph

It must have been his photograph which triggered the dreams that would eventually follow years later.

One afternoon remains so vivid in my memory that I can close my eyes and revisit the experience. I was still in my twenties and I'd hidden his picture at the bottom of my dresser drawer. It had always been my secret, the photo and what it represented. Studying his picture wasn't unusual for me, but for some reason, that particular moment stands out, although it was one of so many.

Holding his picture, wishing to reach through to the image and touch his face, I gazed at the soft dark eyes looking off dreamily into the distance. They conveyed such a thoughtful sadness. As I studied his features, familiar yet not so familiar, I longed to hear his voice. Was it stern yet kind? I felt the old yearning along with that sense of being lost.

I desperately wanted to reach back in time and draw him out of the photograph and back into my life. He had been part of my life for such a short time. But there was also something dark, even evil in the photo that always haunted me.

I heard footsteps in the outside hallway and hurriedly, guiltily replaced the beloved photo beneath my clothes in the dresser.

It may have been that same night when I had one of the few dreams I've had of him: two arms extended through the heavens. Long black gloves covered the hands. They were reaching for me and I felt a paralyzing, terrifying evil power that wanted to pull me to the other side. I tried to avoid them, but couldn't resist their strength. The black gloves portrayed his dark side, but the instant our hands touched, I sensed an overwhelming force of love and peace and I believe he was communicating with me.

Once, long ago, I was instructed to forget his name and everything about him, denying any connection between us. The more I thought about him, the more questions I had. If I could just step into his photograph and look around, trying to fathom reasons why he rose to the top, why he was ever associated and had volunteered to join such a sinister organization? He became a major part of Hitler's human machinery, and this in itself both horrified and fascinated me. It was the source of my greatest shame.

But the secrets of our lives, those we find most significant, don't allow us much respite. They keep rising to the surface until we acknowledge them. He was my secret, the most disturbing factor of my hidden past, the cause of my quest, but he was also the focus of my search for the truth about myself.

I vividly remember that night so long ago. I was already asleep when my oldest sister Brigitte gently woke me and gave me the photo, pressing it secretly into my hand whispering her emotional farewell, 'I will always love you. Don't ever forget us.'

It was early December 1956 and I was thirteen years old, accompanied by my recently adoptive parents and a three-year-old brother, facing a whole new future. With my biological mother hospitalized, and without my father's presence, I had been placed as a foster child with the Poune family who decided to adopt me after three years.

We left Nuremberg for the seaport of Bremerhafen, traveling by train arriving several days later. I always loved riding on trains and it was thrilling to actually experience the encounters of the sleeper and dining cars. Courteous porters wearing tight-fitting dark blue uniforms with round pillbox-type caps were eager to assist us. Crisp white linen tablecloths decked the dining car just like the trains portrayed in my favorite old black and white films.

When we first reached the seaport of Bremerhafen where the USNS *Henry Gibbins* was docked, the ship appeared ominous through the misty gray fog and cold rain – almost threatening, like an enemy warship. I recall the fascination because never before had I been this close to such a vessel.

We boarded the army transport ship, our floating home for the next two weeks, cautiously walking up the long gangplank hauling our carry-on luggage, wondering how many people before us had done the same. Launched in 1942, she had seen service in the European Theater during the Second World War, and under an order signed by President Franklin D. Roosevelt in 1944 she carried 1,000 Jewish refugees from Italy to New York.

After the war, the *Gibbins* transported war brides from Europe to the United States. Later she was renamed *The Empire State IV* serving as a training ship for the New York Maritime College. However, this December 1956 she was once again returning servicemen and their families to the United States.

It was foggy and raining as we set sail, waving farewell to the people on the dock while an American military band played *The Stars and Stripes Forever*. Despite the weather, the scene was breathtaking. But as we pulled out of the harbor I was torn by clashing emotions that overwhelmed and confused me. I felt optimistic excitement about the new country I was headed for, but also there was sad hesitation about allowing myself to feel excited and happy. I was leaving behind my entire past, everything and everyone I had ever known, abandoning the child I had once been.

Like many others in my circumstances, I had already lived a lifetime of upheaval and hardship. I realized I would never see my biological family again, and in my mind I replayed the bittersweet scenes of my mother, my two older sisters with me, and all we had lived through together. I found myself yearning for the mother I had to leave behind, but foremost remained the many unanswered questions surrounding the mystery about the father I never knew. As any 13-year-old I didn't dwell on these thoughts and soon they were forgotten, although only temporarily. Through the romantic eyes of this young girl I was about to experience a true life adventure on the high seas.

Being a military ship, it was far from what one could call a cruise. However, captured through my own far-fetched schoolgirl imagination, the *Gibbins* became a beautiful sailing ship and surely the captain had to be a handsome swashbuckling pirate. Somehow that fantasy was rudely shattered early each morning when we were awakened by the loud gong of the reveille, and a deep voice could be heard shouting throughout the ship's corridors: 'Reveille and it's time to get up!' Each morning I grabbed my pillow and covered my ears, but soon it became a familiar routine and if we wanted breakfast we had to jump up and get to the dining room. There, our waiter named George greeted us at our assigned table with a friendly smile as he served the delicious food prepared in the ship's galley.

Every day was a new adventure for me. We children on board even decorated a Christmas tree in the lounge. I was wearing my favorite aqua and white striped knit top with a hood when I went off exploring the corridors by myself, but soon realized I had ventured too far when I stumbled upon a large group of sailors. A little frightened, I hurried back to our cabin as one of them called after me, 'In a few years you're going to be a beautiful young lady!' In the tiny bathroom of our modest stateroom I looked at my reflection in the mirror wondering what it was he saw?

The sea was furiously turbulent throughout our voyage as we hit one fierce storm after another. The tremendous force of the huge swells battered the ship so severely that part of the massive bridge section was torn off. I heard rumors that this was the *Gibbins'* last ocean voyage because she was not seaworthy to make another Atlantic crossing. However, she would continue to operate as a transport ship until 1959.

We were tossed up and down relentlessly by the waves and it seemed we would be swallowed up into the deep. At such times it was difficult to walk around and we were not allowed on deck. I never became seasick but my new Mom spent a great deal of the voyage in her bunk unable to eat, while my new little brother was extremely seasick hooked up to IVs in the infirmary.

We safely weathered these storms, but the rough seas made it a much longer voyage than anticipated. Everyone on board was hoping we would arrive in New York before Christmas.

Finally, on 21 December, the USNS *Henry Gibbins*, who had once again bound across the briny deep, entered the port of New York and I became initiated into the Royal Order of Atlantic Voyageurs. We children received a colorful document pictured with sea serpents and mermaids, proclaiming our official Atlantic voyage, signed by the guardians of the deep, King Neptune and Davy Jones.

On deck, in awesome absolute stillness, we all caught sight of the magnificent Statue of Liberty, an unforgettable experience sensed with unusual pride by me, even at the age of thirteen. Historic Ellis Island, called The Gateway to America, which millions of immigrants had passed through, had closed its doors only two years prior to our entry. We had to wait for a few hours to come into port while the *Queen Mary*, who had priority to dock, processed her passengers to disembark. Finally, we were allowed to leave our ship and immediately entered the large nearby immigration building.

I clearly recall waiting anxiously in several different lines with my new parents going through all of the customary immigration procedures. My new Dad and brother being American citizens were processed through quickly. My Mom and I were detained by customs and patiently went through their routine of bureaucratic red tape. Ursula looked pale and much thinner than when we first boarded, still not feeling too well, and I sensed she was nervous, keeping her red sweater jacket wrapped securely around her. I was holding on to my adorable little blond-headed brother's hand, still weak, looking bewildered and shy, yet his chubby little cheeks gave way to a faint smile as he looked up at his big sister for assurance. For some reason I was focusing on his polished little white oxford shoes, thinking he too must feel insecure sensing our apprehension. Still in the line for immigrants I nervously clutched my German passport, yet feeling like an American. I was wearing my favorite blue jeans with the turned-up cuffs that were lined with red flannel plaid material with matching plaid shirt, white Bobbie sox and brown-and-white saddle shoes.

But it was especially alarming and I was terribly fearful when the inspection official asked to look through my small, brown leather suitcase. I nodded, but my trembling hands were perspiring. With a great sense of relief, I observed that he barely glanced through the contents.

Had he looked further toward the bottom, under the layers of clothing, he might have found an old album in which I had hidden that very special photograph my sister Brigitte had given to me weeks earlier. The old photo was of my father, and the unmistakable design of his particular uniform carried staggering implications about the officer whose identity I would not be willing to reveal for years to come. The photo surely would have divulged my background and I feared that I might end up rejected, or even worse, sent back – deported – by myself.

After long hours of anxiously waiting, and with my greatest fears laid to rest, my new family and I passed the final inspection. The process was complete and we were allowed to enter New York City. The skyline loomed in the distance, those tall buildings including the Empire State Building, which I had heard so much about.

The first and lasting impression I had as that young girl in my new country remains clearly defined in my memory. I was filled with intense excitement, everything seemed so vast and overwhelming, yet it also felt safe as though I had always belonged there.

Another part of me – the part I would try so hard to silence – was confused and sad. From here on out there would always prevail a secret, inexplicable longing for those kindred souls I had left behind, and they would have to remain mere ghosts from my secret past.

It was cold and already late afternoon by the time we took off on the New York turnpike. As we drove toward our final destination in upstate New York, my eyes followed the road with great curiosity, as around each turn I imagined a whole new life beginning to unravel. Without any warning it started to snow and with a sudden shiver of excitement I remembered that it was almost Christmas – my first Christmas in America!

I was the youngest daughter of Arthur Liebehenschel, one of his 'other children'. It was a term he had given those of us who were from his first marriage. From my adoption at age thirteen, I had to cast off my old identity and found myself living a life of secrecy. I now had a new identity to hide the shame of my father's name, and it was only the beginning for a child who had no preconceived idea of what it would be like having to live a life of secrets and lies, shrouding the truth of her past.

That December of 1956, as I came to America from Germany, I was leaving behind that child, who during her brief existence had already lived a whole lifetime of human experiences. I left behind a childhood in foster homes and my biological family, with the lingering grief over my mother's hospitalization in a mental institution. I also resigned myself to bury the many unanswered questions concerning my absent father.

I learned at an early age that I must please in order to belong, so I knew it was necessary to shed the first thirteen years of my life, erasing that part of my identity as if I had somehow died or never existed. This began the secretive cover-up, the inner turmoil that would become part of my everyday life, and the mystery that surrounded the family I had been born into.

As an adult, I spoke English without an accent. I became an expert at personal subterfuge. I hid the facts of my life, deftly evading questions and always covering up the truth. My two children knew very little about my past.

But I lived with an inexplicable sadness and longing to know who I really was. I carried this burden silently within me, and it would be four decades before the child I had left abandoned on the shore of that distant continent would eventually reappear and search for her true identity.

I've heard that it often takes a crisis to make us look deeply within ourselves, to face what we find with total honesty. It took the death of my older sister Brigitte, diagnosed with breast cancer, and the end of my twenty-eight-year marriage, to finally thrust me into the mirror. I had to understand myself, to achieve that self-knowledge that begins the path of growth and discovery. This quest had to begin with knowing my father, for it was he who had fostered the shame that had lead me into hiding.

My sister Brigitte, after a year of chemotherapy and radiation, preceded by a radical mastectomy, was told that the cancer had gone into remission. But seven years later, the cancer returned even more virulently than before.

At the same time, I watched helplessly as my husband sank deeper and deeper into an alcoholic haze. Gone was the handsome, responsible man I had loved and married. In his place was a distant stranger. Adept at concealing ugly truths from years of practice, I kept my two children from knowing just how serious their father's drinking problem actually was. I retreated into devoting my time caring for Brigitte. I watched in despair as my sister, who had been the strongest one in the family, grew weaker and smaller and more dependent.

She didn't know it, but we each – for different reasons – were helpless during that painful time. I felt as though everything was crumbling around me. A sick feeling in my stomach constantly plagued me, reminding me that this was not a bad dream. This was reality.

On the afternoon of 30 December 1988, two days after her fifty-sixth birthday, I left Brigitte sleeping and kissed her goodbye about 3 p.m. At 9:30 that evening, her husband Heinz called to tell us she was gone.

On a beautiful crisp day in January 1989, I stood on a boat that would take Brigitte's ashes to their final destination. Thirty-two years earlier my first ocean voyage had taken me far away from my beloved oldest sister. Once again I found myself on a ship taken out to sea, but this time to say my final farewell to Brigitte. I looked out over the ocean as the water displayed blues of every hue while a biting wind pierced through me.

As the relentless waves tossed the boat up and down, the shoreline vanished and reappeared with an almost hypnotic rhythm, lulling me into memories of Brigitte: as a beautiful sixteen-year-old with gleaming black hair, pirouetting across the dance floor at the Eva Weigand Ballet School; as the determined young woman who courageously rescued me when I was a starving child; as a vivacious woman sitting with me on the beach at Sea Cliff not far from here, sipping champagne with strawberries as we watched the sun sink beneath the horizon.

Heinz and their son Kye cast Brigitte's ashes along with some rose petals over the side of the boat. I watched the trail they left until they were carried away by the waves, quickly disappearing, leaving nothing but the reflection of the early afternoon sun bouncing off the blue water. Suddenly I felt terribly alone.

A frightening realization suddenly gripped me. I could no longer hide in the shadows, feeling safe and secure behind Brigitte's urgent need for me. I had to face what was left of my own life.

I would make one final effort to save my marriage, but to no avail. It was the second loss in a very short time. Our divorce was final in March of 1991.

Twenty-eight years together, and now my husband and I parted, each leaving the Ventura courthouse in tears to go our separate ways.

I can still hear his last words to me when I moved out of our new home on Riviera Court. As I walked out into the snow and climbed into the moving van he called out to me, 'Have a nice life!' But divorce is death. I'll never really get over it.

Now, at age forty-seven, I began my self-search with the photograph. As I reached for it I heard – or rather felt – a voice deep inside of me command: 'This is a part of who you are. You must get it back.' It wasn't my own voice, but rather one with authority and conviction, a voice in touch with the deepest part of my soul. I had never heard this voice, but it wouldn't be the last time it spoke to me. Perhaps it came to me at that moment because for the first time in my life no one could control me or force me to deny who I really was.

I looked at the picture in my hand, fragile from years of secretly grasping it, and an overwhelming need to protect it propelled me into action. I rummaged through other pictures I had, searching for a frame, something that would give his photo the importance I thought it deserved. At that moment I wondered about the significance of ships in my life because I chose a silver frame which held a sketch of a sailing ship.

I again studied his soft eyes and gentle expression. What was he looking at as he gazed intently into the distance? Like all photos of soldiers, the image projected strength and pride in the uniform. But this was not just any uniform. If you looked closely, you would see the forbidding death's-head insignia of a German SS officer. It was this insignia and what it stood for that had been the evil haunting me for so long.

The SS officer in the photograph was my father, one of Hitler's elite, Arthur Liebehenschel, Second Kommandant of the Auschwitz Concentration Camp during the Second World War.

And so it was, that the special photo which my sister Brigitte gave to me when I was just thirteen before coming to America – the photo of the handsome man whose features resembled mine – the Nazi officer wearing the black uniform – the same photo I would keep secretly hidden and wouldn't share with anyone all these years was, as Brigitte told me, my Papa.

Whenever I took the photo out of my dresser, gazing at his face, tracing his features with my fingers, I saw in his eyes my own eyes, in his nose, my nose. What permitted him to rise to the top of such a loathsome organization? Was there something so dark and sinister inside him that could also exist within me as well? If so, I had never known it. Wouldn't any child of an SS officer ask the same questions?

His photo reassured me that I had once belonged to a family who bore a resemblance to me. It was my only tangible evidence that I had actually had a father. He left my mother, my siblings and me when I was only nine months old, as he was deeply in love with another woman. Life's lessons and maturity allowed me to forgive him for that. When I looked at his photo, I didn't see the officer, but the man – I didn't see the Kommandant, but my father.

The near collision of the two events which tore my life apart – Brigitte's death and my divorce – compelled me to acknowledge that I had no personal history to rely on. It was time to get to know my father and thereby know myself. Though I never actually knew him, he has shaped my life profoundly.

My search was never with the intention of exonerating him.

Chapter One

Party Member # 932766
& Family Man

I remembered that Brigitte had recorded some audiotapes of our family's history shortly before she died. Until now, I had had no desire to listen to them, not wanting to revive the pain of losing her. But now I was ready.

I had married young, at age nineteen, and since my twenty-eight-year marriage had come to an end, I found myself alone for the first time in my life. At my small apartment I picked up the telephone, and with a trembling hand dialed the number of Brigitte's son, Kye. Without telling him the reason for my request, I asked him for the tapes. He readily agreed to make me copies. I hung up the phone and immediately felt that I had made an important decision.

Because I had no plan beyond listening to the tapes, I had no way of knowing that I had just taken the first and easiest step in what would be an eight-year quest before I would eventually find some of the answers I sought. This journey would be filled with frustration, disappointment, emotional turmoil, conflict and countless dead ends.

It was later that year in 1991, on a hot, sunny afternoon, that the search for my father actually began. With a mixture of excitement and trepidation, I sat down alone to once again listen to Brigitte's melancholy voice as she spilled out her recollections of our family's history of which I'd known only the most rudimentary of facts. She brought into sharp focus some memories that had grown faint throughout the years, but mostly she revealed details about my family that I'd never heard before.

I took notes as I listened to the tapes, writing on a large yellow note pad with a pencil that would soon be worn down to a short stub. And then it was not until some time later that I finally retired the old typewriter and replaced it with a computer.

My father was born on 25 November 1901 as the illegitimate son of Emma Ottilie Liebehenschel and Anton Heinrich Weinert in Posen, Poland. It was not unusual for these ethnic Germans, known as 'Reichs-Germans', to live in Poland. His mother named him Arthur Wilhelm Liebehenschel because Anton was already a married man and denied paternal responsibility, even refusing to give him his name.

Anton, a teacher as well as a railroad official, soon deserted them, leaving Emma to raise her only son by herself. Arthur held a deep, loving bond with his mother, who worked hard as a seamstress in order to survive. His adoration for his mother often was expressed throughout his writings. As a seamstress, she worked diligently to keep her child, but barely making ends meet.

There never was any mention or evidence of his own father, and one senses through this a deeply hidden void, creating more hurt than resentment. His father abandoned him before he was even born and never acknowledged him as his son, even in later years.

In Arthur's journals, he spoke of a stepsister Helene whom he wished he could have met, but never knew. Little is known about his actual childhood but he mentioned several times in his journals that it was a difficult one and the good memories were those of his beloved mother.

The First World War had ended with Germany defeated in August 1918 and disarmed by the Treaty of Versailles. That was under the Weimar Republic, in power from 1919–1933, which tried to establish a democratic parliamentary regime. From testimony given by my father on 7 May 1947, he stated:

> My mother came from a family of Inn Keepers from East Germany and my father was a Railroad Official, a low ranking civil servant working as Secretary of the Railroad in Posen, Poland. He was a teacher by profession. His background stemmed from a line of mill workers in Prussian Silesia. I was raised in a religious atmosphere. My father was Catholic but I was raised solely by my mother who was a devout Protestant.
>
> I have fond memories as a child of our neighbors, the Polish family known as Glowinski to whom I owed much in that time. Their family consisting of ten children was very prosperous and life was much easier for them than for my mother and me. I spent a great deal of time with these people and was often given generous gifts.
>
> I was an only child. My father lived to be seventy-four and my mother died at age fifty-one. I had been a member of the Lutheran Church.[1]

After finishing high school Arthur studied public administration and economics. As a young man he joined the 'Freikorps' (Free Corps) where he served as a 'Border Guard-East' from January 1919 to August of that same year. This newly formed illegal military authority came into power after the defeat of the First World War, consisting mostly of idealistic activists who had been members of the armed forces; many of these men later also became members of the Nazi Party. It was brought into being by those who were of Hitler's generation who shared his enthusiasm to defend Germany from the Bolsheviks.

In October 1919 Arthur joined the army – the Reichswehr – at age eighteen. It was known as the '100,000 Men Army' as this was the maximum number allowed after the First World War. The military seemed to offer some measure of security as well as the chance for a patriotic young man to serve his country.

In 1920 the National Socialist German Workers Party, known as the 'Nazi Party', derived from 'Nazional', had a mere sixty members. Adolf Hitler was the head of this new political party, the NSDAP. He promised, among other things, to return Germany's colonies to her, which had been lost at the time of defeat. War reconstruction and payments to the Allies were among the great economic pressures. With the country in such turmoil and politically unstable, Adolf Hitler became the dominant figure. His hypnotic speeches had an extraordinary effect on the people.

In the Reichswehr my father was in the Infantry for two and a half years and then became Master Field Sergeant in the Medical Corps. His rank in this army was 'Sanitaets Oberfeld-Webel' at the time of his marriage to my mother, Gertrud Baum, on 3 December 1927 in Frankfurt-Oder.

I unfortunately have little information about my mother's background or childhood. Hers, too, was not an easy life – the sadness reflects in all of the photographs which I have of her. She was born in Zuellichau, Poland on 3 October 1903, a small pretty woman with hazel eyes. My parents, both ethnic Germans, met when she was working as a secretary for a college professor in Zuellichau. Evidently she worked closely for a number of years with a Dr Rudolf Hanov, the author of a book on the history of a local students' group. It was published in 1933 and he dedicated this book to her:

> Dedicated to Frau Gertrud Liebehenschel, the former Gertrud Baum, for her longstanding loyal assistance. In fond memory of our collaboration toward matters concerning the subject of Burgkellerei – by Dr. Rudolf Hanov.

My sisters remembered that our mother often spoke highly of this old friend and wondered if they had been romantically involved at an earlier time.

Still living in Frankfurt-Oder on the Polish border, my parents' first child – my oldest brother Dieter – was born to them on 2 September 1928. At the time, my father had also been attending secret underground meetings and became very involved with the Nazi movement. As with so many other people, he was overwhelmed by the powerful speeches of promises to reunite Germany and to return the people's dignity and economic welfare.

By the end of 1929 unemployment had risen to three million, and inflation was rising making circumstances even more favorable for Hitler and his party. On 30 January 1933 the forty-three-year-old painter from Austria was appointed Chancellor of Germany.

After twelve years of duty in the Reichswehr, father was discharged as Master Sergeant, a non-commissioned officer, on 3 October 1931. Throughout the following months after his discharge he remained unemployed. In 1932 my father went to work for the Finance Office in Frankfurt-Oder.

After my brother Dieter was born, Brigitte arrived four years later on 28 December 1932, followed by my sister Antje, who was born 7 April 1937. It was extremely cold that year, and Brigitte remembered my mother saying that there had been little money for coal. They had no heat and 'could scrape the ice off the inside walls' of their small apartment. To keep the new baby warm, Mother and Father placed her between them in their bed, but were afraid to move for fear she might be smothered during the night.

One of the first major breakthroughs during my research came when I finally received word from the Berlin Document Center that all existing reference material had been moved to the National Archives in Washington DC. Grateful that I could now correspond in English – and after the usual bureaucratic red tape – I located the transcripts taken at Nuremberg of Father's pre-trial interrogations.

I received the transcripts on microfilm, which I took to the local library to view. As I threaded the film onto the ancient machines, I was filled with a strange mixture of happiness at receiving this tangible piece of evidence and fear of what I might learn.

As I read, a knot formed in the pit of my stomach. Some of the testimony was damning – not only from witnesses, but also from my father himself, who was clearly lying about what he knew. I left the library, my head reeling. Was my father really responsible for the murder of hundreds of prisoners as the witnesses claimed?

As with most of the documentation that I would accumulate throughout the next few years, these transcripts were in German and I began the diligent, lengthy and incredibly emotional task of translating my father's testimony into English. It was as though I found myself back in time at the Nuremberg Palace of Justice with my father, and I can almost see him on the witness stand. In my mind's eye, I am experiencing these dramatic hearings. I wonder if his obvious lies are due to the oath he had pledged to Hitler, promising obedience, loyalty and of course the code of secrecy. Here was his testimony about the beginning.

Transcripts of Pre-trial Interrogation at Nuremberg:
U.S. Military Chief of Counsel for War Crimes/SS Section
Taken Of: Arthur Wilhelm Liebehenschel – by E. Rigney
Date: September 18, 1946 – 10:00–11:30 a.m.

Q: Did you ever belong to any other political party before 1930?
A: No.
Q: Did you ever belong to any other political organization other than the Union?
A: No.
Q: When did you join the NSDAP [Nazi Party]?
A: 1932.
Q: Did you ever hold any leading or subordinate office within the NSDAP?
A: No I joined the SS.
Q: We're now talking about the 'Party'. Did you ever hold any official position in the party?
A: No.
Q: Never?
A: No.

Q: What other formation within the party did you belong to?

A: I joined the general SS.

Q: Since when?

A: Also since February 1, 1932.

Q: With what rank did you start in the SS?

A: I started as private in the SS.

Q: I'd like to go back to the question of the 'Party'. You said you held neither rank nor a position in the 'party' itself. Did you ever hold any official functions in the party?

A: No.

Q: Did you have personal friends that were members of the party?

A: That I don't know. I had virtually nothing to do with the party itself. The SS was automatically assigned to the 'party'. We had little or no involvement with the party. We paid our dues.

Q: So the answer then to my question from a logical point of view would be: 'Yes' that your friends within the SS were also members of the party?

A: As you wish.

Q: What was the general reason that you joined the SS?

A: This is how it was at that time: Since I was unemployed after twelve years, one needed to seek an occupation, but there was no employment for some time. I wanted to have some activity; something to keep me occupied. That is why I joined the SS. At that time the SS was still seen as a military branch with decent people.

Q: That's a matter of opinion. We are not here to discuss our ideas.[2]

Later, when Dieter and Brigitte had whooping cough and Antje was just a tiny baby, mother was afraid Antje would also become infected. Therefore, they were sent on a train with identifying name tags to Zuellichau, to Oma, our mother's mother. Oma lived alone in a large old house in the city, as our grandfather had died in June of 1936. Dieter and Brigitte found her apartment fascinating. It was quite dark inside as the bedroom had no windows. The heavy overstuffed furniture was of old craftsmanship. The large dining table was beautifully carved wood covered by an old-fashioned, long-fringed tablecloth that nearly reached the floor.

Brigitte recalled how Oma was very strict, but a wonderful lady. She stood for no nonsense concerning picky eating habits, something Brigitte was known for. My sister preferred eating snacks between meals and Oma warned her that if she didn't clean her plate, she'd have to wait until the next meal. My sister showed her rebellion by taking a newspaper under the table and proceeding to eat it piece by piece.

Oma could not get angry when she found Brigitte pouting and peering through the long fringes of the tablecloth. But she too was headstrong and made no attempt to offer any snacks! I suppose there was a lesson learned, but who was the teacher?

It was 6 January 1929 and Hitler appointed Himmler 'Reichsführer SS'. Himmler was placed in charge of the original SS troops, the black corps which were the elite guards, a select group of young men eighteen to twenty years of age, pledged to protect Hitler with their own lives.

Himmler, as most of the youths of that era, including my father, seemed to be driven by a strong belief in complete order and discipline. History tells us that after the war many Nazis testified 'they were only following orders'. In the interesting book *Hitler's Elite* by Louis L. Snyder, the author cites that historians who have researched the psychological aspect of this behavior, have called this conduct the 'obedience syndrome'. The foremost golden rule was to respect authority and to obey law and order.

Adulation of the government and complete subservience to authority was the sign – and expected of all model citizens. It was not only taught within the home and family, but even the educational system of that time was indoctrinated by teachers spreading the philosophy of Georg Hegel. Disobedience was considered betrayal to the Führer and the Fatherland.

At the onset of Nazi rule, Himmler was involved with the earliest concentration camps, which had been constructed at Dachau near Munich, then Buchenwald and Sachsenhausen by Berlin. These 'correctional institutions' were soon turned into death camps. Later, the Reichsführer would be the one to make life exceedingly difficult for my father.

My father joined the general SS as a private in February 1932 and became 'Party' member # 932766. He became a part of this elite and powerful organization, which Himmler built into a private army and police force by using highly specialized training. In 1933 the ranks of the SS had a membership of 52,000 men, escalating Himmler's power, and soon he had complete control of the German people. The Death's Head Units of the SS (*Totenkopfverbande*) were established and its members were primarily employed as concentration camp guards.

> At the time I joined the SS, I automatically and also voluntarily, became a member of the NSDAP [Nazi Party], in which I never held any official offices. In accordance with the propaganda of the SS at that time, I informed my superiors in 1938 that I had relinquished my faith and religion and was no longer affiliated with the Protestant Church. In actuality, however, I remained a member of my congregation and continued to pay my dues. I never officially acted out my separation from the church. I hid the truth from the SD to avoid their punishment.[3]

The young and most able were formed into a specialized battle unit in 1940. The 'Totenkopf' Division became part of the Waffen SS (Military Division). These troops were not involved with the concentration camps. Those members who were wounded or elderly, unfit for the front, were – as in my father's case – put in charge of the concentration camps.

My father took the oath of 'nobility and honor', the same oath taken by the military forces:

I swear before God this holy oath, that I should give absolute pledge to the Führer of the German Reich and people, Adolf Hitler, the Supreme Commander of the Wehrmacht, and as a courageous soldier will be ready at all times to lay down my life for this man.

With Hitler in power, Joseph Goebbels, the ambitious Minister of Propaganda, waged his skillful campaign by showing the Führer kissing babies, children bringing him flowers and playing with his animals, and showing him on newsreels in theaters to convince people of his fondness for children and his goodness of heart. These clever lies built Hitler's national image, and fooled most of the public.

It was during this time of desperate economic decline that to many – those who chose to join the Nazi Party or the SS – it was merely a job. In a bleak time of unemployment, hunger, bankruptcy and despair, Hitler had come along with the answer to regain economic strength. One has to wonder how many people would have chosen to participate in Hitler's 'workers' party' had they known the extremes of the end result, as we know it today.

Those people, however, who were not sympathizers of the Nazi Regime, were threatened to enlist against their will. In order to keep their jobs many became non-active but paying members.

It is easy to comprehend why my father made the choices he did at the time. He must have sensed renewed hope with the Nazi regime and was readily caught up to Hitler's ideas of a more prosperous Germany. The army had been his career for twelve years and he was drawn toward the strict military discipline of the SS. Joining this organization seemed the right thing to do at this point in his life. Brigitte recalls him as 'a gentle man who saw only good'.

When Father started his career in the administrative part of concentration camp duty, the camps were set up more like penitentiaries for political prisoners. Later they became the death camps, as we know them today. Did my father realize the horrific implications connected with this organization when he joined? I will never know the answer to this nagging question. Later my father confessed to my brother Dieter and sister Brigitte that, had he known in the beginning what he knew then, he would not have taken the path he did. He also did not want his son Dieter to join the SS.

In the beginning of Nazi rule there were some positive things happening for the general good of the country's economy. The economy was slowly improving with numerous jobs created through the construction of the Autobahn, which was completed in 1937; factories were booming and building construction put thousands of people to work. Every family consisting of two or more children was subsidized twenty Marks per child, which was finally putting food on their barren tables. Even special care benefits were given, like free summer camp for children from poor families. Because of this upward movement, people were obviously fooled and convinced that Hitler, who seemed to be liberating them from their crisis, was the suitable leader for Germany.

Since August 1934 Father was no longer working for the Finance Office, but became adjutant and head of staff personnel of the 27th SS Regiment, serving for the Kommandant in the Lichtenburg Concentration Camp. At the same time he was Section Chief of the Politische Abteilung at Columbia Haus in Berlin. Columbia Haus was a concentration camp, which held prisoners under interrogation at the Gestapo headquarters. It became infamous for the torture methods used there.

When we lived in Prettin, on the river Elbe, he was part of the unit SS-Wachtgruppe 'Elbe'. Here he was the adjutant to the Kommandant of the Lichtenburg Concentration Camp. From July 1937 he was department head and part of the staff of SS-Obergruppenführer Eicke until 1940. It was here in Prettin that my sister Antje was born in 1937.

The ancient Lichtenburg Camp had once been a monastery which was built during the fourteenth century, in the time of the Renaissance. In the years 1575–81 Prince August of Sachsen occupied the three-winged structure and it became his palace. Before it became a concentration camp it was used as a penitentiary for political prisoners. My parents lived across the street and my brother recalls how he used to squeeze through the large iron gate at the entrance. He made it a habit to always wander off and would be found playing inside the courtyard.

Dieter started grade school here, and Brigitte's memories are of the tinker man, who came around with an old small rickety truck. He would trade old newspaper or tin foil with the neighborhood children in exchange for small gift items. Once Brigitte had saved a huge stack of newspaper and in return she was given a blue 'pearlized' glass necklace. It was her special treasure she would keep for many years.

It was also at this time, by orders of the SS, that a complete genealogical history of my parents was documented. It traced back to the year 1800 and proves their ancestry stemmed from 'pure Aryan', non-Jewish blood. This was absolutely mandatory for all SS and party members.

My father became gravely ill at this time, diagnosed with an infection of the heart muscle. Doctors gave him little hope, but having a very strong will for survival, he miraculously pulled through and recovered. Apparently his heart was left damaged and he was to suffer from this the remainder of his life.

As a result of the weak heart disability he was permanently reassigned to administrative office divisions, within the framework of concentration camps. Incapable of performing his duty regularly during the three-year period of his illness, he was, however, paid 250 Reichsmark monthly by the SS.

At some time throughout his career my father was awarded the 'Orden & Ehrenzeichen' (Medals & Decorations) of the Wartime Cross of Merit I & II. He was also given the SS dagger and ring.

Transcripts of Pretrial Interrogation at Nuremberg:
U.S. Military Chief of Counsel for War Crimes/SS Section
Taken Of: Arthur Wilhelm Liebehenschel – by E. Rigney
Date: September 18, 1946 – [continued]

Q: Now we come to your first office position within the SS, after you left the Finance Office in Frankfurt-Oder in 1935, is that correct?

A: It was 1935.

Q: At that time you started a position in the SS. What was the position?

A: Head of Personnel and Adjutant of the 27th SS Regiment.

Q: Where?

A: In Frankfurt on the Oder.

Q: Who was your superior?

A: Lt-Colonel Gerlich.

Q: Until when was Gerlich your superior?

A: Until the end of February 1934.

Q: How long did you work for the 27th SS Regiment?

A: Approximately until March 1935. Then I became ill.

Q: How long were you ill?

A: Almost three years. I had severe pneumonia, a relapse, and also an infection of the heart muscle. I was unable to work for almost three years.

Q: Were you in the hospital?

A: Yes several hospitals.

Q: What did you live on for three years?

A: I received a salary of 250 Reichsmark from the SS.

Q: Monthly?

A: Yes.

Q: What was this equivalent to, as far as rank?

A: At that time it was not about rank. It was simply a legal settlement according to individual status.

Q: When did you resume your duties? In 1938?

A: In 1938 I started working for the SS Main Office (Hauptamt).

Q: Under what title?

A: Department Chief.

Q: In which section?

A: In the Department of Weapons and Equipment.

Q: How long were you at the Main Office in Berlin?

A: Until I was transferred to the Economic Administration Department in January of 1942.

Q: What were your functions within the Main Office?

A: There, I was in the section for Weapons and Equipment.

Q: What was your duty?

A: My tasks were checking the books of various units, keeping files and count of weapons and equipment.

Q: Were there any other tasks within the Main Office, leading or subordinate duties?

A: I was only assigned to do office duty, as my health would only allow.

Q: I didn't ask you if you did office work. I asked if you performed other duties within the SS Main Office?

A: No.[4]

Father's health was slowly improving and he was promoted to Chief of the Political Department at the SS Main Office, Columbia Haus in Berlin. My family moved from Prettin to # 45 Hoeppner Strasse, Berlin, Tempelhof. Father's superior officer at that time was Captain Weinhoebel who was later killed at the front.

In 1938 my family moved once again, this time to Sachsenhausen. It was our first actual home, a small two-story house, a definite step-up from previous apartment living. It was located in a housing tract for SS officers.

Rudolf Hoess was the Protective Custody Commander at this time at the camp Sachsenhausen, and would later become the first Kommandant of Auschwitz from 1940–43. He and his family lived next door to us in Sachsenhausen. My sisters were never fond of him or his family. Their two sons 'were mean and cruel' according to my sisters, who were always invited to all the boys' birthday parties. My parents insisted they attend but usually against their wishes.

Across the street was a beautiful forest of mixed trees, pines, birch and others, a wonderful playground for the neighborhood. The Hoess children used to tease and chase Brigitte in this forest. One day they chased her, causing her to run so fast that she fell and badly cut her knees. Bleeding and crying she headed home. Father comforted her and told her after he washed and bandaged her knees that he would teach her to ride her new two-wheel bicycle. He held on to the seat, assuring her 'Brigittchen you can do it!' while she peddled faster and faster. Soon she no longer heard his voice and when she turned around and saw him waving to her from a distance, she realized she had been riding on her own. She had forgotten all about her painful scrapes; however, the scars that were left on her knees would always remind her of those wicked Hoess boys!

Our home was only a short distance from the Sachsenhausen Concentration Camp, which had been established in 1933. Among the captives were political opponents, churchmen, communists, homosexuals and Jews. Many of the Jews had been sent here after the 9 November 1938 twenty-four-hour street violence known as 'Kristallnacht'. This was the destruction of synagogues, the breaking into of thousands of Jewish shops, and the demolition of dwellings and homes. Countless books on philosophy, history and poetry were burned. Those arrested were released two to three months later, but many had already perished.

For some time the Sachsenhausen Camp was also set up as an extensive Brick Works. Prisoners were forced to work to meet the availability of building materials for the many elaborate projects planned for the rebuilding of the empire – the Reich – according to Hitler's dreams, and were carried out by his architect, Albert Speer.

After the war the Sachsenhausen Camp, like numerous others within the area, was established as a 'Special Camp' by the Soviets. Over 60,000 civilians were incarcerated there, intended for long-term imprisonment. Among them were low- to mid-ranking Nazis, members of the German Army, Soviet concentration camp prisoners who were accused of being traitors, and even victims of totally arbitrary arrests. These people included over 2,000 women, who were required to perform forced labor for the development of the Soviet Union.

In 1946–7 in this camp alone over 12,000 died of hunger and disease, and were buried in mass graves within the camp's perimeter.

Our grandmother from Zuellichau came to stay with us for a few months while we lived in Sachsenhausen. She was not well and our mother was going to look after her. Bedridden with a heart condition, she unbelievably 'smoked like a chimney'. Brigitte was her favorite and when Brigitte went in to visit her early one Sunday morning, Grandmother was still sleeping. Brigitte wondered why her arm was hanging down to the floor. Brigitte told Mother, 'Oma must be feeling better because she's still resting this morning.' Yes, Oma was resting … but forever.

Antje was two. She also found Oma lying very still in her bed that morning. She climbed on top of her and with the chocolate bar from her nightstand, she went on to feed Oma and herself the sweet, rich chocolate bar. When they discovered her she was sitting on Oma's chest, whose entire face was covered with chocolate and only Antje's large expressive eyes were recognizable, looking back at them with sheer delight.

As was the custom, Oma was laid out in the parlor in her coffin and Brigitte was made to kiss her goodbye. Into adulthood, the traumatic memory of Oma's cold body remained to haunt her.

It was about this time that Antje really started talking and could not say 'Brigitte'. One day she looked at her and called her 'Gitscha'. She was Gitscha to all of us until she passed away in 1988.

By 1939 the threat of war was imminent, due to Hitler's aggression toward Germany's bordering countries, and before long the First World War would rage throughout Europe in earnest. Any desire my father had for a normal family life was soon shattered by the overwhelming demands of war.

Chapter Two

Oranienburg

The year was 1939 when my father was relocated and the family moved to Oranienburg near Berlin, a short distance from Sachsenhausen. Here in my imagination, I can picture the man in the photograph as he walked the streets of quaint, historical Oranienburg; as he sat at his desk, working on the endless stacks of paperwork of the Third Reich; at home as he hung the glittering tinsel on the family Christmas tree while my mother looked on. And I see my siblings as happy children totally unaware of what fate their tragic future held.

German troops marched into Czechoslovakia on 15 March, and Hitler announced, 'Czechoslovakia ceases to exist!' Poland was invaded and occupied by German forces in September of that same year. The war had begun.

In Oranienburg my father worked in the notorious T-Building and was assistant to General Richard Gluecks in the office of the Concentration Camp Inspectorate. Gluecks had authority over all concentration camps as of 1939, after Theodor Eicke, under whom my father had previously worked, was promoted to Commander of the SS Death's Head Division. The 'Concentration Camp Inspection' moved its headquarters from Berlin into the so-called 'T-Building' in Oranienburg, after its completion in 1938. It was built by prisoners from the neighboring Sachsenhausen Concentration Camp. It derived its name from the T-shape of its three-winged structure. Theodor Eicke, who had been the first inspector here, was ordered by Himmler in 1934 to dissolve existing smaller camps and reorganize them into larger remaining camps. These camps were under the jurisdiction of the Death Head Units of the SS, making Eicke one of the key figures of this known 'System of Terror'. Theodor Eicke met his death as his plane was shot down by Soviet troops over Demjansk on 23 February 1943.

In January 1941 General Gluecks requested my father's promotion from SS Major to SS Lt-Colonel, praising him as his 'valuable assistant'. After the WVHA was formed in 1942, incorporating what had been the former Inspectorate of Concentration Camps, my father was given the position of Chief of the Central Economic Administrative Office. This section, the DI Central Office, was in charge of prisoner affairs, equipment and arms for camp personnel and personnel training. Father was here until his transfer to Auschwitz in 1943.

In Oranienburg we moved into another SS housing area. There were smaller homes such as the one we had left in Sachsenhausen, and eight to ten larger villas. Since our father had just been promoted again, we moved into one of the villas on Adolf Hitler Damm # 76, reserved for the higher-ranking SS officers. Our neighbors on the street were all professionals: Dr Hildebrandt, Dr Wolf, Dr Loritz and Wehrmacht (Armed Forces) Chief of Staff Wilhelm Keitel.

Brigitte recalls fondly that it was a spacious two-story home with lovely yards and terraces. From the front entrance, swinging doors led into a large foyer that had marble-like floors, covered by a red carpet runner; on the right, a dining room with sliding doors. On the left side was a spacious living room with a large fireplace and a door leading to the basement, where we took shelter at night from bombing attacks. Off the kitchen was a storage pantry room. Upstairs were the bedrooms and large bathrooms. We had beautiful furnishings and elegant draperies to match. There were intricate decorative pieces throughout, like lamps, whose bases were hand-carved figures that held musical instruments. There was a family piano of which I later had memories. Dieter and Brigitte took lessons, which neither one of them appreciated, and they often played hooky whenever they could get away with it. There were models of ships and, as expected of all loyal officers of the Party, a picture of the Führer decorated the living room.

After the war, when the Russians occupied East Germany, these homes were severely damaged, but today they still stand, privately owned and have been dedicated as Historical Landmarks. The street name has now obviously been changed from Adolf Hitler Damm.

My parents planned an addition to the back of this house. It was to be a 'Winter Garten', a glassed-in solarium or sun room that would eventually become home to various thriving green plants, many of which were given to my parents at the time of my birth, filling over one quarter of the room.

Antje was almost six, and vividly remembers the prisoners in striped uniforms wearing their caps who worked on the construction of the new room. She looked forward to and waited in the morning for the two men who came every day for several months. She followed them around with her 'braids flying' (my father's expression), watching them work and with childlike curiosity asking all sorts of questions. They came from the Sachsenhausen Concentration Camp and were more than happy to talk to her. One of them in particular took a liking to Antje, which was not hard to do, as she was a lovable precocious child. It was as though she reminded him of his own child he might have had. He would pick her up and carry her around with him on his shoulders and promise her he would build her a playhouse like the one she'd always dreamed of. My parents were not concerned, trusting the men, never discouraging the contact between these two concentration camp prisoners and their daughter.

My mother baked large sheets of 'Streusel Kuchen' (a traditional German cinnamon crumb coffee cake) for the prisoners, and my father asked her to add generous amounts of meat into the stew which she prepared for them. At noontime every day Antje brought them from the back yard building site through our formal dining room, where they followed her and smelled the wonderful aroma that drifted from the kitchen. There they ate with ravenous appetites around our large wooden table.

My parents welcomed them into our home, but Papa insisted this be done discreetly without anyone's knowledge. The grateful prisoners expressed their gratitude to my mother, complimenting her baking, and she told them that the recipe for the 'Streusel Kuchen' was her own mother's favorite family recipe.

To Antje they became old friends but one day, when the sunroom was finally completed, she realized with sadness that her friends would never return. She has often wondered what fate befell them.

At the end of our street, following a short path, sat the T-Building, where Papa's office was located. He had a magnificent, roomy office on the second floor. The officers' heavy boots, walking the opulent marble floors, were heard echoing throughout the long corridors. The room of the main office consisted of a beautiful wooden desk; in front of it sat a dark leather chair, and in the corner next to it thrived a big potted rubber plant. On the wall to the right hung a large ostentatiously framed picture of Hitler, and on the opposite side of the room the entire wall was covered with shelves stocked with books. Two grand windows behind the desk looked out onto a tree-lined street bearing little traffic. In an adjoining room there was a sofa, where Papa could rest when his heart condition caused him to feel debilitated of physical strength.

On many occasions Antje would venture to the T-Building to meet Father – usually without my mother's knowledge – and walked home with him for the 'Mittagessen' (main meal at noon). She'd wait for him in the smaller connecting room on the sofa watching all that was going on with immense pride and awe. Men in uniforms and polished black boots came in and out, respectfully addressing my father with the 'Heil Hitler' salute, clicking their heels together and politely bowing their heads. To help pass the time father would send Antje to the 'Canteen', a lunch-room on the first floor, with 20 Pfennigs, where she always bought herself a favorite dried fruit and nut snack.

Antje worshipped my father and it was evident she was the special sunshine of his life. Many mornings when Papa arranged to be driven to the office by his chauffeur, Antje would slip into the back seat and hide, still wearing her night-gown. Papa let her ride along and then sent her back home with his driver. On one such occasion they were going to pick up the Chief of Staff Wilhelm Keitel, stopping in front of his house at the end of our street. Antje observed him from the back seat as a tall man who walked out wearing a long leather coat, but as he headed toward the car he suddenly collapsed in front of them on the path. He would, however, live through to the end of the war, becoming one of the infamous twenty-one defendants at the Nuremberg Trials.

Today, this once busy office on the second floor of the T-Building has been turned into an Exhibit and Documentation Center of the Inspectorate of Concentration Camps. The building has been remodeled and given a fresh clean face. However, some things have remained in their original state. The light-colored marble floors still run from the entrance of the building, upstairs to the second floor and continue throughout Father's former office. The window sills and radiator-type heaters are framed with dark contrasting marble just as they were years ago at the height of Nazi power.

Detailed biographies portray its former staff members like my father. A large photo plaque of him in uniform and black boots can be seen beside a copy of his handwritten Lebenslauf or résumé, as well as many other documents bearing his signature. The large framed picture of Hitler, which hung in father's office, is of course no longer displayed. After the Russian occupation the Germans found they had painted over the canvas, but the original portrait of Hitler had remained unharmed, hidden under layers of whitewash.

It was while father was working within the Economic Administrative Office that he became acquainted with Anneliese Huettemann, the young blond secretary who worked in the outer office for General Gluecks, and was my father's superior. General Glueck's main office was also on the second floor of the T-Building and inevitably father and Anneliese saw each other on a daily basis.

The general lived in a small house near the offices of the administrative building; it was surrounded by trees located on Adolf Hitler Damm between our house and the T-Building. Antje remembers visiting the general in this house, whom she recalls as a kind man who loved children.

Anneliese was able to see our house from her office, and remembers on many occasions at lunch time seeing Antje sitting outside in front of our house, looking in the direction of the T-Building with our dog Ossie. On those days when Antje didn't meet father at his office she always waited there for him to come home. Anneliese didn't know our father too well at this time, but asked him, 'Who is that child who always sits in front of the house with that dog?' And he said with pride, 'That is my daughter Antje.'

Ossie was not a pure-bred German Shepherd, but she had two beautiful puppies named Max and Moritz, who our parents gave to the SS Dog Training Academy to be trained as police dogs. Ossie would leave our house on a daily basis and show up at the Academy to visit her 'family'. It would never fail and there would be a call from the man who was in charge of the training center to tell my mother: 'Frau Liebehenschel, your dog Ossie is here visiting Max and Moritz again!' Ossie also eventually ended up at the Academy, and our family pet was more than likely turned into one of the aggressive SS police dogs.

In 1940 our mother joined the NSDAP – the Nazi Party. This was just a formality; she was a non-active member, but it was a requirement as the wife of an SS officer.

By February 1943 Hitler's Sixth Army lost the fierce battle of Stalingrad to the Soviets. The Russians captured 91,000 prisoners of war of which only a few thousand returned to Germany. It was a devastating turning point in the war for Germany.

Things seemed to be going well for our family. Our parents leased a beautiful piece of lake-view property in St Gilgen, Austria, overlooking the lake Wolfgangsee about fifty miles from Salzburg, with breathtaking scenery as seen in the film *The Sound of Music*. It was a ninety-nine-year lease, and they began building a vacation home. Papa took the family to see it in its various building stages.

Brigitte claimed that it was built by laborers taken from the nearby concentration camp, however, there seems to be no documentation at Ebersee, Austria, confirming that prisoners were used for the construction of our house. We can therefore only speculate that perhaps they were used for the final cleanup of the construction site. Brigitte told me of her mysterious psychic experiences related to these prisoners who worked on our house. She always was a very spiritual person. She told me, 'When we lived there, I used to be awakened by a loud clanking noise. When I sat up, there at the foot of my bed stood a vision of a man's figure surrounded by light wearing the striped concentration camp uniform; shackled, he was holding and shaking the chains making the terribly loud noise that woke me.' She had this same 'vision' many times, but it seemed no one else heard the noise and she was told it was just a nightmare. It was many years later when she found out that the workers who built our house had been prisoners from the concentration camps.

The house was built on the side of a small mountain, and right below was the road and across it the lake Wolfgangsee. Along the shore of the lake ran the railroad tracks of a small local passenger steam locomotive. I can still smell the thick black puffs of smoke and hear the shrill whistle as it would chug along, laboring as it pulled its weight over the rolling hills.

A long sloping wooded path led up to the rock stairs to the front gate of a typical Bavarian type, two-story chalet. It had a wooden balcony and shutters with a garage under the house. The large terrace in the front had a beautiful view overlooking the lake, and behind the lake rose the well-known Schafsberg mountain. There were trees, ferns, mosses and all kinds of wild flowers, and berries such as wild blueberries, strawberries and raspberries. In the forest they picked mushrooms, learning which were the non-poisonous, edible kind.

With the house situated against a fairly steep mountainside, in the winter there was always the fear of avalanches. There was also a smaller building on the property. I remember it as the 'Block Haus', a sort of log cabin. Boxes of fruit were stored inside and I recall the heavenly aroma of pears, apples and raisins. To this day these fragrances and flavors remind me of that time and place.

There was no wiring yet for electricity, so we used oil lamps and had a generator in the basement. Water was drawn from a well and I recall a huge barrel in the back of the house which caught the rainwater. It was always full and the fragrance of the water was clean and fresh.

The interior was relatively small. Through the front door entrance a long hallway reached straight across to the back end of the house, where a door led down into the cellar and from there to the garage. A narrow winding staircase rose to the upper level from there. Before the stairs, on the right side, the girls' large bedroom was located where Brigitte and Antje slept in wooden bunk beds. A sofa also sat in this room near the window, which was covered only with a pretty valance, as wooden shutters on the exterior were secured every night for warmth and privacy. On occasion, our mother slept here on the sofa, with my sisters when they had nightmares or became frightened during the night.

Next to their room was another bedroom furnished with additional bunk beds and used as a guestroom, which was usually occupied by Ilse, who was our nursemaid. Across the hall on the left behind the stairwell were the kitchen and a bath. From the front entrance a door on the left led immediately into the living room. It was the largest room in the house and its homey alpine decor gave it a warm cozy feeling. The whole room was wainscoted; faced with dark natural wood panelling, while the top half was painted white creating a striking contrast.

A piano sat against the left wall directly in the corner. Across the room, still on the left side, the entire corner consisted of windows. Nestled within this nook was an L-shaped seating bench and situated in front of it sat the large dining table and chairs made of both light and dark wood. On the opposite side of the room next to the 'Kachelofen', a serve-through window made the kitchen easily accessible. Against the far right wall the grand, dark wooden hutch sat like a showpiece, and was where mother stored our dishes behind colorful, stained, leaded-glass panels. The only means of heat for the entire house was the centrally located large, square-tiled stove, the 'Kachelofen'. It was heated from the kitchen side with wood or coal. It had a bench attached to it that reached all around its circumference. Located in the living room and also facing the kitchen, it extended up to the ceiling, made of light blue decorative and hand-painted tiles; it made the living room a cozy gathering place to warm up after coming in from the snow. This type of heating and stove is typical of Bavaria and the Alps, and dates back to the twelfth century. Long after the fire is out the tile retains and radiates the heat, making it very efficient.

Upstairs was the master bedroom, and from here French doors opened to the wooden balcony. Right next door was our brother Dieter's bedroom. A gun cabinet in the master bedroom held a number of rifles and other weapons which were occasionally used for recreation purposes by our father and Dieter. A small storage chamber was also located on this level and another staircase led to the attic.

It was the summer of 1942 when the house was completed and the whole family went to St Gilgen for vacation. My mother was expecting me. In the fall, she and Antje stayed on, while our father left with Dieter and Brigitte so they could return to school in Oranienburg.

Despite its outward success, my parents' marriage was not a happy one. But whatever had gone wrong in their relationship, our father was making a genuine attempt to save what was left, or so it seemed. He wrote our mother numerous letters to Austria, and when she and Antje returned, there were baskets of flowers to welcome her home, but it seemed more like a final farewell ... as his heart already belonged to someone else.

It was also in 1942 that Papa gave Anneliese a beautiful ring, an expression of his love for her. It was of white gold, with a large oval-cut aquamarine blue stone. He had it made by his aide, who in his private life had been a jeweler and goldsmith. It was passed on to my sister, Antje, just recently, as promised to her by Anneliese many years ago.

My mother's thirty-ninth birthday was 3 October 1942. She and Antje had recently returned to Oranienburg from St Gilgen. Mother was five months pregnant with me, but still fitted into her floral print traditional Dirndl dress. Antje was playing in the foyer at our house and watched mother as she was standing in the dining room entrance; Papa was congratulating her for her birthday. He gently hugged and kissed her and then handed her a small wooden box. It was of light polished pinewood. The top was hand-painted with bright pink and yellow alpine flowers, including blue Enzian and white Edelweiss. It had a small lock with a tiny skeleton key, and carved and burned into the lid on the top was the inscription St Gilgen. She unlocked the box and within it she found a pair of earrings. They were of white gold, and the long dangling teardrop was a beautiful blue aquamarine cut stone. Mother was deeply moved and wept bitterly as she knew their relationship was already in trouble. At that time, however, she was completely unaware of the existence of a matching promise ring which father had already given to another woman, along with his love.

15 February 1943: This morning, our mother asked Dieter, Brigitte and Antje to get their own breakfast. She was not feeling well, and told them that maybe they'd have a new brother or sister later. Dieter was now fourteen, Brigitte ten and Antje six years old. When they came home from school, the doctor and midwife were there. Papa asked them to be well behaved. They waited and by early evening heard the cries … I was born.

I have so often thought of the irony of it all, as at that precise moment, at camps like Auschwitz, people were being herded into the gas chamber and tiny new-born babies like me were never even given a chance to live.

They named me Bärbel Ulrike. Then they were all allowed into the room, to see me for the first time.

Until the year she died, Brigitte would tell me this story every year on my birthday: When they saw me, I looked like a doll to them. Then my brother said I was looking at him but Brigitte insisted it was she that I had looked at first. Finally it was a heated argument over who held my attention first. They were 'escorted' out of the room by the midwife, still quarreling. When Brigitte turned to look at mother from the doorway, mother looked very sad and Brigitte felt she had been neglected in the midst of all the excitement. Brigitte ran back into the room, sympathetically throwing her arms around our mother's neck, and gave her a loving kiss on the cheek. Mother gently smiled at her.

I think of this story that Brigitte used to tell me every year on my birthday, and long to hear it just one more time …

Today is your birthday little sister, and I remember how happy I was when I took my first look at you forty years ago. Nothing has changed. I love you very much and only hope we have many more years together.

Your big sister, Brigitte
February 15, 1983

After all these years, I have discovered the reason for my mother's sadness on the day of my birth. Divorce documents found in my father's SS personnel file, disclosed that at that time, although still together in our home, my parents were no longer living as husband and wife; they slept in separate rooms.

After my birth the NSDAP presented my mother with the 'Mutterkreuz', a bronze medallion called the 'Motherscross', an honor awarded by Hitler to German mothers who bore four or more children. Those mothers who bore six or more received a silver medal, and eight or more children was honored with a gold medal. Making children for the Führer was the future of the Fatherland; the parents of large families were highly praised. Of my few precious keepsakes from the past, remains only the original blue and white striped ribbon, from which once hung the bronze metal given to mother in 1943.

Antje remembers being very jealous when I was born. Our mother was still recuperating and she'll never forget how tender and affectionate Papa was with me, as he bathed, diapered and even fed me. I think she had always been his favorite and received more attention, naturally, having been the youngest.

However, my arrival must have been a painful event rather than a joyful occasion for my parents. This was a very heart-wrenching discovery for me. Apparently, I had been conceived into a union as a final attempt to save a love that was already lost.

Chapter Three

The Last Embrace

Ilse came to work for us as a nursemaid in Oranienburg after my birth. She was to become a significant person in our lives. Our father took her out of the women's concentration camp at Ravensbrück. The reasons for his choice were apparent, as she was beautiful, with raven-black hair, big blue eyes, and long black eyelashes. She was a Jehovah's Witness and refused to work in the armament factories. She also had a little girl named Mia who had been taken from her; she had no knowledge of where her daughter was.

Ilse's mother had already perished in a camp. Being the same age, I took Mia's place and she loved and spoiled me endlessly and I was drawn to her as well. Even at that early age, I recall the closeness and spiritual bond that drew me to her. I remember her beauty and the love she had for me. I called her 'Ecke'.

While working for us, Ilse went to have some dental work done at the nearby camp Sachsenhausen. The camp dentist was a prisoner named Rudolf (Rudy). Rudy was a non-Jew; a political prisoner who had performed illegal abortions. Coincidentally, he and Ilse happened to have known each other before their incarceration, and had even been engaged to one another. After her dental appointment at Sachsenhausen they remained in touch.

Oranienburg was the only place we were all together as a family. My brother and sisters have memories of happy family times, but also the frightful realities of the war. My brother recalls that even though it was wartime, their lives as children were relatively unburdened. He pushed me around in my wicker carriage until I would fall asleep.

Children occupied themselves in ways to fit into the times. There were regular air raids in the mornings and evenings. Shrapnel from anti-aircraft was scattered all over the streets and yards, and children would gather some of these pieces into baskets and trade these treasures for other unusually shaped pieces of shrapnel.

One day, an English bomber was shot down near our house. Dieter and Brigitte watched as it spiraled aimlessly through the air, losing altitude, before it crashed to the ground. They saw where the smoldering plane landed in a field and immediately took off in that direction on their bikes. A large crowd of people had gathered and they took the charred pilots, placing the bodies in their parachutes.

Nearby, Dieter spotted a helmet and also picked up a few special new pieces of shrapnel to add to his collection, which he hoarded in our basement.

This was a time when life was completely unpredictable, when air raids forced us into our bunkers at a moment's notice. There were air-raid bunkers in every schoolyard, and the children were drilled and trained on going underground.

In 1943 a bunker was constructed at our house. It was located in the front yard; covered with dirt and sod, it looked like an igloo. We had suitcases in there with personal belongings, valuables, important papers, water, food and other supplies. It was a favorite place to play. My sisters and brother often took potatoes and would roast them over the small stove. One day, during an air raid, Dieter and Brigitte crept out of the shelter. The sky over Berlin, which was about thirty-five miles away, glowed a crimson red from the flames of burning homes while the shrapnel sizzled through the skies. When Papa finally found them, they were playing on the swings. Several of their close school friends and their families were killed during these attacks.

Although there was a war going on all around them, people tried to continue with life's simple pleasures and live a somewhat normal existence. My father had a passion for music; he was very fond of folk songs of the Rhine region, but his special love was the classical composer Händel and his favorite piece was *Largo*. The melancholy tune could often be heard playing throughout our house on the old wind-up Victrola phonograph.

Our parents attended the theater regularly, and were at the opera in Berlin one evening when they found themselves caught in the midst of several air raids. When they failed to return home, everyone feared for their lives. They finally arrived home safe and unharmed after having spent many hours in the extensive street shelters of Berlin.

There were also steady bombings in Oranienburg. American and British bombers were looking for the hidden Heinkel Aircraft Works, located somewhere in the forest of the surrounding area. It was the plant that manufactured Germany's most modern jet fighter plane, the Me-262. It had two jet engines, a speed of over 500mph and a fighting capability far superior to any enemy aircraft at that time.

This whole generation of children, especially the age group of my brother Dieter and sister Brigitte, were senselessly robbed of their childhood, seduced by Hitler's youth movement where they were molded into future soldiers and mothers of the Fatherland. Baldur von Schirach, the Hitler Youth Leader, organized special Adolf Hitler Schools where many German boys were trained on warfare and how they could conquer the world as the master race. These were prep schools for the SS, to which only boys of pure Aryan family trees were accepted. Completely brainwashed, these children even turned against their own families. Later in the war they were conscripted and thousands of young boys were killed or horribly wounded. The young cries for their mothers were heard across the battlefields. Antje's husband Ernst was one of them. He lost a leg.

Willingly removed from their homes and drilled on principles of National Socialism. Their individuality stripped away in an effort to create the ideal man ...

strong, obedient, racially pure and prepared to make the ultimate sacrifice for Hitler and the Fatherland.[1]

Dieter was not sent to attend one of these special schools, but joined the Hitler Youth as required of every Aryan boy at ten years of age. They all wore short pants with brown shirts and ties. He participated in the extensive after-school curriculum of physical strength training; later he became part of the enemy anti-aircraft auxiliary fighters.

Brigitte was a member of the BDM (Bund Deutscher Madchen), the Federation of German Girls. Their hair was woven into braids and their uniforms consisted of dark skirts and white blouses with ties. Brigitte recalls marching through the forests singing old German folk songs, following the high-waving symbol of the swastika depicted on the red and black Nazi banners which they carried. Large numbers of children gathered in sport fields, exercising together in an almost hypnotic state; expressing their youthful enthusiasm and their dedication to Hitler who had become their idol. Girls were said to have been 'hypnotized by their charismatic leader, told they were the crown of creation, the mothers of future soldiers.'

Every German girl was to stay chaste and pure, saved for motherhood, as their main task in life was to bear children. The boys and girls alike were sworn into their organizations with the same oath as the soldiers, pledging their allegiance to Hitler.

In the schools, Nazi ideology became most important and was introduced into every subject. Children were weighed, measured and then classified by character-istics such as their shape of head, nose and eye color, which determined their level of racial purity. At the top of the list of propaganda was Rassenschande – racial defilement, shame inflicted toward anyone who was not of pure Aryan blood.

Teachers who were hired by the state planted the poison seed, influencing the children against Jews, gypsies and people of color. They were educated with special cynicism and hatred toward Jews who, according to them, were considered the criminals who would eventually destroy mankind. Pictures in their text books depicted the good and bad races; Jews being of an ugly, evil race in contrast to the perfect Nordic types.

As part of their community service the children also had to go door-to-door to collect sweaters, socks and blankets for the German soldiers on the Russian front. Women unraveled knit blankets in order to knit sweaters and socks for the soldiers.

Religion was shunned, but Hitler's regime had its own answer to what would have been Dieter's confirmation into the Lutheran Church at the age of fourteen. At this time of his coming of age he was initiated into what was called the 'Jugend Weihe'. It seems Dieter had quite a celebration, coming home inebriated and singing merrily. Our father, however, was not happy with Dieter's disgraceful behavior and clearly uttered his disappointment.

Dieter staggered upstairs to his room while father's gaze followed him from the foot of the stairs and with an increasingly raised voice continued to express his disgust and disbelief at his conduct on this special day of solemn commemoration.

Our mother, however, felt it was an innocent initiation into the ways of an adult world and she tried to mitigate our father's reaction.

Food and supplies were getting scarce. Many people suffered from hunger at this point in the war. Our family seemed to manage with food stamps, and our father was able to obtain staples through the black market, but the SS also looked after the welfare of its 'family' members.

As children, and with me only a baby, we were totally unaware of the horrors going on around us or what our father's involvement was. He tried to talk about this subject and expressed to my older brother and sister that he didn't want Dieter to go into the SS, and if he had known the direction Hitler was going to take, he himself would not have joined the SS; but it was too late. He'd made his commitment and chosen his path and there was no turning back, if he valued his life. On several occasions he voiced his disapproval of the SS and its policies.

Once, he was gone for four weeks, and our mother told my siblings that he went on a vacation by himself to recuperate from his heart condition. The 'vacation' was the result of accusations Papa had made against Heinrich Himmler.

On another occasion there was a party at our house. Brigitte watched from the staircase with awe and excitement. Ladies were dressed in beautiful gowns and men were in uniform. Our father, whose inhibitions had given in to a few too many glasses of Champagne, threw a drink at the Führer's portrait, which hung in our living room. As he turned to face his guests he caught a glimpse of Brigitte sitting at the top of the staircase and their eyes met. Brigitte recalled he seemed taken off guard. The pleasant party atmosphere immediately turned into an uncomfortable silence and then the room was quickly filled with apprehensive nervous conversation.

Later, disciplinary actions were taken by SS Lt-General Oswald Pohl, who was not only Himmler's close associate, but also his informant. He was father's immediate superior and would cause considerable problems for him in the future.

Reichsführer Himmler was outraged and sentenced my father to four weeks of solitary confinement. Brigitte recalls when he came home he was thin, pale and ill.

Oswald Pohl was also in charge of the labor camps over which the SS used its power to promote economic expansion for the Reich. Foreign workers were arrested for trivial violations and transferred to these camps, which were predominantly armament factories. Pohl was also responsible for handing over the wealth and belongings of concentration camp prisoners to the Reich. His colleagues later testified that Pohl promoted this with 'particular zeal'. He had at his disposal a workforce of more than half a million concentration camp prisoners; some were even 'leased out' to industry.

In father's dossier file there is other evidence of 'SS Disciplinary Actions' brought against him, as he noted on September 1941: '3 days detention, resulting from submissive negotiations with the Wehrmacht.' This was regarding his lenient stipulations with the armed forces concerning Russian POWs. More of this will be referred to later, as part of his stated testimony.

Our mother was a good homemaker and parent, usually preoccupied, always cooking and baking, and looking after our welfare. Papa spent as much time as he could spare with his children, time in front of the fireplace telling great ghost stories, walks in the forests and around the lakes of our neighborhood. Those times he walked with my brother and sisters they were so proud of Papa, so handsome in his uniform, feeling safe and secure as he held their hands. Of course they had no way of knowing what threatening implications that uniform actually carried.

Christmas was his favorite holiday, and along with our mother, they made it very special. The tree, which we were not allowed to see until Christmas Eve, was beautifully decorated with real candles for the lights, delectable sweets, wonderful old-fashioned, decorative, hand-blown glass ornaments, and the tinsel which was hung ever so straight, made of heavy lead in those days, hung by our father in single strands.

Hitler's officers were not allowed to attend church. Therefore, on Christmas Eve, Papa would change into civilian clothes, and take the family to church services across town where he wouldn't be recognized. He had a deep faith in God, which would be his salvation through many difficult times in his life. Hitler also didn't acknowledge this to be the celebration of Christ's birth. It came to be called the Yule-Fest or Winter Solstice; this is when the sun is at its greatest distance from the celestial equator. It was their celebration of the sun soon coming closer to speed the winter along; the looking forward to longer summer days once again. Father continued to call it 'Weihnachten' – Christmas, the birth of Christ. To this day, Christmas has a special magic for me as well and will always be my favorite holiday.

> It was wonderful when I could tell you Christmas stories and it was wonderful when I could spread the Christmas Holiday Table with goodies. You helped carry so many of my worries through your happy childlike eyes, you my dear children …
>
> *Father to Brigitte, Dec. 1945*

Yes, Oranienburg was the place we were all together as a family, but it was also the final turning point toward a life without Papa and a family soon to be torn apart.

It was the beginning of 1943. Our father said he had to make a trip to Austria to check on our house in St Gilgen. The truth was that it was actually a romantic rendezvous with the woman he loved. Someone revealed this to our mother and she found out that he had been seeing the pretty secretary, Anneliese Huettemann, and that they had planned to meet in Austria.

My mother decided to follow my father to St Gilgen and left a few days later. She never suspected him and wanted to find the truth out for herself. She traveled on the little train and arrived at our house on the Wolfgangsee to find my father and Anneliese there … together. Mother caused a terrible scene.

Antje remembers when our parents returned home from Austria together that she was wearing her favorite dark blue dress with embroidered pink roses. Our mother had a dress made of that same material; I recall her wearing it often. From that time on our mother was always crying. Antje would frequently find our parents in the corner of our dining room on a sofa, in the dark. Father talked to her quietly, but mother was crying. Antje's curiosity kept drawing her back to the room to see what was wrong. They consoled her and promised everything was all right. But everything was not, and they separated.

Papa left our house on Adolf Hitler Damm and took an apartment. I was only a few months old. He wanted Antje to go with him and she really would like to have gone, but she felt so sorry for our mother.

Anneliese also lived within our neighborhood. Brigitte at this time showed her deep hurt and total resentment toward Anneliese by calling her names and sticking her tongue out at her whenever she walked near our house. Brigitte even talked her little sister into joining in with her, which Antje found to be a fun prank, even though she didn't understand the motive behind it. Shortly thereafter Anneliese moved from Oranienburg.

Since I've read my father's journals I understand how deeply he was in love with this woman. I suppose he did what he had to do at that time, but nevertheless, he left my mother and us, 'the other children', as we were referred to in his journals, with a terrible void, abandoned in the midst of war.

My father had an important job in Oranienburg within the central office of the Concentration Camp Inspection. As a part of the Branch D-I he was responsible for dispatching orders directed to all concentration camps, which originated from Reichsführer Heinrich Himmler. Since my father was made chief of this department after the WVHA was established in 1942, his signature was required on these communications sent to the various concentration camps. Records show that these documents bore my father's signature.

His definition concerning coded numbers and letters used on official documents was part of a statement given by my father in court on 8 May 1947, in Krakow, Poland. He said:

> The letters DI in the letterhead of written matters, pertained to the DI office of which I was Chief. Circulars were addressed to all Kommandants of Concentration Camps and denoted in the letterhead e.g. Az. 14d3, which in this case would be the belongings of deceased prisoners. The information from these documents was then entered into Journals in consecutive numbered entries, designated as [Tageb. Nr.] The description DI/Az. 14d3/OT-Geheim Tgb. Nr. 38/43 meant that a circular was sent regarding the remaining belongings of prisoners [Az. 14d3] and that this was entered into a 'secret' Journal under the Nr. 38/43.
>
> The DI office kept one Journal for general purposes and another Journal for secret matters in which the incoming and outgoing correspondence was entered. The secret affairs were considered those that were not made available to anyone else within the DI office, with the exception of the Chief who in this case was me. This was the formal criteria and regulation of this division.[2]

These following communications signed by my father were concerning Russian POWs, a matter which would come back to haunt him during his trial.

Oranienburg Nr. 2719
Nov. 14, 1941 – 1639 -WAT-
To the Kommandant: Gross-Rosen Concentration Camp:
Requesting the names of all those SS members that were involved with the executions, who will be eligible for the 'Kriegsverdienstkreuz #2 with sword'

I.V. gez. Liebehenschel
SS-ObersturmbannFührer

Oranienburg Nr. 2786
Nov. 20, 1941 –1845 -RI-
To the Kommandant of the Gross-Rosen Concentration Camp:
With the list bearing the names of SS members who were involved with the executions and are to be awarded the Kriegsverdienstkreuz; the following reason is to be given: 'Durchfuehrung von Kriegswichtigen Sonderaufgaben' [given for the Enforcement of Special Wartime Assignment]. The word 'Execution' is not to be used under any circumstances.

I.V. gez. Liebehenschel
SS-ObersturmbannFührer

On 21 November 1941 a list of twenty-two names was sent by the Gross-Rosen Concentration Camp; a formal proposal for the decoration of these men – who participated in the execution of Russian POWs – whose commemoration was to be awarded in the form of a medal. The reason given: 'Enforcement of Special Wartime Assignment'.

SS-Fuhrungshauptamt
The Inspectorate of the Concentration Camps
Pol./Az. 14b 18/ot./u.-
Geheim Tgb. [Secret] Nr. 73/42
Subject: Distinguishing mark characterizing Russian POWs
Reference: Copy of communication from OKW
Az. 2f 24/73 1 POWs Allg. [Ia] Nr. 539/42 of 1/16/42
Dispatched: To the Kommandants of the following Concentration Camps:
Da., Sah., Bu., Mau., Neu., Au., Gr.-Ro., & POW camp Lublin.
Enclosed find a copy of the given order, regarding the acknowledgement and enforcement of the administering of distinguishing marks for Soviet POWs.

I.V. gez. Liebehenschel
SS-ObersturmbannFührer

The following was the original communication of the order that came from the command of the Wehrmacht (Armed Forces) regarding the Russian POWs, dispatched through my father's department.

Duplicate

General Headquarters of the Wehrmacht

Az. 2f 24/73 I POWs Allg. [Ia] Nr. 539/42

Bln.-Schoeneberg I, I/16/42

Badensche Str. 51

Subject: Distinguishing marks for Soviet POWs

Since most Soviet POWs who escape, make every effort to rid themselves of any distinguishing marks and are often not recognized as POWs or especially as Russian POWs, it is therefore ordered: 'Every Soviet POW is to be marked with an X on the underside of the left forearm; with *Hoellensteinstift* [tatoo].'

> Dispatched by: Kdo. I–XIII, XVII, XVIII, XX, XXII
> with duplicates for Oflags, wwwwStalags pp.
>
> Chief of General Hdq./ Armed Forces
> Order of: sig. Dreyer/f.d.H.d.A.
> SS-UntersturmFührer

Duplicate

Dispatched to: Departments II, III, IV

Oranienburg FS. Nr. 903 3/24/1942 – 1259 -HE-

To the SS-StandartenFührer-Koch

Kommandant of the POW Camp Lublin:

Subject: Jews from Czechoslovakia

Concerning the 10,000 [ten thousand] Czechoslovakian Jews destined for the POW camp at Lublin, as previously informed, will be shipped out on special transports on March 27, 1942.

Each special train will carry 1,000 [one thousand] prisoners. Each train will pass through the train station at Zwardon [OS] where they will arrive at 6:09 in the morning and after a two hour delay, will continue and be escorted by the accompanying Commandos of the Schutz Polizei under the supervision of the State Police of Kattowitz.

The head of the Commandos will have a list of names and the schedules of the first 4 transports have been arranged as agreed upon by the Reichsbahn as follows:

DA 67 on 3/27, DA 69 on 3/30, DA 70 on 3/31, DA 72 on 4/5, on these days the time of arrival in Zwardon is 6:09, departure from Zwardon at 8:20, arrival at Lublin at 6:30 the following day.

You will be informed at a later time of schedules for the remaining 6 transports, as in the given order in FS. Nr. 886 of 3/23/42.

The supplied provisions should be sufficient for the duration of the transport and as instructed must be reported immediately upon arrivals through the FS.

> Chief of the Central Office
> gez. Liebehenschel
> Fd. Rd.-Abschrift
> SS-OberscharFührer[3]

Among other circulars referred by the Department of the Reich Criminal Police, which were dispatched and signed by my father, was the one of 14 November 1942, stating that the common practice of sterilization performed on criminal prisoners, usually determined by the ERB/Gesundheitsgericht, would now be under the jurisdiction of the acting camp doctors. Also, that the 'Sonderbehandlung 14 f 13' (killing of ill prisoners/euthanasia) would be stopped and determined by camp doctors only in the cases where these prisoners were no longer capable of work performance. Those that recuperated and were again capable of work detail would not fall under the jurisdiction of 'Sonderbehandlung'.[4]

Transcripts of Pretrial Interrogation at Nuremberg:
U.S. Military Chief of Counsel for War Crimes/SS Section
Taken Of: Arthur Wilhelm Liebehenschel – by E. Rigney
Dated: September 18, 1946 – [continued]

Q: When did you start at the Economic Main Office?
A: In January 1942.
Q: Which sector were you in?
A: Sector D.
Q: Were you chief of sector D in 1942?
A: No.
Q: Who was chief of sector D in 1942?
A: The supervisor was Gluecks.
Q: What was your position under Gluecks?
A: I was in charge of the so-called 'Central Office'.
Q: What section was this?
A: 'I'.
Q: When did you become Gluecks' acting deputy?
A: I was actually never considered his acting deputy.
Q: Would you like to reconsider your answer?
A: On paper I was acting deputy but otherwise that was not my position.
Q: Did you ever place your signature on letters or circulars that went to the other Kommandants of the concentration camps? You may answer this with yes or no, as you know this as well as I do.
A: I had orders and commands but never …
Q: What did you sign?
A: General Inquiries concerning my position.
Q: But you were authorized to sign letters when Gluecks wasn't there. Is that not correct?
A: No, only general matters, all others had to wait.
Q: I repeat my question: You were however authorized by Gluecks, in his absence, to sign for him 'as instructed'?
A: As instructed only through general exchange of correspondence. Important matters had to wait.

Q: We are not at this time discussing important or unimportant matters or correspondence of section 'D' of the Economic Administration Main Office. This is not what we're concerned with at this time. We are discussing first of all in general: Were you authorized to sign documents for Gluecks as instructed?

A: No, I repeat; only unimportant documents nothing else.

Q: What would you say if I produced and brought forward letters stating your signature?

A: You can submit these, they would only be a confirmation of what I testified.

Q: And they do confirm this, but we will get back to that. How long were you at section D?

A: Until November 15, 1943.

Q: What was Gluecks' position in section D?

A: He was Group Section Chief.

Q: What was the task of Section D?

A: Supervision over all concentration camps.

Q: And also over foreign concentration camps – correct?

A: What do you mean by foreign?

Q: Outside of German territory, for example, Poland.

A: Auschwitz.

Q: Any other camps?

A: Auschwitz and Lublin.

Q: Who was Gluecks' acting deputy?

A: Lt-Colonel Maurer who later became supervisor.

Q: Since when was Maurer Gluecks' acting deputy?

A: Actually always, even when I was signing documents.

Q: You must admit that your last answer was a contradiction that any child could conclude.

A: Why?

Q: You say it was Maurer, but on paper it was you, yourself. You know for a fact that you were Gluecks' acting deputy.

A: Acting deputy is the wrong term.

Q: Tell me how would you phrase this?

A: Acting deputy only when he was absent, but even then I had no authorization to make decisions independently.

Q: Gluecks took a vacation, what year was that?

A: Summer of 1943, at which time I went to Pohl twice a week for signatures of important matters.

Q: What sort of matters were these?

A: Important orders that pertained to the camps, various orders or directives. I was not authorized to give commands or orders.

Q: Before Gluecks took leave did he say approximately something like this: 'If any important decisions come up while I'm gone, concerning section D, I want you to go to Pohl; go to him with these matters'?

A: I had to go there twice a week.

Q: Was that the only time Gluecks was gone?

A: He was gone a couple days when he'd visit the camps.

Q: I didn't ask how long he was gone during the week, but I wanted to know if the summer of 1943 was the only time he was gone?

A: He only took one long vacation, the short vacations …

Q: In other words, is it a fact, that Gluecks arbitrarily, as Inspector of Concentration Camps took numerous trips to execute his business as Inspector of Concentration Camps?

A: That is correct.

Q: In such cases you were the person who took his place, and when important matters came up, you took these to Pohl for a decision?

A: I had to present him with every matter.

Q: Can you answer this question with 'yes', as I have phrased it?

A: Yes, but they were not my decisions to make. I was more like a staff supervisor – supervisor over personnel.

Q: So it is actually incorrect, Liebehenschel, what you said to me before, that Maurer in Gluecks' absence, would go to Pohl to discuss these matters?

A: This he also did, as a matter of fact Maurer was there when he took over as deputy.

Q: When did Maurer become official deputy?

A: Officially the moment I left for Auschwitz.

Q: In what year?

A: November of 1943.

Q: So November 1943, Maurer took over your position and became Gluecks' deputy?

A: Officially.[5]

Papa's farewell letter written to us in Oranienburg:

November 9, 1943

Dear Brigittchen, Dear Atilein, Dear Bärbel,

Now I have to leave you and don't know when I'll see you again. How I'd like to have taken you into my arms and given you a great big hug but you went to the theater today of all days, when I have to go away. I had forgotten that the performance was today. Now I have to leave without seeing you once more. That hurts so much, because I love you with all my heart and will hold you always within my heart and soul with great love. Stay good and dear as you always were and don't create too many worries for your mother.

You my dear Brigittchen, will soon be a grown up girl and will understand later, as all people, that life can be troublesome and many people who are not bad have to go along a difficult path through life. This is how you must also look upon my life, the life of your father, who always did everything for you and who will be there for you always and forever, my dear children. If you ever need me in any way, I will help you where I can, as before. If you yearn for me then come to me. My door to my house and heart will always be open to you.

Turn into good and upright Germans as I have always tried to be. Don't forget me. I will never forget you. And when you fold your innocent little hands in prayer, then ask God that I may stay healthy.

I take you firmly into my arms and give you many heartfelt kisses. Stay healthy, dear and good.

Always, Your Papa

Papa did manage to see us one last time, but it was a sad day when we said goodbye to our father. He had sent tickets for a stage play of *Hansel and Gretel*. Brigitte and Antje attended the afternoon matinee. Father had forgotten it was the same day he was to leave for Auschwitz. He didn't want to miss saying goodbye and so sent his large official car with his chauffeur, who came to pick up my sisters from the theater before the performance was over.

Antje didn't comprehend then that it was a final parting and that we would not see Papa again. At that time all she could think of was to return to the theater to see the end of the play. On the way, they stopped to pick up Ilse and me. I was recovering from a near-fatal infection of chicken pox, but they bundled me up in a blanket and we all drove to Papa's apartment. It was a very affectionate farewell, but being only nine months old I have no memories of any details, or how I may have felt during these last moments with my father. I only know what I've been told.

My father enticed me, holding up a candy bar as he stretched his arms out toward me; from across the room I toddled over into what would be our last embrace. Today I still wonder, and the same question fills my mind: did he look at me with regret and longing or was I simply one last detail to be attended to? And finally, is the repeating dream that I have had of my father later in adulthood some kind of contact from our last meeting?

Two arms extend through the heavens, long black gloves cover the hands. They are reaching for me and I can't resist their strength … the instant our hands touch, I sense an overwhelming force of love and peace and I believe he is communicating with me.

Orders for father's disciplinary transfer to Auschwitz came as the result of my parents' divorce and his 'illicit love affair'; this was not considered acceptable behavior for an SS officer.

Dieter went with our father; he felt sorry for him but also hoped our parents might reconcile and we would reunite as a family. Father and Dieter left for Auschwitz that evening. We three girls would never see our father again after this night.

Chapter Four

Auschwitz

Your father was a dear and admirable human being, ambitious and very intelligent. He would suffer with excruciating headaches and become very ill every time a new transport of prisoners arrived at Auschwitz-Birkenau. As Kommandant he had to watch the misery as the trains arrived. He would take long showers, as if to wash away the filth and horror ... he could no longer face the ugly realities of the word ... his world ... as Kommandant of Auschwitz.

Anneliese, May 1994

By 1995 I had moved into the small house in Lake Elizabeth, California. The years following my divorce would often prove to be very trying, but every day seemed like a new learning experience and it was a time of tremendous growth. Writing and research was a daily occurrence. Often the circumstances in my personal life seemed confusing and doubtful while the vulnerable child within me silently cried for safety and security – reason enough for me to give up. However, an inexplicable driving force kept me focused in only one direction – to write my book – and nothing was going to stop me. Gradually my self-awareness evolved, as I began to embrace the truth of my past.

The audio tapes my sister Brigitte had recorded lacked the documentation and facts I needed to fill in the gaps about my father's career. So began my quest, and through my intense research I have developed a substantial record of my father's life and deeds. I pursued inquiries with Holocaust research centers, museums, archives in Germany, Poland, Israel as well as the United States. I combed the transcripts of the testimonies given before the tribunals at Nuremberg and Auschwitz. Soon I was corresponding with camp survivors and later we would meet.

I became progressively more efficient at translating many of the documents into English. However, much to my disappointment, the transcripts from the Auschwitz Archives arrived written in the Polish language and consequently there were more delays. A translator had to be found who would render the witness testimonies into German, which I then translated into English.

I was horrified when I read that several of these witnesses recalled my father as just another SS officer, an oppressor in an ironed uniform and polished boots; yet I was filled with a sense of relief, knowing others remembered his lenient policies and claimed he gave them hope and even saved many lives. In addition, I poured through every book I could lay my hands on, at the library and the book stores, that recorded the Second World War in Germany, and some mentioned my father. Often my sister Antje would send me newly published German releases about the Nazi era. Although knowing him as a father was still an impossible goal, he was gradually becoming real in my eyes.

The transition from a life of secrecy to openness was slowly unfolding. Through my correspondence with numerous archives I had no choice but to candidly admit, for the first time in my life, that I was the youngest daughter of Arthur Liebehenschel. Surprisingly, it was easier than I had anticipated. That was the first time in my life I found that I was not ashamed to disclose that I was the Kommandant's daughter, and each new piece of information brought my father into sharper focus and defined my own life more clearly.

Transcripts of Pretrial Interrogation at Nuremberg:
U.S. Military Chief of Counsel for War Crimes/SS Section
Taken of: Arthur Wilhelm Liebehenschel – by E. Rigney
Date: September 18, 1946 – [continued]

Q: When did you start your position at Auschwitz?
A: November 15, 1943.
Q: Why were you transferred to Auschwitz?
A: It was concerning a family matter. It was a disciplinary relocation.
Q: Will you briefly explain this?
A: Must I answer this question or may I remain silent?
Q: No. You held a position in section D that would be considered a good position within the administration. You had a position, and you yourself said you were acting deputy of the section D Group Leader. One could rightfully say, that your transfer to Auschwitz was not a promotion?
A: And that it wasn't, I had said it was a punishment.
Q: Why were you disciplinarily relocated?
A: I had an unhappy relationship with my wife, and I wanted a divorce. That is, my wife divorced me.
Q: Is that also the reason you received no further promotions?
A: Yes, first of all that, and presumably also because I ran Auschwitz differently than the others.
Q: As you arrived in Auschwitz, how many Camp Kommandants were there?
A: Three Kommandants.
Q: That was in November 1943?
A: Yes.
Q: Did each of these Kommandants have equal authority?
A: Each man was independent in his own camp.
Q: And to whom did these three Kommandants have to answer to?
A: First of all Group Section D and then Pohl.

Q: Describe your duties as Camp Kommandant of the Camp I in Auschwitz?

A: There were rules that had to be followed according to the Camp regulations that every Kommandant knew, that is the high command of the camp. What specifically did you want to know?

Q: Alright, so let's not pretend ignorance. You said that the camp had rules and regulations, that is obvious. I want to know: what direct duties the Camp Kommandant was commissioned to carry out, which specific duties?

A: The camp Kommandant had to see to it that the prisoners were cared for and were designated their work detail. He was responsible for their clothing and billeting, and for their decent treatment. He had to follow up on these things and it was a daily task. This is what I did at Auschwitz; that is proven not only from me but many prisoners who came of their own free will, not people I called. They were foreigners, Germans, Jews, even Jewish prisoners who were not only in my camp but have also spoken for me at Dachau.

Q: How many inmates did you have in camp I?

A: Fluctuating between 13,000 and 14,000.

Q: You say 'fluctuating', between what numbers did it fluctuate?

A: Often they needed forces to go to the new armament camps and it was sometimes 300 to 400 that were taken; when this happened they were also pulled out of camp I, the original camp.

Q: Camp I was the 'original'?

A: It was the 'Original Camp', the best camp.

Q: Do you want to explain the concept 'Original Camp'?

A: It was the first camp, it was the camp established first.

Q: Are you saying that camp I was the main camp?

A: That is not what I'm saying, it was not the main camp.

Q: Why was it called the 'Original Camp'?

A: I just explained that.

Q: That was not the official description?

A: No, the official description was 'Camp I'. When I came to Auschwitz, camp II was Birkenau and camp III was Mederitz.

Q: In which of these three camps did the 'gassing' take place?

A: Camp II had the facility.

Q: What sort of facilities were there?

A: There was a crematorium there.

Q: When was this crematorium built?

A: That I don't know.

Q: Think about it for a moment.

A: That had to be there when I came. It had to be built earlier.

Q: Who drew up the plans for this crematorium?

A: I don't know that either.

Q: That is not true, and now I'll tell you exactly why it isn't true. I'll tell you exactly why you know of this. The crematorium, as all equipment for the concentration camps, was under the supervision of section D. You weren't just part of section I in Group D, but you were part of the staff, and for this reason you had to know what was going on. You sit here and mean to tell me, that you didn't know who drew up the plans for the construction of the crematorium?

A: No, I didn't know that. As a matter of fact, it wasn't section D; it was built by section C.

Q: Then it is a known fact to you, that section C was responsible instead of section D, for the building of the crematorium?

A: I only had outside contact with Section C.

Q: I repeat: Is it a known fact to you, that section C was responsible for the construction of the crematorium?

A: No, I don't know that.

Q: When you were there who was supervisor of section C?

A: SS Brigadier General Kemmler.

Q: At Auschwitz, did you see the trains that came from the east, and other points of Europe?

A: No.

Q: How long were you at Auschwitz?

A: From November 15, 1943 to April 5, 1944.

Q: And at that time four to five trains came weekly into Auschwitz, which held 1,500 to 2,000 people, that were sent to the Auschwitz gas chambers?

A: At that time there were no trains.

Q: And you were Camp Kommandant and want to tell me now, that you never saw any of the trains?

A: I was there for four and a half months, and at that time no trains came. Hoess was still there the beginning of December, what he did I don't know. I didn't concern myself with it as he had his special assignment. At my time the 'Action Hoess' let up. Someone else was to be appointed and after I left there then this whole matter resumed. In any event, I was not involved with this.

Q: Did you know Hoess well?

A: Mostly through the take-over of the camp.

Q: You took over the Camp I from Hoess?

A: He had the combined command of all three camps at Auschwitz.

Q: So it is assumed, that he briefed you on your position there?

A: For the Camp I, of course, this is the camp I took over from him.

Q: Did you have the jurisdiction over the other two camps?

A: No.

Q: Why not?

A: That was ordered by Berlin, before I went there.

Q: Who was responsible for that?

A: Pohl, he placed each commander and gave each their assignment.

Q: So, the new organization at Auschwitz was assigned by Pohl?

A: Through him or the motivation of the Reichsführer.

Q: You just said it was Pohl?

A: Specifically Pohl, he gave us this assignment.

Q: To make this clear: It was Pohl's actions that the camps were separated?

A: That the Auschwitz camp was separated.

Q: Were you a personal friend of Hoess?

A: No.

Q: How long have you known Hoess?

A: I knew him only through hearsay.

Q: How often did you see him?

A: When he came to the conferences.

Q: In Berlin?

A: That's where we were sent.

Q: Pohl sent for you?

A: Pohl and Hoess.

Q: How often did you speak with Hoess?

A: I don't know that.

Q: Briefly describe how the gassings were done at Auschwitz?

A: That I don't know, I didn't experience this.

Q: You're trying to tell us that at the time you were Camp Kommandant that not one single human being was gassed?

A: In any event, I had nothing to do with this.

Q: That was not the question. The question is: to your knowledge at this time, were there any people sent to the gas chamber?

A: That I don't know, I have no knowledge about this.

Q: Now we come to the end of your assignment at Auschwitz. How was it you left Auschwitz?

A: I was discharged April 5th.

Q: Who was your successor?

A: SS Captain Baer, adjutant to Pohl, succeeded me.

Q: His first name?

A: I don't know.

Q: Why were you discharged?

A: I had already said it was concerning a personal family matter. I then had met a woman I wanted to marry. Pohl would not grant me permission to marry, as the woman had been imprisoned by the Gestapo after having been picked up by the secret police, as it was apparent she had a relationship with a Jew. The actual case was: that she had grown up with Jewish children, and when they were reunited in 1935, he and his sister met with her in a cafe, at which time someone informed on them. I was not granted permission to marry her, and the reason for denial in their eyes was the fact she was not worthy of being the wife of an officer and a high leading official. Shortly thereafter came my discharge.

Q: That was April of 1944?

A: Yes.

Q: Then what did you do?

A: Then I had a relapse of the heart condition and was treated at 'Kattowitz' for three weeks, and then was sent to Lublin.[1]

Together with her audiotapes, Brigitte had compiled a file consisting of photos, father's letters to us children, and an article out of the old German magazine, *Welt Bild*, dated 23 December 1960. The article was called: 'The Biggest Crime of our Century' by Thomas Gnielka, naming SS officers still pursued at that time for crimes perpetrated at Auschwitz. A full-length photo of Father in uniform was captioned: 'The most humane of the Kommandants at Auschwitz.' Excerpts from the article cited:

> Rudolf Hoess was transferred to Oranienburg. To take his place came Obersturmbannfuehrer (Lt. Colonel) Arthur Liebehenschel, as Kommandant to the camp. Before Hoess was hung, after his trial in Warsaw, he wrote this about his successor, Liebehenschel. Hoess' records make it clear that after Liebehenschel's arrival, there was a sense of 'breathing easy' among prisoners. Hoess talks of Liebehenschel being a paper pusher, and not having practical knowledge, therefore was a 'failure'. For Hoess to call Liebehenschel 'A Failure as Kommandant' is very clear, as Hoess was under Heinrich Himmler's orders to keep the exterminating machinery of Auschwitz flowing continually and in Hoess' eyes, Liebehenschel was the one who poured considerable sand into the gears of his perfect works.

The article continues:

> It is of ironic fate that Liebehenschel, particularly this 'The most humane Kommandant of Auschwitz', should be caught in the trap of his own system. Therefore the improvements for the prisoners were not of long duration, as Liebehenschel's personal destiny would be entwined with those of his Jewish prisoners. His problems stemmed from the Nazi crime of 'Rassen-schande' [race-defilement]. In the beginning of 1944, the new Kommandant asked permission to marry, going through the high command of the 'Reichssicherheits-Hauptamt'. Research done by the 'Rassenamt', the Race-Bureau, found a stain. The SS found proof that his fiancée, this girl, had previously been in close relationship with a Jew, in Cologne. She was picked up by the Secret Police and brought to a Gestapo Interrogation Cellar. She was kept all night until she was physically and mentally broken, to confess to her friendship with a Jewish boy. As a result of this 'race-defilement', she was sent to prison where she had to spend quite some time. Richard Baer was sent to talk some sense into Liebehenschel, but did his best not to, as Baer himself wanted the position of Kommandant of Auschwitz. It was a frustrating situation for Liebehenschel to continue the relationship with this woman, as Baer's reports and Liebehenschel's refusal to cooperate, offended the SS and the Gestapo. Baer's report was soon in their hands (he was not willing to give up this woman) and as a result Liebehenschel had orders for a disciplinary relocation to Lublin.[2]

Consequently Rudolf Hoess, formerly the Kommandant at Sachsenhausen and our neighbor there, was also father's predecessor at the Auschwitz camp. Hoess was transferred to take a higher position in Oranienburg and our father took over as Kommandant of Auschwitz I in November 1943. Without particular under-standing or tolerance for one another, the lives of Rudolf Hoess and my father would strangely parallel throughout their careers within the ranks of the SS and the framework of concentration camps.

Rudolf Hoess, the pioneer of Auschwitz, was praised by his superiors for his 'great contribution'. In 1941 Himmler, having risen in rank within the Party, appointed Hoess for the 'secret' task of establishing the Auschwitz Concentration Camp, in an isolated area in Upper Silesia, to deal with the 'Jewish Problem'. The Führer presumably ordered the 'Final Solution' in 1942 at the Wannsee Conference and it was to be carried out by the SS.

Hoess constructed the extermination facilities, gas chambers and ovens. He even planted trees and flowers around the crematories. He was very pleased with his own accomplishments and Berlin showed its appreciation by promoting him to Obersturmbannführer-SS, Lt-Colonel.

He said in his autobiography: 'I was trained to obey orders without even think-ing, and disobeying never occurred to anyone.'[3]

Above the main gate entrance to the Auschwitz camp was a large sinister inscription that read 'Arbeit Macht Frei' (Work Will Set You Free). A four-meter high electric-charged barbed-wire fence surrounded it. Auschwitz was one of the largest of the Nazi concentration camps, thirty-seven miles west of Krakow, in Polish eastern Upper Silesia. It was the most extensive of the forced labor camps.

In October of 1941 the second much larger section of the camp was built. It was 1.9 miles from the original camp and it was called Auschwitz II, or Birkenau. Surrounding villages were destroyed in order to build additional sec-tions of the Auschwitz camp. It covered an area of 15.5 square miles, which was declared a prohibited area. Extensive work was started on the barracks and other facilities of Auschwitz II-Birkenau. This camp was known for its most cruel and inhumane conditions. The crematoria and gas chambers were located at Birkenau and it had its own Kommandant. A quote by Sim Kessel, who wrote *Hanged in Auschwitz*, mentioned: 'Auschwitz I – main camp had a relatively good reputation among prisoners in satellite camps, known was the climate of terror in the nearby Birkenau.'

In June of 1940, the first transport of prisoners arrived at Auschwitz. Among that transport was Janusz Mlynarski, age seventeen, who I have come to know and respect. The most feared and insidious of buildings was Block 11, for the more severe punishments. Next to that building stood the 'Black Wall', where regular executions of prisoners took place.

The Kommandants were instructed to follow orders for camp procedure set forth by Himmler and most of them had no problem to do so in order to win his approval. The original camp was known as the 'Stammlager' or Auschwitz I. My father was made Kommandant of this camp.

When my father became the Kommandant in November 1943, documentation shows that he released many prisoners from this Block 11 and put an end to the executions against the Black Wall. He stopped the routine 'selections' and relaxed camp discipline, not only in the interest of work productivity, but it also appears he cared about the prisoners. He shortened roll calls and gave orders that night-shift workers were not to be deprived of sleep during the day and the barbaric standing cells were demolished.

There is no doubt, however, that Father felt a great loyalty and pride toward the SS and believed in the strict military standards of the movement. He was a patriot with a true love for his country. Although he respected authority and did follow certain standing orders and regulations which were set forth for the Kommandants by SS Headquarters Berlin, he took it upon himself to initiate some new rules and laws of his own, which made life easier for his prisoners, but for which he himself would suffer retribution.

Auschwitz I consisted of twenty-eight red brick barracks, of which four were Krankenbau (Infirmaries). The prison hospital (HKB) was where prisoner Wladyslaw Fejkiel, a Polish doctor, spent four years in the 'Stammlager' (main camp), first as caretaker, then as doctor, and later as elder of the HKB. He testified at my father's trial, stating that conditions did not improve at the hospital while my father was Kommandant. It was here that Fejkiel became acquainted with prisoner # 355 Janusz Mlynarski, who was also a caretaker at that time, and with whom I was fortunate enough to have an interview in the fall of 1998.

These so-called hospitals were overcrowded, with unbelievably primitive and unhygienic conditions. Block 7 in Birkenau was called 'the waiting room to death' where the stench of excrement came from the overflowing urinals. The most common cause of death here came from widespread dysentery. The quarantined sections held patients with infectious diseases such as typhus, spotted fever, TB and more. Many of these people recovered only to be sent to the gas chamber at a later time.

There was also the camp kitchen, a canteen, offices, an officers' club, even a brothel. The prostitutes were younger prisoners. It was patronized mostly by the SS and some privileged Capos (German former criminals). Orders were to pay two marks; one was to go to the prostitute and one was deposited in a special Reich bank account. Taken from official bulletins written by my father, it cites he gave the strictest orders that the Bordello of Auschwitz was off limits to all SS officers, punishable by arrest.

The warehouses, known as the 'Canada' section, held stocked crates of the personal effects which were taken from the incarcerated prisoners. They contained gold, silver, rich clothing, diamonds and other precious stones. The Capos were in charge of sorting these valuables and every one of them was guilty of stealing and trading. This made the camp, as well as the Third Reich, very affluent.

Prisoners were made to work unloading freight cars stacked with cabbages and turnips. Many women worked at various nearby poultry farms, but the main objective was the forced labor in the armament factories. The Buna Works was a synthetic oil and rubber factory at Auschwitz III. The laborers were from Birkenau.

An ordinary day for the prisoners was waking at dawn, straightening their pallets, morning roll call, journey to work, hours of hard labor, standing in line for a meal, return to camp, block inspection, and evening roll call. The Kommandant's and the staff's working hours were nine-hour days, four and a half hours on Saturday, and Sundays off on rotation. The prisoners' diet consisted of, in the morning, hot colored water called coffee; noon was rutabaga soup and at night a chunk of black bread, sometimes with a bit of sausage or margarine. The Kommandants and staff ate relatively well. The officers' club was stocked with Champagne, beer and wines.

In the earlier years in these camps, living conditions, housing, food and working conditions were tolerable. Then, the inmates consisted of opponents of the Nazi regime. Hitler wanted to 're-educate' them to his ideological indoctrination. The goal was to have these opponents support their Nazi movement. They may have started out as 'educational camps', but later came the criminals, prostitutes, homosexuals, vagrants, gypsies, clergymen, Jehovah's Witnesses and pacifists, who were all considered a threat to society.

The arrest and imprisonment of Jews, merely because they were Jews, did not happen until the pogrom of 10 November 1938 known as 'Kristallnacht'. The largest number killed in the camps were Jews, but many of the prisoners were not Jewish.

In 1942 the Auschwitz and Majdanek Concentration Camps were set up as extermination facilities, to comply with Hitler's 'Final Solution'. Special freight trains with prisoners started arriving at Birkenau daily. They stopped at a siding track that was built within this camp. Jews and others not fit to work were exterminated. Epidemics and starvation also claimed thousands of lives.

This issue will always remain the most disturbing in my mind as my father did have knowledge about the exterminations at the camp. Evidently his authority was limited and even though he tried to dissuade his superiors in Berlin, which did delay the actions of their orders for a time, it was they who made the final decisions.

Oswald Kaduk later testified using information given to him by camp doctor Wirths: 'Liebehenschel at that time went to Berlin to make an effort on behalf of the prisoners, to keep the transport from going to the gas chamber, but Berlin ordered them to be gassed. The Selection was carried out by Arbeitsdienstfuehrer Sell.'[4]

The camp command consisted of several departments which were divided into those of Administration, Personnel, Communication, Transportation, Equipment, Mail, Supplies, Kitchen, Health and other matters. The camp Kommandant had assistants with the titles of deputy, adjutant, master sergeant, medical and education officers and a legal and fire officer. His success as Kommandant depended a great deal on the supervision of his staff. The Nazi staff was aided by a number of privileged prisoners who were offered better food and conditions and had more chance of survival.

Among those chosen for these special assignments were those for the 'Sonderkommando'; this group was made up of strong young men selected at the ramp upon their arrival. It was their job to transport the corpses to the ovens of the crematorium. In many cases these men even came upon the corpses of family members and friends which they also had to place into the ovens. In order to exist and function they became less than human themselves, left with little feeling or sensitivity.

Those prisoners who gave the deadly Phenol injections were rewarded for the gruesome task with extra food and bonuses of alcoholic beverages. The prisoners were driven to the lowest form of humanity, to an animalistic sense of survival. It was not unusual for one prisoner to kill another for a piece of bread. The frail, emaciated, almost skeletal, prisoners known as 'Muselmann' were a familiar sight as they moved like the walking dead around the camp. Completely drained of their physical vitality they had lost all human desire for life.

Each prison compound had its own commanding officer. Each living quarter or 'Block' had its 'Blockführer' or corporal or sergeant. A deputy oversaw the prisoner division and was in charge when the Kommandant was absent. Capos were the German convicts in charge of the prisoners and they were categorized by the SS according to national origin. Each category was identified by the color of the badges: Political–Red, Criminal–Green.

My father's aide was named Zoller, whom he knew and requested to be transferred from Mauthausen Concentration Camp; he was known to be brutal. SS deputy Franz Hofmann was put in charge of the prisoners, and it was said that he and my father together caused a sense of 'breathing easy' among the prisoners.

Kommandants were responsible for everything that occurred in the camps, except the Political Department, which operated as an extension of the Gestapo. As of 1942, they were no longer responsible for the physicians and medical staff who had become independently responsible for the Selections. Much of the Kommandant's time was spent dealing with administrative matters, endless memoranda and reports. Many of the camps' Kommandants later claimed to have just done their duties, by following the written laws and guidelines for the camp as delegated by Himmler, and this gave many an outlet for their sadistic perversions and brutalities.

By 1943 there were 18,000 prisoners at my father's camp Auschwitz I, as compared to the 140,000 prisoners at their neighboring camp, Birkenau.

The Kommandants' salaries were generous, but not excessive. Their residence, uniforms, board and that of their family, were supplied by the camp. My father had available to him the services of cooks, servants, gardeners and drivers. The housing was usually better than some on the outside. Part of my father's income went for alimony payments and child support, which was awarded to my mother after their divorce.

My father's SS personnel file contained several documents, which showed other wages paid to him by the SS. A subsidy of 260 Reichsmarks was paid after my birth, in February 1943. The document stated my name and that I was his fourth child. 110 Reichsmarks was paid to him after the birth of my half-brother Hans-Dieter, stating he was his fifth child, and my father received a 500 Reichsmark bonus for Christmas, known as the 'Julfest', in 1943. As a result of the evacuation of the Lublin Concentration Camp, my father was no longer eligible for the 200 Reichsmark expense account he was receiving monthly.

Himmler would come to make regular inspections of the camp. In 1943 he made it every Kommandant's duty to watch every execution at his camp. My father stopped the executions and soon became known as being 'too soft' in the eyes of his superiors.

The investigations by Konrad Morgan into the corruption of the concentration camps had started in 1943, another factor which contributed to the change of camp personnel and my father's take-over, and from there on more lenient camp regulations were initiated.

When my father began his new assignment he quickly came to realize it was not simply commanding a concentration camp, but it was also about politics and the domination of power among the ranks of the SS and the prisoners as well. He was faced with what would be an ongoing struggle for authority within the camp.

Under Hoess' leadership the SS Political Department (Politische Abteilung – an extension of the Gestapo) had been given the power over the prisoners. They used this power to terrorize the camp and the fate of the prisoners was left in their hands. This encouraged and reinforced the organization of the underground resistance movement. This movement consisted of prisoners and their various groups of conspirators who worked together with the Polish resistance and their contacts outside of the camp. The group of resistance prisoners leaked news to the outside world of the exterminations and crimes committed at Auschwitz which prompted Himmler to transfer Hoess to another position.

Stanislaw Dubiel was the prisoner-gardener at the Villa Hoess at Auschwitz who testified at the August 1946 hearing that he overheard pieces of a conversation between Himmler and Hoess in the garden. Himmler mentioned at that time that Hoess had to leave Auschwitz because the British Broadcasting System had aired too much on the murders of prisoners at the camp. Max Grabner testified from the Krakow prison that Hoess, although praised for his accomplishments, had to leave for 'political reasons'.

Release of the prisoners in Block 11 upon my father's arrival in November 1943 caused a definite dispute between him and the SS Political Department, who had been responsible for the incarceration of most of these prisoners in this bunker. As a result, SS men were prohibited from putting prisoners into Block 11, or arbitrarily killing any of them, without the consent of their Kommandant, and so the capacity and influence of the Political Department within the camp was considerably decreased.

Among those prisoners released by my father was the communist Ludwig Worl, a political prisoner incarcerated in concentration camps for many years and confined to the bunker in Block 11 since 28 August 1943. My father made Worl an Elder Capo calling him 'a quiet and decent man'. In the book *Auschwitz* by Bernd Naumann, Worl was quoted as stating: 'Liebehenschel was replaced by the SS because he was too soft. He stopped the 'selections' and had the notorious standing cells demolished.'[5]

The acting director of the Political Department, Grabner, was arrested, which was the result of the findings of Konrad Morgan's investigation into camp corruption, and he was replaced by my father with SS Second Lt Schurz. Further investigations also uncovered widespread corruption under Hoess at the Auschwitz Camp. Gold was smuggled by members of Hoess' staff.

Prisoners belonging to the resistance movement cooperated with my father, making available the names of informers and spies for the Political Department. The widespread conspiracy involved informers for the Political Department and members of the resistance movement. Among them were the prisoners named Stanislaw Kowalski and Stanislaw Dorosiewicz; the latter was the well-known and feared Block Elder of Block 15, the head confidant of the Political Department. The political prisoner Hermann Langbein of the Resistance was also the office clerk to the garrison doctor, Dr Wirths, and was very active within the resistance movement.

The day before Langbein was released from Block 11, Josef Cyrankiewicz, member of the underground resistance, was placed in the bunker after a wig and street clothing were found hidden in his bunk, and it came to the surface that he had planned an escape. He related to Langbein his knowledge of the informer network, their methods and of the informer Dorosiewicz, who was behind the intended escape. Langbein, who was the secretary to Dr Wirths, with whom he had a good relationship, confronted the doctor. It concerned his inside information that was told to him by Cyrankiewicz. He secretly hoped he would be able to help the cause of the resistance. Dr Wirths listened eagerly about the conspiracy and how the informers were causing unrest within the camp. Wirths then asked Langbein to write down what he knew, saying, 'I believe this will be of great interest to Lt-Colonel Liebehenschel'. He then took the report written by Langbein and drove off, but returned shortly saying, 'I saw the Kommandant and he was pleased with your statement. He is against the use of informers. He wondered what you suggest should be done about the concerned informer.'

Josef Cyrankiewicz from Block 11 was asked to report to the Kommandant, my father. Cyrankiewicz knew that the Political Department was instigating a plan to discredit my father's lenient policies, which would then recover authority for the Political Department throughout the camp.

On 21 December 1943 the planned conspiracy by the Political Department was carried out with the help of two prisoners, camp Capo and informer Stanislaw Dorosiewicz and a Jew named Hersz Kurcweig, both from the 'Canada' section. As arranged in advance, they made their escape and murdered SS Private Peter Jarosiewitsch who had accompanied them. This provocation was to and incite repression and retaliation against the prisoners to implicate my father's 'soft' policy.

Hermann Langbein wrote about this incident in his book *Menschen in Auschwitz*. He was born in Vienna in 1912. A member of the Spanish Brigade in 1938, he ended up as a prisoner at Dachau and in 1942 was transferred to Auschwitz, where he spent two years as a leader of the International Underground Resistance Movement within the camp.

The following quotations come from Hermann Langbein's book; recollections of his personal contact with my father:

> The next day there was heated excitement throughout the camp. It is now known that Dorosiewicz escaped and the entire area was being searched.
>
> Dr. Wirths asked Langbein with nervous excitement, 'Have you heard? It is the informer that you wrote about yesterday in your report which I took to the Kommandant.'
>
> Later Dr. Wirths telephoned Langbein from the Kommandant's office. He was told to come immediately and to bring his shorthand pad, that the Kommandant wished to see him.
>
> Langbein: The Sergeant in the outer office takes me at once into the Kommandant's office, through padded double doors, 'Prisoner # 60-3-55 reporting for duty'.
>
> Inside [there is] dark furniture, a large, dark desk, behind it sits Kommandant Liebehenschel, across from him Dr. Wirths with his back to me. I feel my heart pounding. My nerves are not what they used to be.
>
> Kommandant: 'So there you are. The information you gave me yesterday was very valuable.' A short pause, then Wirths says: 'Langbein, tell the Kommandant about the informer in the camp, as you told it to me, yes, go ahead and talk'.
>
> Langbein: 'Lt.-Colonel I have a favor to ask first.'
>
> Kommandant: 'What is it?'
>
> Langbein: 'May I speak as though I were not a prisoner?'
>
> A small pause, but not too long.
>
> Kommandant: 'Yes, speak freely.'
>
> Langbein: 'Then I request not to be asked where my information came from. We prisoners know many things that we are not supposed to know.'
>
> Kommandant: 'I am not interested in that.'
>
> Langbein: 'This informer is not only today responsible for the escapes of the Poles, but for some time now has been intimidating and blackmailing them with his threats. I don't know if you can prevent this Lt.-Colonel, the Political Dept. has many varied methods. I myself have been in the Bunker for two months.'
>
> Kommandant: 'Why were you in the Bunker?'
>
> Langbein: 'Because there was suspicion of a political action.' The Kommandant frowns.
>
> Langbein expressed his concern that his testimony would become known by the Political Section.
>
> Kommandant: 'You forget that I am Kommandant.' He is annoyed and continues: 'Nothing will happen to the Polish prisoners, I myself will see to that. As long as I am the Kommandant, you are not going to be returned to the Bunker.' He says to Dr. Wirths: 'Captain, if anything should happen, inform me at once.' Wirths nods his head, 'Jawohl'.

Langbein described to my father the methods and activities of the Political Department and the involvement of the camp informers.

Later, Wirths told Langbein that the Kommandant wanted a list of all the informers known to him. A list was compiled and a few days later a transport consisting of all the named informers of the Political Dept was scheduled to be shipped to the Flossenburg Concentration Camp. No one understood how this came about, especially not the informers. Then a sense of 'breathing easy' was felt throughout the camp. The action was known throughout the camp as 'Explicit orders of the Kommandant'.[6]

In a letter sent from the resistance movement within the camp to the PWOK (Committee for the Assistance of Concentration Camp Prisoners) in Krakow, it was said, 'There is in progress a quiet but bitter struggle between the Political Department and the Kommandant.'[7]

It was my father's intention to put an end to the network of spies within the Political Department and hinder their brutalities toward prisoners. The result of Dorosiewicz's escape and the murder of the SS man did not bring any repercussion for the prisoners, as promised by my father to Cyrankiewicz and Langbein. Cyrankiewicz was released from the bunker. Both of these men survived their Auschwitz ordeal. Langbein went on to write several books on Auschwitz and the resistance in the concentration camps and Cyrankiewicz was premier of Poland for several terms, the last from 1954–70.

Word came in January 1944 that there was to be another 'Selection' of many Jews. One thousand Jews were in the 'bath barracks' waiting to be sent to the gas chamber. Hermann Langbein intervened with the help of Dr Wirths, who then went to take this up with my father. Wirths said to Langbein, 'The Kommandant was aware of the transport. It was not done behind his back as you suspected, Langbein. The action was a direct order from Berlin, from the "Arbeitseinsatz". There was a communication that there were too many prisoners in the camp who were unable for work detail.'

Langbein writes, 'It is unfortunate that the successor of Hoess, Arthur Liebehenschel didn't write memoirs as Hoess did when he was imprisoned. It would have been interesting to hear what this man of high command perceived of the annihilation camp, whose impact was made clear by his predecessor.'[8]

Hoess testified at the 1947 trial, 'Through the destruction of the informer network in the camp, Liebehenschel had helped the prison resistance movement and given it the means for further development, making him unsuitable for his job.'[9]

With the onset of my father's command at Auschwitz, he posted written ordinances revised every several days in the form of an official bulletin. He established specific procedures and conditions, which were in accordance with strict military regulations. Some were merely notices of social events to take place within the camp, all of which gave a broader picture of what daily life was actually like for my father and the others who made up this world within the walls of Auschwitz. With a few obvious exceptions, as one reads through these pages of his routine camp regulations, it is almost believable it could have been a military prison camp anywhere.

Here are some of the various topics taken from official documented bulletins written by my father during the time he was Kommandant, the months of November 1943 through April 1944.

From the Senior SS Officer
Location: Auschwitz
November 11, 1943

Standortbefehl Nr. 50/43
[Official Ordinances]

1. As of today, by orders of the Reichsführer SS-Chief of the German police, I take over the command of the Concentration Camp Auschwitz from my predecessor SS Lt.-Colonel Rudolf Hoess.
The order set forth by the Chief of the SS Wirtschafts-Verwaltungshauptamt, SS Lt.-General and General of the Waffen SS Oswald Pohl, for the division of the Auschwitz Concentration Camp into three separate Camps

Camp I (Original)
Camp II (Women)
Camp III (Satellite)

will be carried out within the next few days.

2. Furthermore to go into immediate effect is my position of duty as SS Senior Officer of the SS Standortbereich (domain) Auschwitz.

The SS Senior Officer
SS Lt.-Colonel
A. Liebehenschel
Adjutant – SS Captain Zoller

November 17, 1943

Addressing the Kommandant:

It has come to my attention that Officers, Non-Commissioned Officers and Enlisted men are addressing me as Kommandant. I prefer to be called by my rank only.

Special Collection for the WHW:

I have been notified that the members of the SS [Totenkopfsturmbannes] as of Nov. 9, 1943 collected an amount of RM 15,221.60.
I hereby want to fully acknowledge the members for their proud accomplishment. Also this action reveals the spirit of the troops.

Entertainment for the Troops:

The following events will take place during the month of November 1943.

Tuesday, November 23, at 20:00 hrs.

Performance in the State Theater of Marish-Ostrau, 'Der Strohm' – Play by Max Halbe

Friday, November 26, at 20:00 hrs.

Performance in the Operahouse Kattowitz, an opera by Walter Kollo, 'Die Frau ohne Kuss'

Sunday, November 28, at 15:30 hrs. Matinee performance for the children of SS Families of 'Der Gestiefelte Kater'. Admission – 50 RM

Monday, November 29, at 20:00 hrs.

The Symphony Orchestra of the city of Kattowitz, will perform 'Beschwingste Musik', in addition to several vocal soloists.

Commendation:

I commend SS-Sturm. Basil Malaiko, 2nd Company, for his prudent observation and action, which prevented the escape of several prisoners. As reward Malaiko is given 5 days of special furlough.

Distribution of Vehicles for Camps I II & III:

Various Vehicles are assigned to each camp and are to be used for official business only and its use to be determined by the camp Kommandant.

[example of vehicles made available for the officers and the senior officer, at Camp I]

3 – Mercedes

1 – Opel Kapitan

1 – Opel Admiral

3 – Simca

1 – Wanderer

1 – D.K.W.

December 7, 1943

Christmas Trees:

The Commander's Office of the Concentration Camp Auschwitz will be available to take orders for Christmas trees until 14:00 hrs. on Dec. 12, 1943; for the various companies, their departments and sections.

The Auschwitz C. Camp I has hired 6 women who belong to the ranks of the SS. I expect them to be treated properly with utmost regard by all its members.

Prohibiting the shooting of Stray dogs:

To go into effect immediately.

Living Quarters of SS Women:
Are off limits to male personnel. Visiting hours remains until 22:00 hrs. in the recreation room.

A member of the SS is killed by a Prisoner:
Resulting from the murder of SS Private Peter Jarosiewitsch, orders came from SS-General Oswald Pohl
   a. Guards keep a distance of 6 paces from each prisoner.
   b. Those with weapons are to carry their loaded and secured arms along with their ammunition shells under the right arm only.

Vacation-Homes at the Front for Waffen SS & Police:
In September 1943, the first three such homes were made available in the Protectorate of Boehmen and Maehren, as another in the Steiermark; all for members who wish to meet with their wives and children and also newlyweds and those families who have lost their homes during bombings and have no possibility to take a furlough in the Heimat.
For reservations contact the offices in Berlin-Grunewald, Douglass str. 7–11.
Prices are as follows: Each room/full room and board
One Bed – 6.00 RM, Two Beds – 11.00 RM, Three Beds – 15.00 RM, Children – 3.00 RM.
In special cases allowances for a reduced fee can be arranged.

January 1, 1944

My wishes go out to all SS Officers, Non-Commissioned Officers and Enlisted men, Women of the SS, Civilian employees and all employees of the district of Auschwitz, for a happy and fortunate 1944.
With the firm belief in our hearts, and faith in the Führer, let us take every minute and give all our strengths, together, to contribute towards victory.
Whatever our given task may be, it will be fulfilled relentlessly: never say, 'I cannot'.
Every person is to do their duty with complete cooperation for a victorious 1944.

SS Lt.-Colonel Liebehenschel

Installation of Electric Fence around Crematoria I & II:
The electric fence starting at the Women's camp was extended to Crematoria I, and from the men's camp to Crematoria II. To touch this fence is of life threatening danger.

Horse-drawn Carriages:
I have been made aware repeatedly and must establish the fact that horse drawn carriages (sleighs at this particular time) have been driven with extremely high speed,

to the point of putting stress on the horses, leaving them exhausted which is not tolerable especially in this particular time. I request that all drivers act on my advice so that the horses may be spared and remain fully capable to work.

Standortbefehl Nr. 6/44

Transportation of Prisoners:
February 7, 1944

When we have to transport people [prisoners] from one location to another, there are necessary conditions that must be met so that the work forces don't suffer as a result of the transit. I hereby order the following:

a. It is the personal and complete responsibility of the camp Kommandant to see to the proper departure of each Transport.

b. The examination will be performed by the camp Dr. in the presence of the Schutzhaftlagerführer and the Haftlingseinsatzführer. The Schutzhaftlagerführer is responsible for the preparation of the prisoners until the time of departure. Consisting of Sufficient Supplies, accompanied with arms [M-PI]. The larger transports should consist of [more than 4 Train Cars] and should be accompanied by a Transport Officer. Likewise the allotted dress and supplies to be taken for prisoners. The traffic conditions and time must be taken into consideration and appropriated. More is always a good rule. Once in the cars the prisoners are not to be left without care. The floors of the rail cars should be lined with excelsior. Each rail car will have a kettle with hot water or tea and a sanitary receptacle and a safety light [Stall-Lantern]. During very cold weather the rail cars will be accommodated with heaters, supplied by the Reichsbahn. During moderate cold weather it will be sufficient to wrap their feet and upper bodies with newspaper.

Top Secret – Special Command:

Tgb. Nr.36/44 geh. **February 14, 1944**

Every German, especially the men of the SS know what the goal is for this the 5th year of war. All available work forces and every available hour is subject to the armament of our forces and through this victory.

To follow through with this challenge the solution must be found and determined as to which area and section is of most importance. It must be dealt with accordingly but there has been enough discussion about this subject.

We have to begin immediately within our own camp. There are available to us in Auschwitz 41,000 prisoners who are capable to work so it seems unjustified that 12,000 are employed and utilized for the maintenance of the camp.

Through extensive personal observance and research, I came to the conclusion, with the exception of the armament factories, that all other work places have far too many prisoners appointed to their sections and as a result of this incompetent selection of work details, they are not utilized to the full capacity therefore through inadequate supervision we are actually inviting loafing as a means of education. In the meantime the armament factories are expected to increase the performance and output on a daily basis.

As of today this concept has not been grasped by those responsible for the various departments throughout the concentration camp. I will therefore put a stop to this and as the SS Führer responsible, will order the employment of only the least number of able-bodied workers for the various workstations within the camp.
With the increase in numbers of the work force in the armament factories the goals should be achieved and even increased.

Those officers who are not able to accomplish this, should contact me and I shall take over their command for a few given days and prove without a doubt that the goal can be achieved with the increase in the number of working prisoners.

I ask the Camp Kommandants of camp I & II, to proceed so they may reach their goals as well.

It goes without saying that with an increase of working prisoners we also need added security, many guards have various duties including tours to the front and other important assignments, so we need to help ourselves.

I hereby order that anyone working in offices be asked to volunteer several extra hours a day for special guard duty.

For continuous work productivity, I reiterate that everything must be done to maintain the strength of our prisoners. The most important rules are:

1. One roll call per day only, no longer than a 10 to 15 minute duration.
2. Free time and sufficient sleep of the workers is of the utmost importance. Offences or any chicanery or unnecessary stress of this sort will be met with strictest punishment.
3. Each prisoner has the right to his allotted board, accommodation and supplies. The distribution of packages plays an important role. In the course of two and one half months a number of one million packages have been received. Perishable contents not able to be consumed are to be distributed among the less fortunate.
4. Continuous supervision of the condition of prisoners clothing, especially their footwear is required.
5. Ill prisoners are to be placed under doctor's care in the hospital, in order to have the healed return to their workstations.
6. Diligent workers are to be rewarded in every way, until the day of their given freedom, the lazy individuals who show no improvement will be strictly punished within regulations.

I have once again brought attention to this pressing matter, but do not have the time for any further written notification. I will have a personal meeting with the Kommandants of camp I and II and will discuss with conviction how to swiftly carry out this order. I'm hoping everyone will act on their own accord and do what is required of them.

gez. Liebehenschel
SS-Obersturmbannfuehrer

                 -end of ordinances-[10]

When my father was found to have had an affair, Richard Baer wasted no time taking this opportunity to have my father relieved of his post, as Baer himself hoped to take over the duty as Kommandant of Auschwitz.

Members of the SS were considered a part of a noble privileged 'family'. They informed my father that Anneliese was not of suitable character to be the wife of an SS officer because she had not adhered to their code of strict virtuous morals – which her past confirmed – as she had been sentenced to prison for an alleged affair with a Jewish man. This broke the Nuremberg laws, which were passed on 15 September 1935, prohibiting marriage or any sexual contact between Jews and non-Jews.

Divorce was frowned upon and the affair which prompted my father to divorce my mother was inappropriate and unfit behavior, inciting them to launch serious actions to bring an end to their relationship. Oswald Pohl, the supervisor of concentration camps, sent his deputy Richard Baer to Auschwitz, in order to deal with what they felt was an unpleasant, embarrassing incident. Baer reported:

I arrived at Auschwitz on the given day at 22:00 hours with the confidential letter in my possession. I sat with Liebehenschel in the ante room at the Officers Club. After we spoke of a few matters concerning the job, I gave him the letter [from Pohl] and told him that I had instructions to do my best to help with his problem. [The letter spoke of Anneliese's arrest and imprisonment and the rejection to their request for marriage.]

Since Liebehenschel is known as a melancholy and sensitive man, I was told to carry out the conveyance in a sparing manner. After reading the letter maybe two or three times, Liebehenschel broke into tears. When he recovered somewhat, he tried to cast doubt on the information I had brought. I told him that Fraulein Huettemann had signed a confession confirming the content of the letter. I added that, in light of the circumstances, I had been sent to arrange matters.

Liebehenschel spoke of his loyalty to the SS and the Führer and afterwards said that he understood the matter and would act as befit an SS officer. In his emotion he ordered champagne and drank large quantities which I fully understand considering the circumstances. Afterwards I spoke with Fraulein Huettemann, promising her and her mother assistance in finding an apartment and work. I found no reason she should not marry whomever she wished, even an officer of a government agency, but through the findings by the SD there was no possibility for a future marriage, not to a member of the SS. She then claimed that her signature was taken from her under duress and false pretenses. I said that, based on my long experience in concentration camps, no one signs a confession against their will. Liebehenschel claimed that the Gestapo has methods of squeezing confessions like these from people. I told him that this was a serious charge and required proof. With the champagne bottle emptied I suggested we continue our discussion the following day. We parted under most agreeable circumstances.[11]

Richard Baer later replaced my father at Auschwitz, and ran the camp between May 1944 and January 1945, strictly by the book, as it once was. Without my father there, 'to pour considerable sand in the gears', Hoess' 'perfect works' were once again flowing. 'Action Hoess' continued, as in June 1944 Hoess himself returned to coordinate and carry out the murder of 430,000 Hungarian Jews at the Auschwitz camp.

SS Corporal Oskar Kieselbach compared Kommandants Liebehenschel and Baer. He testified: 'Baer was stronger than his predecessor Liebehenschel, but the latter was popular with members of the SS as well as the prisoners. The same cannot be said about Baer.'[12]

I found further information on this matter in Father's SS file, disclosing his total devastation. He returned home after the meeting and awoke Anneliese, confronting her with, 'You've told me terrible lies and deceived me from the beginning'. She adamantly denied these accusations. The following day Father asked Baer into his office to further discuss the problem. Baer went on to report my father as saying:

> Your disclosure yesterday, befell me as a man who'd been hit with a hammer. He must first fall before he can then get back up and so it was with me. After our discussion yesterday, I confronted Fraulein Huettemann at that time, I begged her to tell me the truth, and swore to her that no matter how she answered, I would never leave her. Yet, her answer remained the same, even through the embarrassment of these intimate questions.
>
> Now I know and am convinced that this has determined the truth and the SD has based its findings on inaccuracies not fact. The notarized statement also confirms this. I will now request the Reichsführer, for permission to marry.

Baer continued:

> Concerning me, Liebehenschel expressed I have not spent enough time in Concentration Camps to know of the methods of persuasion used to obtain confessions from prisoners. My reply to him was that if he succeeds to show evidence against the accusations of the interrogating Police, that it would provoke a Revolution in the history of the SD.[13]

A notarized statement by Anneliese declared that she never had any relations with the accused Jewish boy, and that they were only childhood friends. Also that her confession was taken under 'duress'.

Notarization (under oath) by Dr. Alexander Hoffmann
April 21, 1944

In 1935 I was arrested by the State Police along with my girl friend and Kurt Stern. We were imprisoned for over three weeks. There never was any romantic involvement, affections, kisses or sexual relations with the Jewish boy. We were merely acquaintances. If I signed a statement confessing to a relationship, it was taken under duress.

sig. Anneliese Huettemann[14]

Hermann Langbein noted in his book:

A look behind the scenes of the SS moral standards is clear to see, Pohl wanted to minimize the fact that Hoess had taken one of the prisoners as his mistress and then wanted to eliminate her as the affair came to surface. Hoess was also investigated in the concentration camp corruption case but this was dropped in the end. It was Baer who answered the judges stating he found out about the female prisoner with whom Hoess carried on a love affair and Hoess had told Baer: 'Through the chimney with her.'

Hoess was promoted nevertheless. But the legality of Liebehenschel's connection with a woman who was supposed to have had an affair with a Jew, was in the eyes of Oswald Pohl like a misalliance and therefore enough reason that Liebehenschel could not remain as Kommandant of Auschwitz, even though the woman held a trusted position with a high ranking SS Officer.[15]

My father's SS personnel file did not contain a great deal of information on his actual career as an SS officer or his activities at the Auschwitz and Lublin concentration camps. There was, however, extensive documentation of numerous communications sent through, from the various chains of command within the SS organization, about Anneliese, about her involvement with the Jewish boy when she was eighteen and her relationship with my father. There were even photos of her in his file.

The notarized statement by Anneliese, along with a letter pleading for the consent of marriage to my father, as she was pregnant with his child, was sent to the Reichsführer, Heinrich Himmler himself.

Most Honorable, Herr Reichsführer – SS
Heinrich Himmler – Berlin
May 13, 1944

I beg your forgiveness, that I dare to turn to you for help with a personal matter in a time when all strengths must serve toward victory.

Through the procurement of documents for marriage the SD uncovered my signed confession stating I had previous relations with a Jew, for which I spent 3 weeks in prison. This is not the truth and was signed under duress.

I was asked by Lt. Col. Liebehenschel to be present so I could myself hear the accusations against me, from SS Captain Richard Baer who is adjutant to Lt. General Oswald Pohl. As I contested, I was ridiculed in the most vulgar manner by this 'noble' SS Führer.

In light of the situation it was suggested for me to leave the city of Auschwitz as quickly as possible. I answered that I worked for the city, was a free citizen who had not committed any crime and had lost everything as the result of a bombing raid in Wuppertal and therefore had nowhere to go. He replied there were still sufficient accommodations elsewhere within Germany. I then informed him that I was pregnant and couldn't roam aimlessly throughout the world with my unborn child, and also had to care for the son of Lt. Col. Liebehenschel, to which this rude insensitive person replied 'You can give the child up and find a job elsewhere'. As I broke into tears from those sordid inferences he added 'Your tears only confirm that you're lying, you can marry anyone but not an SS Officer'.

Herr Reichsführer, should an expectant German mother be humiliated in this way? I don't want to marry just anyone, but the man I love and who I will love until I die, as he has the character, integrity and principles, from which even Herr Baer could learn a great deal and use as a good example.

I do not want to denigrate him in your eyes, but for me he no longer exists.

I ask you please Herr Reichsführer to make a fair decision, as an expectant German mother I want to give many more children to the German nation, with this man I love.

Heil Hitler!

Anneliese Huettemann[16]

Throughout the pages of the old historic documents one hears the cries of desperation – the great passion which was alive and existed between Father and Anneliese. It also proves the fanatic obsession of the 'Jewish Question' on the part of the Reich and how my father's 'illicit love affair' with Anneliese had caused quite a sensation throughout this elite SS system.

This is the letter sent by Oswald Pohl, father's superior, to Rudolf Brandt, who was Himmler's assistant, after receiving a copy of the letter of 13 May 1944, sent to the RF office by Anneliese.

To: Dr. Brandt – Reichsführer SS/Personal Staff
From: Oswald Pohl/Tgb.Nr.530/44/secret/Berlin/June 6,1944
Re: SS-Obersturmbannfuehrer Liebehenschel

I find it completely unbelievable that Baer would have behaved toward Frl. Huettemann in the manner she described. I know Baer well and trust him. SS Lt. Colonel Liebehenschel apparently had an affair with Fraulein Huettemann, who also worked for the Amtsgruppe D, but this was not made known until after his divorce. Fraulein Huettemann spent three weeks in prison in 1935 as it was found out she had sexual relations with a Jew named Stern, which she now denies.

I personally saw her confession, the records that bear her signature. Even though she was only 19 at the time, it had been two years since the Party came into power and she, as a German girl, should have known what her responsibilities were. She can't use youthful ignorance as an excuse for her actions.

Liebehenschel was then given the opportunity to view these documents in Duesseldorf himself but at that time they were located at the RSHA office in Berlin and he saw only copies of the documents signed by Frl. Huettemann. He even went so far as to question the authenticity of the documents at the STAPO office and threatened the head of the STAPO, that he would file a complaint at the Reichssic herheitshauptamt

After my findings of Fraulein Huettemann's past I was unable to give my permission for Liebehenschel to marry Fraulein Huettemann and I have since transferred Liebehenschel to Lublin. Of course it was not possible for him to remain at Auschwitz.

Please inform me of the Reichsfuehrer-SS's final decision on this matter.

Heil Hitler!

Oswald Pohl[17]

After my father was given direct orders by Oswald Pohl to end his relationship with Anneliese, he told them: 'Throughout my life I have experienced many disappointments. The one woman I loved more than anything was my mother. My married life with the woman I divorced was unhappy even though we had children. In Fraulein Huettemann I've found the essence of being closest to my mother.'

My father made his final request for their marriage in August 1944, going through the required SS chain of command. It was suggested to him by Dr Joachim Caesar, who was in charge of all agricultural operations at Auschwitz, that he should direct his request to SS Brigadier General Heider. Caesar was a personal friend of my father and Anneliese. Caesar's first wife had died of typhus in October 1942 and he also contracted the disease shortly after her death. He was not investigated after the war and died in 1974.

SS-ObersturmbannFührer

Arthur Liebehenschel

Auschwitz, August 30, 1944

Hauptstrasse 33

Reference: Required Documents for the application of marriage of SS-Obersturmbannführer Arthur Liebehenschel and Fraulein Anneliese Huettemann.

Enclosures: -9- [2 R&S Amt Questionaires/1 sealed letter including 4 sheets of medical data/1 letter/1 Family History & 4 Documents/1 Schuldenerklaerung/4 other miscellaneous Documents]

To:
Chief of the Marriage Bureau
Rasse u. Siedlungshauptamt
SS-Brigadier General Heider
zur Zeit-Rosslau/Harz
Kyffhauser Hotel

Brigadier General!

I am enclosing the necessary documents for the consent of my marriage to Fraulein Anneliese Huettemann and request that the Reichsführer-SS would grant immediate approval for the license.

I request the most urgent attention to this matter as Fraulein Huettemann is expecting my child in October and it should of course be given my name.

The delay is the result of circumstances that were uncovered regarding Fraulein Huettemann from which stipulation came the rejection by my previous superior SS-Obergruppenführer Oswald Pohl.

All other particulars were enclosed with the application sent by Fraulein Huettemann to the Reichsführer-SS in her correspondence through his Personal Staff on May 26, 1944, made evident and passed on to the Rasse u. Siedlungshauptamt.

The events and allegations against Fraulein Huettemann are explained in the Notarized Statement sent to the Reichsführer-SS.

Anneliese Huettemann has led an unblemished and decent life. She and her parents who have lost everything during an air raid bombing are known as respected citizens in Wuppertal-Elberfeld. Her father today at age 60, is still serving at the Eastern Front, where he has been since the beginning of the war. Her sister is married to an SS-Unterführer who is at present in the Waffen-SS.

If my belief and trust in this German woman was not 100%, then as a man of the SS I know precisely what the consequences would be.

In the difficult times during my divorce when everyone disapproved and through all the associated unpleasant circumstances, she stood by me and my son as my loyal comrade.

It was brought to my attention through my acquaintance with Lt-Colonel Joachim Caesar, who advised me to make my request through you Brigadier General. I only ask for fair and somewhat benevolent treatment and that you come to a final conclusion and express this to the Reichsführer-SS.

May I once again ask for speedy expedition so that the marriage can be performed before the birth of the child in October.

Please send notification to my bride, Anneliese Huettemann/Auschwitz O/S, Hauptstrasse 33, and send a teletype message to me, presently at the High-SS & Polizeiführer in Triest, Italy. After examining the enclosed documents and diplomas, please have them hand delivered to me in a sealed envelope so as not to lose them in the mail as they will be necessary for the civil ceremony at the Registry Office.

Brigadier General please help us!

Heil Hitler!
Arthur Liebehenschel
SS-ObersturmbannFührer[18]

In October of 2000 my sister Antje and her husband visited the Harz region, this town of Rosslau to which my father had addressed and written his letter to Brigadier General Heider. Located in the former East Germany, once part of Soviet-occupied territory, they now came upon this town in shocking desolate condition. When my father wrote to the general it was August 1944, and Rosslau was then a bustling SS center of operations for the Rasse u. Siedlungshauptamt.

Today, almost sixty years later, it is deserted and in a state of deterioration. They found a dying older generation, caught somewhere between Russian domination and lost within the epoch of the Second World War. Many homes stand vacant on eerie lonely streets, where weeds have long taken over the once green yards and thriving gardens. Sad and depressed they watched these old inhabitants going about their monotonous routines of everyday life; uninterested and unaware they had been trapped in a time warp.

The young people have long moved away, not having any hope for a future and with nothing to hold them there. Antje wanted to look up the Hotel Kyffhauser, once the location of the office of the SS General, where our father's request had been sent. An old woman pointed to a huge rubble pile next to the old train depot. Adjacent to the ruins stood the gutted shell of the large Hotel Deutsches Haus, another former SS Operations Headquarters.

Here, as in so many small towns in the east, there is a stark indication of the former communist influence. Until this time there have been no funds to restore the town or even clean up and haul away the debris, leaving only portions of crumbling walls as haunting reminders, even today, of Hitler's Nazi regime.

Antje and Ernst both experienced a dreadful feeling of emptiness as they left behind the deserted streets and abandoned homes of this town of Rosslau, and carried with them the cold images depicting a lonely, but never forgotten past.

Knowing how this subject still seems to upset Anneliese, I have tried to avoid any unnecessary questioning, in respect for her sensitive feelings. I was, however, unclear about the dates of her marriage to my father, and found the courage to bring up these questions to her over the phone.
She told me:

> I no longer have any documents or data but I believe it was in January 1944. I can't say for sure, I have tried to avoid the subject on all those matters. We were never married in the church. The Reichsfuehrer Himmler didn't want us to marry. We were, however, married secretly, that is to say we were married in Auschwitz at the 'Hotel zur Post'. The proprietor was a man who used to own the 'Hotel zur Post' in

Wuppertal and we knew each other from there. Your Papa, his adjutant and myself were the only ones who attended; we had dinner together, but not a real wedding celebration. It was a civil ceremony, but no one knew about it. I once wrote there, requesting the marriage certificate, but was informed they had all been relocated and were not available. Himmler didn't want this marriage as it was said I had been imprisoned as a result of my relationship with Jews … which was all false, cruel lies. It was a dreadful time for us. After countless communication back and forth, your Papa and I drove to Wuppertal and there picked up the legal certificate, through the 'Kriminal Kommissar', as Himmler had finally consented and all was well. Soon afterward we were publicly and officially married.

Anneliese – September 11, 1999

Transcripts of Pretrial Interrogation at Nuremberg:
U.S. Military Chief of Counsel/War Crimes Section: Heath
Taken Of: Arthur Wilhelm Liebehenschel by Mr. von Halle
Lawyer: Drechsler Stenographer: Roeder
Date: October 7, 1946 – Time 14:30 – 15:15 p.m.

About the Camp:

Q: When you were Camp Kommandant from November 1943 to April 1944 what was the total number of inmates of the entire combined camps?

A: Approximately 70,000.

Q: In your estimation, how many were in camp II?

A: Camp II was the women and gypsies. There were at least 40,000.

Q: How many barracks were in camp I?

A: 28.

Q: How many inmates in each barrack?

A: In each barrack 300, they were brick barracks, two story.

Q: How many were these barracks supposed to accommodate?

A: 300 persons, I didn't allow them to be double-stacked.

Q: But that would only add up to about 8,000 persons. You told us there were 13–14,000 people. Where are the remaining people? Think about it precisely before you answer. How many people per barrack when you were at Auschwitz? They had to be double stacked?

A: One cannot say stacked – one over the other, as in addition the attic rooms contained 60 to 70 persons.

Q: How many administration buildings were in the camp?

A: One large administration building, one Kommandantur.

Q: There was a hospital in the camp, what capacity?

A: The capacity was to accommodate 2,000 patients.

Q: Was it usually filled?

A: No.

Q: When did the inmates go to roll call?

A: It depended on the season, in the winter when I was there, it was shortly before 7:00 a.m. in the morning [sic].

Q: And in the summer what time was roll call?

A: I wasn't there then, I came November 15th, but I think the prisoners went to roll call at 5:00 a.m.

Q: Who informed you when there was a death of an inmate?

A: In case of a death I was notified by the camp physician.

Q: How was this done?

A: A report was sent.

Q: And which contagious cause would be given?

A: We no longer had contagious diseases, thank God.

Q: But you had inmates on whom experiments were performed, and if I proved to you that this was actually the case, would you as the camp's Kommandant consider yourself responsible?

A: I don't know of any such experiments having been conducted at Auschwitz.

Q: I asked if you would consider yourself responsible?

A: Yes, if that was the case, yes.

Q: How many prisoners were transferred, daily, weekly or monthly from Camp I and III, into Camp II?

A: I don't know.

Q: How often did you get together with the other Camp Kommandants, Hertjenstein from Camp II, and Schwartz from Camp III, to compare reports?

A: Daily reports, no. They came to confer with me once a month.

Q: Why you? Does that mean you were responsible for them?

A: No, I had seniority.

Q: You have seniority at the camp and have no idea what goes on there?

A: We only discussed general affairs.

Q: What does that mean?

A: Personnel problems, leaves, etc.

Q: So, you only discussed such things; not about how many people were sent to the gas chamber? Were you clear on that matter?

A: Not during my time. I don't believe this happened, otherwise there would not have been Jewish prisoners, which were sent to Dachau, that declared that I had nothing to do with this. They stated I was not involved in the bad treatment of prisoners.

Q: What did the prisoners receive for breakfast?

A: Soup, coffee, bread and jam.

Q: How much bread?

A: 650 grams daily.

Q: The soup was made from potato peels?

A: No.

Q: How many prisoners were used for labor in Camp I?

A: Very many, approximately 3,000, for each work detail. We had a clothing factory that employed a few hundred, a shoe factory that employed 400 to 500,
   a butcher shop, I'm not sure how many worked there, probably another few
   hundred, a nursery and laundry that also employed a few hundred.

Q: So far we have approximately 1,500 people.

A: The kitchen had about 250 to peel potatoes, these were people that were
   semi-disabled and there were many more for regular kitchen detail.

Q: How many inmates left every morning for work detail outside the camp?

A: 2,500 for Union-AG, about 2,000 for agricultural projects, about 3,000 for
   German armament factories, about 1,000 for construction, and for the mill
   and bakery 100 persons.

Q: How did the prisoners get to their place of work? Did they walk or were they
   driven by truck?

A: They walked, the work places were nearby.

Q: What people were sent from Camp II?

A: That I don't know. I only know that women worked in the textile mill.

Q: In Camp III were 40,000 inmates?

A: Yes, and then there were all the neighboring camps; one was Monowitz.

Q: What were the other surrounding camps?

A: Wyschowitz, Gleiwitz, and Haydebreck, they were branch camps of Camp III,
   and mostly armament camps.

Q: The workers from Buna Works were pulled from Camp III?

A: Yes, partly from III, and when new camps were constructed they were also
   taken out of Camp I. In fact that was ordered.

Q: By whom?

A: From Berlin.

Q: Was that conveyed centrally?

A: Yes, through Berlin.

Q: From what section?

A: Section D.

Q: Whom did Buna have to contact for its work forces?

A: Camp Commander Schwartz.

Q: Did Buna contact you directly for workers from Camp I?

A: Not without the consent of Berlin.

Q: You sent people to Buna?

A: Yes, they were sent first to Camp III, then from there on to Buna.

Q: How often were you at Buna?

A: Once.

Q: What year was that?

A: I think beginning of 1944.

Q: Who showed you through Buna?

A: Director Duerrfeld and several others.

Q: Who else was present and what was the occasion that you went through the
   Buna Works?

A: It was a gauleiter named Ulbrich, who came for inspection.

Q: Were you ever in any of the Textile Mills where the women were employed?

A: No.

Q: If the factory work places were not satisfied with the prisoners, did they report this to you?

A: Yes.

Q: Who reported this to you?

A: The deputy of that section.

Q: And he filed a complaint if the individual prisoner didn't work hard enough?

A: That never occurred while I was there; because all my prisoners were good workers. Especially the night shift prisoners who were given an extra hot meal, according to my orders.

Q: Why do you emphasize how compassionate you were?

A: I don't emphasize this, my prisoners confirmed it many times.

Q: You could never have remained in a concentration camp, if you were so compassionate?

A: And I couldn't either. Did you know that my prisoners have said I made a sanitarium out of Auschwitz?

Q: And as a result of this action, you were not personally incriminated or punished?

A: I was treated like a criminal by my superiors.

Q: How could you remain in your position?

A: After I saw what wrong was done to these people, I felt it my duty to remain at my post and this way at least I could help these human beings as much as possible.

Q: How could you even confer with a person like this Hertjenstein, who was one who daily took people's lives?

A: I don't believe that this happened in my time there. It must have been during Hoess' time there.

Q: How many people died in Camp II when Hoess was in charge? Your prisoners, for whom you had so much compassion and were your personal friends, must surely have told you how many died?

A: They told me of the terrible treatment.

Q: I have a document here that says: once a month all prisoners had to undress and were examined by an SS physician, the ones that were ill or not capable of full work detail were separated and later sent to the gas chamber. The block sergeant had a card, when someone was singled out to be sent to the gas chamber he would place the card on the left side?

A: No, that is not true.

Q: So you think that's a lie? But then you'll find there are many more such lies, in this same form.

A: I can't change that, but in any case that is not true, it didn't happen during my time. I was there from morning until night and always intervened where necessary and was there for every person. I understood the misery of my prisoners because of my own suffering I have endured. You can ask the Jews, they will confirm this.

Q: Why didn't you resign?

A: When I realized that one could do some good in a wretched camp, I wanted to stay as I could maybe save some more lives.

Q: You were in section I before?

A: That was an unimportant matter.

Q: There you had already discovered what transpired in the concentration camps? Gluecks for example knew exactly what went on?

A: The old man probably didn't see much.

Q: Did all prisoners return to the camp at night?

A: Mine all returned to the camp.

Q: At what time?

A: At dusk.

Q: How many nationalities were at Auschwitz Camp I?

A: A great number.

Q: Was there a difference in the treatment of prisoners of the various nationalities?

A: No.

Q: [Showing a photocopy of a label: Zyklon B with Skull] Are you familiar with this?

A: No.

Q: Did you ever see Zyklon B at Auschwitz?

A: No, Zyklon B Prussic Acid, I never saw there.

Q: Do you have any idea how many people were gassed?

A: No.

Q: Did you know that some were gassed?

A: I have just learned about this, I suppose there had been talk about it.

Q: Now we come to the end of your duty at Auschwitz, what was the reason you left Auschwitz?

A: On April 5 I was replaced by Captain Baer, Adjutant to Pohl.

Q: Why were you replaced and what did you do then?

A: I had met a woman I wanted to marry but Pohl refused to give his consent as she had previously been sent to prison by the State Police for an alleged relationship with a Jew. In actuality she had grown up with these Jewish children with whom she met in a cafe in 1935, when she was reported. After my release I spent 3 weeks in the hospital and then came my transfer to Lublin.[19]

Father's role as Kommandant of concentration camps was so unlike his previous administrative duties within the system. It would not be easy for him, as he had no preconceived idea what hardships he would have to endure.

Chapter Five

Austria

In November my father had been transferred to Auschwitz, and by December 1943 my parents' divorce was final. I was ten months old. As a result of the divorce the family was no longer eligible for the SS housing. Mother took us three girls and Ilse and we moved from Oranienburg to our house in St Gilgen, Austria, in early 1944.

When we packed and the movers came, Brigitte was afraid of the uncertainty of our future, as it was the beginning of our lives without Papa.

Hitler was born in 'Braunau am Inn', less than 100 miles from St Gilgen, Austria where my parents had built their vacation home by the lake Wolfgangsee. Hitler thought of himself as the chosen one, sent to annex his Austrian homeland to the German Reich. He invaded Austria on 12 March 1938. German troops were received jubilantly by the Austrians. Villages and houses were decorated with swastika flags. Women and children tossed flowers and there were tears of joy. People lined the streets to welcome this fellow Austrian who was now their Führer. Over 99 per cent of the Austrian voters approved of the 'Anschluss', the annexation of Austria to Germany. Hitler claimed it was the proudest hour in his life.

When our mother, Ilse and us three girls arrived in St Gilgen that February of 1944, the beautiful mountains, rolling hills and trees were covered with thick blankets of glistening white snow. The temperature was below freezing and we fought our way through deep layers of snow up the path to our house.

The well was frozen and we had to draw water from the lake for our daily use. The lake was also frozen over and holes had to be broken into the ice to get to the water level. Drinking water was bought at the neighboring inn 'Gabauer', and it was a long difficult climb up the path through the snow carrying heavy pails full of water.

It was almost impossible to get fuel for the generator in our basement, so we did without the luxury of electricity also. Petroleum oil lamps were our source of light.

Antje recalls the first day we arrived in our new home in St Gilgen. A fire was quickly started in the tiled stove and slowly the cold living room became warm and cozy. Back in Oranienburg, as we were getting ready for the move, our mother had given Antje a box and told her she may want to pack some of her favorite toys so she would have something to play with, as all of our other things would not arrive until later with the movers. Antje felt homesick for her familiar surroundings, which she had known in Oranienburg, and for Papa. Slowly she unpacked the box. Among her things she found her beloved teddy bear and immediately everything seemed easier. This teddy bear, worn smooth with age, has not only survived the war but seen the birth of two following generations, and has been a constant companion throughout her life. Today it occupies a special place in her home. The strong awareness of father's absence affected everyone when we moved to Austria.

The war was still on and people were talking of it all coming to an end. We listened to the radio and the Propaganda Minister Goebbels talked of a secret weapon, soon to bring the war to an end. Our mother had a map of East and West Germany on the wall and pins kept track of the war movement. The Russians were advancing into the east and on the western front the British and Americans were closing in.

As a result of the overwhelming defeats in Russia early in 1944, every German able to bear arms was enrolled into the armed forces. As a result, the law of conscription, which is the exemption of the youngest or only son in a family, was suspended, as they were running out of replacement forces. Even older men were pulled into the war, as well as my brother Dieter, recruited at age fifteen; made to intercept enemy aircraft on the front lines after school.

Everyone has a special place out of their childhood they'd like to return to. This is one of mine, although I only have fragments of hazy memories. In my memory remains the pungent odor and the romance of oil lamps and a feeling of love and security. Our mother and Ilse did laundry by hand and had to carry all the water from the lake. To get to the nearest market, 'Feinkost Schweighofer' in St Gilgen, which has been in business since 1893, we had to ride the train, or in the summer we walked, pulling the groceries home in a little wagon. The winters were most difficult of course, but not through the eyes of children. My sisters recall wonderful childhood memories of beautiful Austria.

All this was hardship for mother, who had three children to look after. She had no time to reflect on how she was left all alone in such a desperate time, stripped of the security she once knew with my father. There is such empathy in my heart when I think of her situation; and to make things worse, she was without the man she still loved and would love until the day she died.

The musical *The Sound of Music* has always held a special kind of feeling for me. St Gilgen is no comparison to the much larger city of Salzburg, which is only about fifty miles away, but the beauty of the countryside, mountains and lakes are the same. In fact, the very beginning of the film shows the scenery of St Gilgen and the surrounding area, with the church dome protruding out amidst rolling green hills and lakes. It never fails to increase my heart rate or make the tears well; moved from sheer emotion for the splendor and special sensitivity I'll always feel for this area.

It was a wonderful place for children, so many things to explore. Every morning my sisters would take the large milk can and buy fresh milk from neighboring farms. The farmers were poor, simple people who became our friends. In the spring they drove their herds to higher pastures in the Alps, just as their ancestors had done for hundreds of years before them. They stayed in the alpine huts and ate off the land. They churned butter and made cheeses and sold their dairy products to the townspeople. Large chunks of butter and wonderful cheeses were wrapped and stored in white sheets, which the farmers delivered to our house regularly.

When they returned to the low land in the autumn, if they hadn't lost any of their herd, they celebrated by making headdresses out of flowers and decorated the animals with large cowbells. They paraded this way through the streets. This told people in the town of their good fortune and prosperity during the summer months. If one's herd was without these ornaments, it meant they had met with misfortune on the steep mountainside, and there was no celebration for them. My family experienced such a 'funeral procession' when a herd returned to the valley without the colorful festive decorations. The lead cow wore a black band on her horns and the whole herd looked very sad. Apparently there had been a fatal accident. This tradition is still practiced today and called the 'Almabtrieb'.

The Wolfgangsee was cold, crystal clear glacier water and we could only swim in it on a few hot summer days. There were many thunderstorms and the glorious smell that came from the damp earth is something I still recall to this day.

My sister Antje wrote a letter from Austria to our father. It was in September and he was stationed in Italy at the time. She was seven years old. Our brother Dieter had recently been taken prisoner by the Russians in Lublin.

Austria
September 29, 1944

My dear Papa,

I thank you for your letter.

We have a horrible teacher. He doesn't know what he wants. So far he hasn't done anything to me. About Dieter, it is so very very very very very sad.

My writing is very very bad, with many mistakes, but you should be happy that I'm writing to you at all.

All Bärbel wants to do is 'toben' romp. Ja ja such is life. It is now night and I'll now go to bed.

Greetings and Kisses
From your Antje

P.S. Papa I pray for you
Great health for my Papa

After all these years, my sister Antje finally gave me an explanation regarding this letter, written to my father on 29 September 1944. It was written by a frightened little seven-year-old who talked about her terrible teacher. She remembers he wore the gray Nazi uniform and was very strict. He never gave Antje any problems, but then he also knew that our father was an officer within the SS.

Antje was in first grade and had a special little girlfriend whose name she has since forgotten. She sat next to her on the bench and her twin brother was also in their class. Both children had big brown eyes with unusual blond hair, which seemed to be bleached. She recalls her friend confided in her one day, telling her that her real name was actually Sarah. Sarah was a shy girl. She taught Antje how to draw the pretty flower basket, which Antje sent along with her letter to Papa. Sarah's twin brother had a glass eye.

The experience in that classroom was a horror story, which Antje has chosen not to talk about until now. One day the teacher singled out shy little Sarah, pulling her out of her seat and making her stand up in front of the class. He proceeded to beat her with his bare fists and kicked her with his polished boots until the little girl fell to the floor in a pool of blood. Without any sense of compassion or remorse he then dragged her limp body to the back of the classroom, placing her in another seat away from Antje and the other students. She remained there that day, traumatized with unknown injuries, until the end of class. Antje and the other students were terrified, afraid to return to school.

The twins never came back after that day and no one knew what had happened to them. Antje never had a chance to say goodbye to her friend.

Very disturbed, Antje told our mother about the incident in the presence of Ilse, which prompted their eyes to meet in silent comprehension between them. Our mother consoled Antje, saying they probably moved away. But today Antje still wonders how the twin brother came to have a glass eye? Was it through a similar incident, and had they moved to the remote Austrian village for that reason? Were they able to flee with their family or did they end up on one of the Jewish transports to a nearby camp?

Rudolf, back in Germany, kept in touch with Ilse. Ilse had no flair for poetic prose and asked my mother to help her write letters to Rudy. Mother composed beautiful love letters, which Ilse sent to Rudy in the camp. Rudy wrote back, touched by her literary style, expressing his passion for her. Ilse shared these letters with our mother and both women would giggle like schoolgirls at their own antics. Ilse received packages from Rudy containing large quantities of gold that he had extracted from the teeth of living and dead prisoners at the Camp Sachsenhausen in Oranienburg, where he was put to work practicing his profession as a dentist. Somehow he was able to smuggle the gold out of the camp and sent it to Austria, instructing Ilse to hide it safely.

Antje and Brigitte accidentally came upon these bundles of dental gold at our house in St Gilgen, which Ilse kept hidden in her room. They were dumbfounded, but at that point in time had no idea what to make of the unusually shaped pieces of shiny gold wrapped in large, crudely hand-sewn cloth bags. Rudy took advantage of his plight and found how one could benefit financially, despite the fact he was incarcerated in a concentration camp.

Accumulated dental gold was sent to the Reichsbank, making it a profitable business for the Third Reich. In charge of this ugly business was General Oswald Pohl, my father's superior.

Since our mother was divorced from father, the Gestapo came calling several times to our house in St Gilgen, attempting to take Ilse back to the concentration camp. Mother tried to convince Ilse to sign the affidavit required by them, stating she was no longer a practicing Jehovah's Witness. Mother wanted her to realize that within her heart Ilse didn't need to give up her faith, that it was only an insignificant piece of paper. Ilse was deeply rooted to her belief and felt it would show betrayal to sign such a document, recanting her religion. Our mother was very fond of Ilse and decided that she herself would forge Ilse's signature in order to save her life.

Antje was hiding under the large dining table where she was so often found and watched with curiosity for several days as my mother practiced tracing and writing Ilse's signature. The day the Gestapo returned, Antje hid behind mother's skirt and saw her handing the forged declaration to the officers. Mother explained to them that Ilse was not at home, that she had been sent to the market, when in reality Ilse was hiding upstairs in a small chamber in the attic. They seemed satisfied and left our house with the fraudulent document. Our mother took daring chances for Ilse, risking her own safety and security, but would not allow the Gestapo to intimidate her or take Ilse away.

My mother at this point in time still showed incredible inner strength and courage that helped her through these fearful times. One instance involved a traumatic wartime experience for my sister Brigitte.

She attended school in the town of Bad Ischl, about one hour away when taking the little train. It was a serene, picturesque ride through the Austrian countryside.

One day, on the way home from school, British bombers attacked the train. The schoolchildren were trained to take shelter under the seats or benches in case of attack, but never to run out of the train. Most of the adults ran out in confusion. The raiding force were dive bombers attacking with machine guns. No one understood why they would attack a civilian train out in the country.

The engineer was hit, but was able to bring the train to a stop. It was a bloody massacre. Brigitte remembered, in particular, a young mother with a two or three-year-old girl. The mother jumped out of the train with her child and she was shot and killed, but had thrown herself over her little daughter who survived.

'There was blood and death everywhere, it was absolutely horrible.' Brigitte went into shock for over a week, unable to return to school or get the picture out of her mind. This was a terrifying experience for a twelve-year-old; she would never forget it.

This little train was replaced by buses a few years later. We found the old train in 1972 on the road to Bad Ischl, saved as a museum piece. It brought back all those past emotions for Brigitte, as she recalled her war-time ordeal, and pointed out the same bench where she had sat and took shelter on that day of the bombing so many years ago.

During the latter part of the war the state required every German citizen to take in homeless families if they had extra room available. In the early part of 1945, a few months before the war ended, my mother took in a woman with her five children. It was a family named Stockreiter who had lost their home in Vienna, where much of the city had been destroyed by extensive bombing raids. There were four girls of various ages and an eighteen-month-old little boy.

They occupied the guestroom and my mother graciously welcomed them into our small home; the house now accommodated two families consisting of a total of eight children and three adults. Mother cooked for all of them and, since meats were rationed, she prepared large kettles of simple satisfying meals like stews made from potatoes or noodles with vegetables and even mushrooms from the forest.

It seems, however, Frau Stockreiter and my mother did not see eye to eye, as in Vienna this lady was used to a more privileged life. Frau Stockreiter used up her rations frivolously and used my mother's kitchen to cook elaborate meals for herself and her children. My mother, who had also come from a better way of life, could not come to terms with this woman of high society who was unable to face the reality of war. Mother coped, however, with the added confusion and the fact that our one bathroom was usually out of order due to frozen or broken water pipes. The family Stockreiter left our home in St Gilgen as soon as the war ended, returning to Vienna. I wonder if they were able to resume their life of pre-war splendor?

It was shortly before the war ended when my mother heard the Americans were closing in on Salzburg. She and my sisters went into St Gilgen to 'Schweighofers' market leaving me at home with Ilse. The store's owners and the town's people panicked, fearful of the American invasion. The proprietors gave everything away, emptying their shelves rather than have the occupying enemy forces confiscate what they had.

We were regular customers and they provided us with flour, butter and all sorts of staples that eased us through the lean months which soon followed. They didn't realize at the time that the Americans weren't coming to loot the civilians, but were actually part of the extensive postwar relief program.

Once again winter melted into spring and we had lived in Austria over a year when the war ended in May of 1945. Germany was defeated. On 20 April 1945, Hitler's fifty-sixth birthday, he was to leave Berlin to move to his mountain home the Berghof, on the Obersalzberg in Berchtesgaden. To escape the inevitable

Russian invasion of Berlin, many of his staff, along with state officials and vehicles filled with papers and files, had already left to prepare the alpine retreat for Hitler. But he would never make this last trip from Berlin to his beloved house in the mountains. The end would come sooner than expected and he declared he would not leave the capital.

On 27 April Berlin was completely surrounded by the Red Army; the flames were visible for miles. In his bunker of the Reich Chancellery Hitler told a group of officers that this was the end and he would remain in Berlin. Hitler committed suicide in his bunker in Berlin on 30 April.

The Third Reich had come to its end.

The world was horrified to discover what was left of the concentration camps and their survivors. Food was distributed to them by the Americans and other Allies who liberated the camps. Many of these emaciated survivors came to be known as 'The Canned Goods Victims' as they were not used to the rich nourishing foods which were now available to them. Many perished from sudden overeating with little strength left to live.

One of the first things my mother did at the war's end was to hide the guns and rifles, stored in the cabinet in her bedroom, which had belonged to our father. Mother and Ilse wrapped the guns in oil cloth and buried them in the forest behind our house. Some time later, when mother felt it was safe, she went to dig up and retrieve the valuable weapons. To her surprise they were gone. Only an empty hole was left hidden among the trees. She suspected it was someone within the neighborhood.

Our mother's fears for our safety after the war proved justified. Even though she was divorced from our father, the people around us knew who he had been. They were not too sympathetic towards the defeated Germans who still lived in 'their Austria'. There was more than just a change in their attitude towards us. The same farmers who had been our neighbors and friends, eager and grateful to sell us their dairy products, came carrying pitch forks, clubs and sticks. They stormed up the path to our house, past the large gate toward our front door. My mother saw them coming and sent my sisters into the house to hide. Like an angry lynch mob, the farmers became violent and shouting they forcefully confronted my mother, threatening to kill all of us.

An unidentified man came out of the crowd to our rescue; he had heard of their intent to harm us and convinced them we were only innocent women and children and should not be held responsible for our father's actions. Slowly the mob calmed down and disassembled, heading back down the path still carrying their weapons. My mother never backed away; she remained composed and stood firm, protecting her family.

After the war American forces occupied Austria and many former Nazis were arrested as war criminals. Many were now fugitives who took on false identities looking for places to hide. One of these men was Ernest Kaltenbrunner, Hitler's former Chief of Gestapo and Reich Security; a brawny 6ft 7in SS General with a scar across his cheek left by a fencing sword. He had made his way as far as St Gilgen.

Having been friends of our father and family, he came to our home wanting a place to hide. My mother turned him away saying she was unable to take on the responsibility. Kaltenbrunner, one of the twenty-one infamous Nuremberg defendants, died at the gallows on 16 October 1946.

Our mother, however, didn't have the heart to turn away a young boy wearing a Nazi uniform, who knocked at our front door asking for food. It was one of those overcast wet mornings at our house in Austria. Here in this beautiful, peaceful little corner of the world there was no physical evidence that a terrible war had raged throughout Europe for the past five years. Water was dripping off the rooftops and puddles were left from the rain which had fallen the previous night, leaving the air with that lingering sweet fresh smell of the countryside.

The small, black steam locomotive pulled past the lake blowing its shrill whistle which echoed through the hovering fog, always visible around the lake on those misty mornings. It was Sunday. There was no school, and hearing the familiar whistle of the train Antje ran to an upstairs window and looked down through the trees toward the lake with curiosity. She watched with surprise as a stranger made his way up the path toward the house. He was a young soldier of about twenty years of age, who walked slowly with great effort, finally reaching our front door. Antje ran downstairs calling to our mother.

'Mutti, Mutti, there is someone at our front door! It's a man in a uniform!' Mother opened the front door and let out a gasp in complete astonishment. The young man in a tattered Nazi uniform was visibly hurt, but she only heard him softly whisper 'food' before he collapsed into her arms. Mother called to Ilse to come and help her take him upstairs into Dieter's bedroom.

They carried him upstairs, and although he seemed thin and frail, they struggled on the narrow staircase. They gently laid him down on my brother's bed. Conflicting thoughts must have run through Mother's mind, knowing full well that harboring a Nazi at that time was a serious offense. To Mother this tall injured boy with light brown hair and strong features in need of medical care, somehow exemplified her own son Dieter. He was also a mere boy when he was made to wear a uniform; fighting in a war that was already lost at that point in time, resulting in his capture by the Red Army at Lublin.

Mother and Ilse carefully removed his uniform. They sponged his body, applied some type of ointment and with clean bandages made from torn sheets they wrapped his wounds, which were luckily only superficial. They dressed him in some civilian street clothes which had belonged to my father, still left in the closet downstairs. The two women then walked behind the house carrying his uniform and a shovel. Looking around nervously they quickly buried the Nazi uniform among the trees in the forest, which was the only evidence that could identify their visitor.

They were not alone, however, because two curious little girls hiding out of sight watched in awe as their mother and Ilse dug through the layers of soft mulch.

Our mother nursed the young soldier with special tenderness until his youthful strength returned. She brought his meals on a tray into the room, which had been occupied by her own son Dieter not so long ago. She did not allow Antje and Brigitte much contact with the young man as she was afraid they would not be able to keep the secret. When he was well enough to leave and return to his own family, my mother was deeply moved.

Months after the war, and still in St Gilgen, my sisters took me for a walk one day, past one of several American army camps in the vicinity. An American soldier called to them: 'Hey, how about trading your cute baby sister for a chocolate bar? I'd like to bring her back to my wife as a souvenir!' The black soldiers were amused and laughed aloud when my sisters shouted 'No!' in horror. The soldiers were still smiling when they gave them a handful of Hershey bars. Brigitte and Antje didn't know quite what to think of these Americans, especially since they had never seen a black man before. Were all Americans of this color, they wondered? The majority of Germans had never seen any people of color. Apparently, the American troops deployed into the Austrian region at the war's end were the divisions that consisted entirely of units made up of black soldiers. During the Second World War the US military still practiced racial segregation.

The all-American Hershey bar, in that familiar brown wrapper, represented the 'AMI' (American soldier) to the children of these postwar European countries, as did Camels and Lucky Strike cigarettes to the adult population.

After the war had ended, the first American convoy to occupy Austria sent ahead a scouting unit to take a general survey of St Gilgen and its vicinity. The jeep carrying 'several black, gum-chewing GIs' was seen entering St Gilgen. The incident that followed made international headlines and turned the local law officials of this small village into a laughing stock throughout Europe. The town's police, apparently unaware that the war had ended, observed this jeep as an enemy invasion and took it upon themselves as a last effort to defend their homeland. The excited Austrians disarmed, arrested and 'captured' the baffled, disconcerted Americans as their POWs, who spent a few hours in the local jail until the rest of the troops arrived. They were quickly released by the completely embarrassed and obviously humiliated Police Department.

The Americans actually found this blunder quite humorous and it turned out to be one of the more light-hearted war stories, which would be heard and repeated for some time to come.

Then Rudolf surprised us when he unexpectedly appeared at our house, and within a matter of days the comfortable life we had come to know and love in this beautiful region would drastically change forever.

Chapter Six

One Son Captured, Another Born

When my father was transferred to Auschwitz, he and my brother Dieter, for a short time, lived in a red-brick house within the town itself on Bahnstrasse. Soon, Anneliese came to live with them. She was a pretty, slim, blond-haired woman. She idolized my father and was very proud and very much in love. She was fifteen years younger than him and was completely taken by this handsome, imposing figure of a man who held a high position. She looked up to him as he gave eloquent speeches without forethought or preparation.

Having worked together in close relationship in Oranienburg, she understood his career and position, thus creating a natural bond between them. Although the SS had tried every tactic within their power to discourage their relationship, making it very difficult for Papa in his career, their love would prevail.

When Anneliese joined my father and Dieter, they resided outside of the camp's perimeter at SS Siedlungs-Haus # 35, which was within walking distance of the camp's entrance. The house was a modest two-story with a kitchen, living room and study on the bottom floor, and two bedrooms and a bath on the top level. Their yard had trees and flowers and a garden where they grew their own vegetables. Doctor Frank and the Kommandant of Birkenau SS Major Hertjenstein, lived across the street from them, as well as other SS Officers.

The Siedlungs-Haus was made available to my father by the SS and was custom built especially for its officers and other camp personnel. The much larger Kommandant's villa, which lay adjacent to the 'Kommandantur' – offices of the Kommandant – was still occupied by the family of Rudolf Hoess, the first Kommandant of Auschwitz.

The camp was located only a short distance from the small town of Auschwitz, which was about eighteen miles from the larger city of Kattowitz where they would do their main shopping. Anneliese recalls passing through the camp's entrance, through the large iron gate, with that sinister inscription across the top 'Arbeit Macht Frei'. Inside were actual traditional shops available to SS members and their families, where they were able to purchase ordinary goods.

Dieter attended school in a nearby satellite camp and Anneliese worked part time for a building contractor. She was usually there when my father came home for the midday meal. They had a woman prisoner, a Jehovah's Witness, from the camp to do their housekeeping and cooking. Often they went to dinner at 'Hotel zur Post', a small quaint old restaurant in town, which was their only source of outside activity in this remote area.

It was here at their residence that the incident occurred with the young Polish prisoner, who had escaped from the camp. Anneliese found him hiding in the cellar of their home. They were both caught by total surprise and both equally frightened, but he never intended to hurt her. She calmed him and spoke to him softly, reassuring him he would not be harmed.

She didn't alert the camp, but waited out in the street for my father to come home. The Polish prisoner told my father he had escaped a few days earlier because he had had one wish, which was to see his mother once again. He had then chosen to return to the camp, coming first to my father's house, as he hadn't wanted to cause any problems for him.

My father had compassion and understood those kinds of feelings and desires to see one's mother again. He did return him to the camp but ordered that he was not to be hurt or punished for the escape, which was also mentioned in his journals.

My father was sworn to secrecy as to what transpired at the camp, but Anneliese was always aware of his feelings.

He was gone many evenings when the trains pulled into Birkenau. He was there … as all officers of authority ordered by Himmler to stand watch, and there were informers who were keeping an eye on him, looking for reasons to betray and disgrace him and to bring him to his end. He had to be there, it was required of him as part of his position and responsibility. He had no choice. He had to watch these frightened people as they arrived at the camp.

When he returned home later in the evenings he was mentally and emotionally broken … physically ill with violent headaches … terribly shaken … he would cry, 'No, my God, women and children!' To ease his mind we would take long walks. I saw him silently suffer this anguish. He would be so distressed he could not eat but would drink to try to forget. He could no longer face the ugly realities of the world … his world as Kommandant at Auschwitz. To him this was a torturous time in his life and emotionally he found it extremely difficult to carry out the responsibilities that were expected of him and it seemed he was pushed to his limit. There were others who felt the same, not like those who took the opportunity expressing pleasure with this type of authority.

He had no hatred for Jews and he never agreed with Hitler's Final Solution.

Of course, when he was interrogated at Nuremberg he denied his knowledge of what he saw … but what he didn't state was the fact that he had made several requests to Oswald Pohl for a transfer out of Auschwitz Concentration Camp, only to be unfairly persecuted by his superiors. He was denied these requests but later was sent to Lublin as another punishment because of my supposed relationship with Jews … He did what he could to improve conditions within his limitations, but was of course also under their constant watchful eye, and to go against them would have been insubordination and would have meant his death ... Later he made me promise never to tell you children about his involvement.

Anneliese
April 1997

Anneliese remembers the pressure he was under as Kommandant, which required much self-discipline. To add to his turmoil he then had to answer their accusations concerning her involvement with a Jew. His already darkened world was now shadowed with their orders for him to rid himself of the woman he loved and who was going to have his child. He looked for peace of mind, trying to forget by drowning his burdens in champagne.

Father and Anneliese went through a dreadful time, waiting desperately to marry, but Oswald Pohl, his commanding general, repeatedly denied their requests.

Hans-Dieter was born to father and Anneliese on 13 October 1944 in the neighboring camp Birkenau. It was there in the hospital section that Anneliese gave birth to their little boy. Our father, who was stationed in Italy by now, came to be there with her, just as he had been there before for the birth of all his children. He said in his Journals: 'Hans-Dieter was a special gift from God, a new life in the midst of where so many had to die.' The other women at the hospital were camp prisoners giving birth to their babies, who would then be taken from them immediately; these women would never see their babies again. They were never given a chance at life. It was a terrible experience for Anneliese and it also had a definite effect on Hans-Dieter later as an adult.

Heinrich Himmler eventually gave his consent, and so it was that Anneliese and my father were finally married officially on 16 October 1944. Their newborn son was three days old. Heinrich Himmler was going against the recommendation of both Richard Baer and Oswald Pohl. He believed it was better to avoid a scandal, as it was feared that it could take only one member to disgrace and blemish the image of the entire elite SS organization.

Earlier in the year Dieter had been drafted into the Luftwaffe as 'Flakhelfer', along with his whole school class – boys over the age of fifteen. This was the anti-aircraft fighter division of the air force, ground troops who had to bear arms to combat the enemy. He attended high school at the camp Myslowitz, and remained at Auschwitz with Anneliese to finish the school year after Father was transferred to the camp Majdanek in Lublin in May 1944. My father's move to Lublin was another disciplinary assignment. After he had gone, Anneliese and Dieter moved to an apartment in the town center of Auschwitz, on Hauptstrasse. However, that Easter of 1944 was the last time Dieter was to see our father.

Father only remained at the Lublin camp for two months. It was the same situation; a severe hard labor camp – today we know it was also a death camp. He didn't want to be there, requesting a transfer; he even volunteered for the front lines but was rejected for health reasons. It was during Dieter's summer vacation that year that he went to visit Papa in Lublin. Father was not aware of

Dieter's intentional visit and, with a strange twist of fate, had just left for Berlin to request a new assignment. Their paths were never to cross again. Dieter was caught in an ambush, unable to escape Lublin before the invasion of the Russian army.

My brother was so mentally wounded by his experience as a prisoner of the Russians that even now, sixty years later, he is unwilling to discuss his imprisonment; he has shared only a few simple facts with me. Between the lines I read the heartbreaking loneliness of a young boy who had lost his youthful innocence, on that day in July of 1944.

> It was here at the front lines that the Russians invaded with 1,000 tanks and many other heavy artillery. I found myself in the midst of this witch's cauldron. We defended ourselves in despair but were overpowered by highly outnumbered forces. On July 26, 1944 many other soldiers and I were captured and sent to Russia for captivity. The great ordeal began. We were all sent to Siberia, transported in cattle cars traveling for three weeks.
>
> Dieter, 1992

A week before my brother fell into the hands of the Russian army, father was still conducting business at the Lublin camp, sending trivial communications about one single escaped POW. All the while, the Red Army was approaching.

Lublin July 18, 1944
To the Commander of the Sipo u.d. SD/Warsaw
Reference: Polish Jew, Wodowski Zelik, born 6/29/'11 in Dabrow/District-Kielce on July 14, 1944, at approximately 18:30 hours.
Wodowski escaped from the concentration camp Lublin, Labor Camp Warsaw. He was committed to the camp by the RSHA-Berlin. For further necessary information from the Personnel staff, please direct questions and contact the SS-Labor Camp in Warsaw [Ghetto].
Please instruct what action to be taken for the search.

> Concentration Camp Lublin
> gez. Liebehenschel[1]

A long death march began for Dieter and his comrades; it was a case of survival of the fittest. Many perished along the way. They were finally herded into cattle cars and arrived in Siberia three weeks later. No one knew of Dieter's fate, whether he was dead or alive. For this reason, father and Anneliese named their new little son Hans-Dieter, so somehow through him our oldest brother would live on.

My father and mother both tried to find some news about him through the Red Cross and later found out he had been placed into a 'silent camp'. These prisoners were positively forbidden any kind of outside contact, with no letters home to even let their families know they were alive. They persecuted Dieter because they had become aware he was a Liebehenschel, and they knew of our father. As thousands of Russian POWs had lost their lives at Auschwitz, our Dieter suffered the consequences. He was repeatedly interrogated into confessing that he too was a member of the SS, which of course he wasn't, as the age to join was eighteen.

He labored in the coal mines and became very ill. For a long time his lungs were affected. It was extremely cold, the food was scarce and for the most part non-existent. Every day some of his comrades would freeze to death and he had to dig into the frozen ground in sub-zero temperatures to bury them. His youth was an advantage; he was strong enough to survive, to make it through – physically.

Dieter was not released until May 1950. The deep emotional scar that was left is still evident today. As a man he has never been able to forget this torturous ordeal and will take the horror stories to his grave. He still has nightmares of the living hell.

As a result we really don't know or understand the full extent of his hidden emotions, but he made it very clear to me, when I tried to find out information for my book, that he was simply unable to discuss it with me. He has a fixation with clocks, probably having something to do with the time he lost in his youth. We do know they were terribly difficult years for him, and those six years of his life he still tries to forget.

From Lublin father was sent to Triest, Italy in July 1944, where he worked in the administrative offices (Manpower Main Office) of the construction battalions 'Baugruppe-Ost'. This was a postcard sent by my father from Italy:

December 9, 1944

Dear Children,

With this Italian Christmas Card I send you heartfelt greetings. How are you? I would have been very happy to hear something for my birthday, dear Brigitte and Antje. I would like to send you a little something for Christmas but don't know how I'll get the package into the Reich, but somehow it will work out. I will also have money sent to you from the Reich. Otherwise I'm not doing so well as my heart often gives me trouble. But it will be all right.

Hopefully the war will soon be over so we can see each other again. I am sending some unused ration stamps that I have saved for you. How is Bärbel? Stay healthy and don't forget me entirely. I think of you often. If only Dieter would come back, that hurts so much, only God can help. Is Ilse still there? Say hello to her.

Loving Greetings and Kisses
Your Papsi

P.S. Did you receive my letter?

This was the only time that my father asked explicitly about me, showing that I was of any importance to him. The picture on the front of the postcard showed a small girl holding a green holiday branch – next to her he wrote 'Bärbel'.

For me this was the most personal loving gesture of acknowledgement. Since he left home when I was an infant, he never really knew me. Anneliese and their baby Hans-Dieter lived with father at this time in Italy. I suspect it was a reminder for him that he had another young child not much older than his newborn son.

Transcripts of Pretrial Interrogation at Nuremberg:
U.S. Military Chief of Counsel for War Crimes/SS Section
Taken of: Arthur Wilhelm Liebehenschel – by E. Rigney
Date: September 18, 1946 – [continued]

Lublin:
Q: At what date did you arrive at Lublin?
A: May 19, 1944.
Q: What was your designated position there?
A: Kommandant of the concentration camp.
Q: How long were you Kommandant at Lublin?
A: Until the Russians invaded.
Q: At what time approximately was that?
A: July 21, 1944.
Q: How many inmates were at the Lublin Concentration Camp?
A: It was evacuated as it was near the front, which was about 80 kilometers away. There were only 450 inmates within the camp who were used for maintenance.
Q: That doesn't make sense. As you arrived the camp was evacuated, but yet there were 450 workers that were to recondition the camp? For the Russians? For the Russians?
A: No one could understand this, including me.
Q: But yet you were the Kommandant?
A: What was the use of my petition? I had stressed upon this matter umpteen times. There were 450 more prisoners employed in several factories in Lublin making a total of 900 prisoners.
Q: How many prisoners were within the camp when you came to Lublin?
A: 450 in the camp and 450 in armament camps in the city, at a special camp.
Q: So you had 900 prisoners. What was the capacity of the Lublin camp?
A: The capacity was 10 to 15,000.
Q: What happened to them?
A: To my prisoners?
Q: No, to the 15,000.
A: They had been sent to other camps earlier.
Q: Who told you this?
A: That information was given to me by my predecessor SS Lt-Colonel Weiss.

Q: Was he there when you arrived?

A: He was there and I then took over the position from him.

Q: To which camps were these people sent?

A: To various camps, the majority was sent to Buchenwald, Mauthausen and Auschwitz, but I'm not certain.

Q: So this Kommandant acted against Himmler's orders? As the order Himmler gave was to exterminate these people when the enemy came?

A: That could be. In any event at that time …

Q: That could be? That was so. And you know about this order, as well as I do?

A: Know of it? Yes.

Q: So we could say that this Camp Kommandant Weiss, went against Himmler's orders?

A: In any case he received and followed the orders to distribute the prisoners to other camps.

Q: Was there not also a crematorium at Lublin?

A: In the concentration camp there was a single oven in a wooden barrack.

Q: And gas chambers?

A: I didn't see any. I was not there.

Q: You mean to say as Camp Kommandant you neglected your duties and made no effort to go around and inspect to see what was actually there?

A: I was not interested in the camp crematorium. I already explained that I performed my duties differently.

Q: As Camp Kommandant? You are like a little child, who has to have every single thing explained to him. As Camp Kommandant when you arrived at a new camp, was it not your duty to familiarize yourself and see what was actually there, or to request of your predecessor a report on the new commission? As you came to Lublin, did the acting deputy inform you about various equipment, or did you find the information yourself?

A: Obviously, of course.

Q: So your answer is yes?

A: Yes.

Q: Then what did you find?

A: A camp with barracks in five fields, the camp was vacant. A short time before the Russians had dropped 80 bombs into the camp, and various barracks were damaged. I had no great interest in Lublin. I had turned in a request for a transfer to which at that time I had no response; after I had already been outcast by my superiors, especially Pohl.

Q: How long were you at Lublin?

A: On July 15, I was ordered to a conference in Krakow. There it was planned to tear down the Lublin factories, in order to build positions against the advancing Russians.

Q: With whom was the conference?

A: With the SS Chief of Economic Administration in Krakow.

Q: Was this a deputy to Pohl? What was his name?

A: Scheelin.

Q: What was his assignment in Krakow?

A: Pohl's deputy for administration and economy.

Q: Was that the first time you ever saw Scheelin?

A: I had seen him once before. As I went to Lublin I had to report in to Krakow

Q: What sort of instructions did you receive from him?

A: The first time or at this conference?

Q: At this one, the second conference?

A: It was concerning how many barracks were to be destroyed, the transportation of remaining prisoners out of Lublin, and through the course of this conference we received communication that the Russians had advanced.

Q: What were you supposed to do with the 900 prisoners that were in your charge?

A: The remaining prisoners [900] were transferred to Auschwitz, by Representative SS Captain Melzer.

Q: How did you know that he sent the 900 prisoners to Auschwitz?

A: I learned this at Auschwitz, as I still had a residence there.

Q: When did you leave Lublin?

A: I have already stated that, July 15th.

Q: Where did you go from there?

A: I then went to Berlin and received my orders for my transfer.

Q: From whom?

A: From group commander Gluecks.

Q: Were you ordered back to Berlin?

A: No, I was following up on my transfer, as I had received no word, and therefore …

Q: And what was Gluecks' reply to this?

A: He said he'd talked to Pohl. I had asked him not to send me to Pohl, as he had already sent me a communication to Auschwitz, stating that as long as my point of view remained the same, concerning my personal affairs, he didn't ever want to see me again; this is what he sent to me in his communication. I begged Gluecks to go to him, which he did. I had to wait for days and then it was decided I would be transferred to the SS Main Operations Office. I had volunteered for the front, but was not accepted because of physical reasons. Then I went to the Staff Department.

Q: What position?

A: Section Chief of Department I, in Triest and Laibach.

Q: You went from Berlin to Triest?

A: Yes.

Q: From when, until when were you there?

A: Until February 1945, the 15th or 16th I came back to Laibach. Until this time I was at Triest.

Q: What was your assignment in Laibach?

A: It was the same in Laibach, another construction battalion. First I was with the construction group east, later to the construction battalion Laibach which was part of German territory.

Q: What specifically was Section I responsible for?

A: Supervising construction of fortification and employment of the work force, mostly old men.

Q: Were they prisoners? What units were they?

A: Besides party members they were also various military units and many others.

Q: Where did these work forces come from?

A: 85 per cent from the native population.

Q: Were they all Italians?

A: There it was all Italians and in Laibach territory it was Slovaks.

Q: Did they volunteer?

A: They volunteered and also received 50 lire per week and flour, sugar and cigarettes.

Q: What kind of work did they perform?

A: They constructed trenches, fox holes, anti-tank positions etc.

Q: Who supervised them?

A: By party members, members of the Reich Labor Service, and the Todt organization.

Q: Were they SA and SS people?

A: No.

Q: What uniform did you wear?

A: The party uniform. Later it was the field gray uniforms without any insignia, except a badge bearing the words 'Stellbau Italien'.

Q: I'm not clear what section this battalion belonged to?

A: It was not part of the Wehrmacht or the SS.

Q: To what administration did you belong, technically?

A: The Construction Battalion, it was part of the party. The party had administrative command of these construction projects.

Q: How long were you with the Construction Battalion?

A: Until the end, May 7th, when I was taken prisoner by the Americans.

Q: And now I'd like to ask you to please give me a short character analysis of Oswald Pohl. How would you summarize this in a few sentences?

A: In my opinion he has committed suicide. It is very difficult for me to talk about him.

Q: Go ahead and take a few minutes to give a short character study of the man and the officer, your former superior Oswald Pohl?

A: The man has destroyed my life, he pulled my wife through the dirt and took away my son, and you want me to give my opinion of such a man? The way he was as a person likewise reflected in his career.

Q: Do you personally consider Pohl an efficient administrator?

A: He acted as though he was.

Q: In your opinion, do you believe the other SS Commanders thought of Pohl as an efficient administrator?

A: I believe only to some extent. In a time where all order has gone and a whole New World is coming onto us, it is difficult to say, as many will voice their insults and abuse against others.[2]

Anneliese, Hans-Dieter and her mother lived with father for a time in Italy, but then returned to the apartment in Auschwitz. When Auschwitz was evacuated she found herself and her three-month-old baby cast out onto the street. On 17 January 1945 she fled to Berlin as the Russians were quickly advancing. On 25 January our father came for a short visit to Berlin, returning to Triest on 5 February.

Anneliese recalled the time of evacuation from the Camp Auschwitz and how she lost all personal identification records, which was a serious problem in those days:

> I no longer have my family records. All documents were taken from me at the time of the evacuation, as we took flight from Auschwitz. They were taken by the man who was in charge of this transport. He held on to all of my papers. The train was to go from Auschwitz to Czechoslovakia. I was to go as far as Czechoslovakia but got off the train in Breslau and was then on my own, although my mother was with me and Hans-Dieter was still a baby in the carriage. Then there came a train carrying soldiers and I turned to an officer for help, who took us as far as Berlin, where my sister was … but this was only because I had ID. Your Papa had given me a written letter stating, if there was any problem, I should be taken care of. I presented this and even though it was against regulations, the officer took responsibility, taking me as far as Berlin. They were German Wehrmacht officers, regular army, not the Waffen SS.
>
> Anneliese
> September 11, 1999

In the waning days of the war, father was once again transferred, this time to Laibach, in the Yugoslavian territory. While there with my father, Anneliese got word that her parents' old apartment, where Anneliese had once lived with them as a young single girl, had been bombed during an air raid and they had lost almost all their belongings. Anneliese's mother was alone in the apartment and ran for shelter into the garden when the bombers attacked. At the time her father was serving at the front lines.

When Anneliese received this news she took Hans-Dieter and traveled home to Wuppertal to be with her mother. With the help of her uncles they moved her parents to another three-room apartment. They were able to salvage a few personal items from the rubble pile, but lost all the furniture.

The three-room apartment was precisely that: three empty rooms; they slept on the floor, but were grateful to be alive. After the war this area was occupied by the British who supplied them with blankets and cots to sleep on.

Anneliese missed my father and soon took advantage of the opportunity to leave the boy with her parents in Wuppertal, while she embarked on a journey to be with my father in Yugoslavia.

When spring arrived in 1945, the defeat of the Third Reich was looming while hope for the promised 'miracle weapon' was abandoned.

Toward the war's end my father and Anneliese fled from Yugoslavia and desperately made their way back to their homeland accompanying a German Army Division, camping out with the troops, traveling along in transport trucks. My father suffered another heart attack during this time and Anneliese cared for him as best she could under the poor circumstances. When they arrived in Wagrain, Austria, Papa surrendered to the Americans who had already occupied the area. At this time Anneliese found work on a farm for food, as their reserve had been depleted. They were less than 100 miles from our house in St Gilgen where my sisters and I were still living with my mother. I would like to believe that our father was on his way to see us, but Anneliese tells me that was not his intention.

It was at this point that my father and Anneliese were finally separated. When she begged the black American guard to let her see my father just once more through the fence, he said: 'If you sleep with me.' She lied, promising him she would, and even paid him some money just so she and father would be able to see one another one last time. Later, the guard came looking for Anneliese at the farm where she had found shelter. The farmer told him Anneliese was no longer living there, but she was actually hiding in the attic.

Father wrote of their heartbreaking departure in his journal on 4 August 1947.

> I think of our last meeting: In the distance from the top of the rise I saw you coming long before you reached the guard's barrier. Then you were before me and your eyes reflected the burden of your soul. I took your trembling hands into mine and with it your heart. We both knew it was the final departure for an undetermined length of time. Few words were spoken, the pain was too intense but all was said with our souls touching and clinging to one another.

Father asked Anneliese to search for and look after us children. She kept her promise to him and eventually found us through the Red Cross.

He was then shipped to several different prison camps and finally all SS people were sent to Bad Aibling. From there father ended up at Dachau where he spent over a year, held prisoner by the Americans.

Anneliese became one of thousands of German women who were known as 'Truemmer Frauen' after the war. These women, as well as children, had been left as the sole work force to clear the devastating ruins. Shoulder to shoulder they removed the debris and rubble piles, sometimes with garden tools, but mostly using their bare hands, salvaging bricks or whatever they could to help rebuild their towns and cities.

Through Anneliese, there remains those last fragile ties, which validate my father's true existence.

While at Dachau, Papa wrote letters to my sister Brigitte for her birthday in December 1945, and to my brother Dieter in April 1946.

In captivity, December 27, 1945

My Dear Brigittchen,

Tomorrow is your birthday and you will be 13 years old. You must be a big girl already. A long time has passed since I saw you the last time in February 1944 it will be two years.

The last letter I received from you was in March of this year. With an ache in my heart I send you my innermost Birthday Wishes, even though I don't know where you are or how you are doing and you don't know where I am. Hopefully you, and all of you, are healthy, everything else is bearable and has to be endured.

So I pray to God everyday for his richest blessings and also for you and your New Year in life. You were always a dear sweet girl and with your given character will make it through life's difficult path. Soon you will be at the age where one looks at everything with clear and different eyes. Do this and judge in peace and fairness for yourself when in a distant time you are moved toward that direction. You will then come to the conclusion that everything in life proceeds in God's designated way and we can't change that. And so is the fate of nations as the life of a single person. Even ours, especially our life, had to proceed the way it has until now. Compare all things precisely and you will realize that all situations had to be as they are for you all, for you and for me. You will then understand what I mean.

Of course there was a time where you only knew of my care and experienced happy childhood days, some of the best times, not just for you but also for me. I always strived to bring you as much happiness as possible and to keep from you all sad and unhappy times, as I had to experience in my own childhood.

You are all in my heart as before and this past Christmas holiday, I envisioned all of your shining eyes and felt your live souls near me.

Then I think especially of our poor missing Dieter and pray to God that we will see him again. Just as I always tried to make Christmas a very special time prepared with every thought and love possible, I give you my confirmation of the love I carry for you all in my heart and always will.

Especially now, my thoughts are with you all in this time of the collapse but I am now a POW behind barbed wire and have become so poor I can't even help you.

I don't know what you have gone through, where you are or how you are, but that God will protect you I do know.

Until now you've been relatively unburdened and sheltered. I tried to take care of that. But now life will look different, as I don't know what will happen to me. One thing is certain; I will have to start from the bottom if God grants me the freedom. I'm not afraid of work and I will always cope with the worries of life. All that is in God's hands to whom I have turned over my whole life. Now you probably want to know what I'm doing? Health wise I am doing poorly. Since the beginning of May

I have been a prisoner of the Americans and because of my four and a half months' time in Auschwitz concentration camp I have been held for interrogation since August, behind bars in a cell. Many Germans, Polish and Jewish former prisoners of Auschwitz that have seen me here again have been good character witnesses and confirmed that I treated everyone good and with decency and inflicted no harm of my own or allowed any harm to come to anyone. Now I will have to wait to see what they will do with me. For those other times when I was not associated with the concentration camps and only did administrative work and when I was often ill, that can't be held against me, as never in my life have I harmed anyone. I only write this to you that you, my dear children, don't have to be ashamed of the name you carry. Maybe you can already comprehend that yourself. I don't want to mention any more about this.

The time I have gone through has been very difficult, even with the correct handling by the Americans. Yet I have endured all with similar fate.

At my side stands a knapsack with my sole belongings. For many months I have known nothing of the whereabouts of my loved ones and still the soul is rich and I have felt a definite closeness to God. It is indescribable what wonderful ways God has guided me with his actual miracles – through so much slander and viciousness. Without these miracles I would not be alive. And I always had to be thankful for the outstanding people he sent my way in the saddest times in my life.

And so even you, dear Brigittchen, can see that the Lord and fate so willed it.

Poor, driven and separated from the new-born Hans-Dieter, my God given life's comrade followed me from camp to camp in the first few months of my captivity. She satisfied our hunger by working at a farm. To bring me a piece of bread she often had to walk 40 kilometers a day to come to me and always with a kind and faithful heart.

The woman at the farm didn't want to let her go as she cared for 12 people in the house, worked in the kitchen and also helped in the fields. And then the worry about her man whom she gave such strength to go on living. Without her I would no longer be and that's why I tell you this here. If you can't understand me today, then read this letter later in years and you will understand. By that time I hope to have spoken to you personally. What yearning I have for you Antje (my dear Atilein) and Bärbel to see you again. Brigittchen, until then don't forget me. Always keep in mind that I never did anything wrong and have never forgotten you, my dear children and will forever hold you in my heart.

Sometimes you thought I didn't love you as much as the other children, that was never so. Especially you, whose character and appearance are so much like my dear deceased mother and will stay forever in my soul, as all of you children have the same place in my fatherly heart, where it remains faithfully with its blessings. Naturally as then the youngest, Atilein received more attention but she always was such a dear little thing and was so very close to me and gave me so much strength through my life's struggle. That's why I send special wishes to her today and give her a loving kiss from me. Has she not forgotten her Papsi? A little kiss for Bärbel too.

How is my Atilein and how might Bärbel look now? Every night you are in my prayers. Am I in yours also? I know God has our future already planned and so I believe in our fate and God's help. Soon all avenues will lead us out of the sorrow and darkness into the light. What I have been fortunate enough to experience in the loneliness of my cell is powerful. You must always have a firm belief in God and all things will work out. I hope I can share this with you in person.

At this time I am not allowed to send this letter and I don't even know where to send it. But I had to write to you on your Birthday. May these lines reach you through the bars and be carried to you as are my daily prayers for you all.

When I am free again, I shall find you through the Red Cross. Until then we will think of one another and pray daily with your little hands folded to God and plead him to help. I want to hold you dear children tight in my arms, especially you and Atilein … Bärbel hardly knows me and I want to talk with you at length. This hope too we shall never give up. As you can see Brigitte I am with you especially today on your birthday and am celebrating with you in spirit. Let's forget the ugly times in life, they don't matter any more and let's bring back the beautiful times in our thoughts.

It was wonderful when I walked with you through the Berlin Zoo, it was wonderful when I told you Christmas Stories, it was wonderful when I could spread the Christmas Table with goodies or walk with you in the forest and tell you secretive myths of the German Forests, or when you all, especially Atilein with her flying braids, would run up to meet me. You helped carry so many of my worries through your happy childlike eyes, you my dear children which you will always be.

And you, dear Brigittchen, try to understand all hardships and suffering, as once all happiness through the Lord as he willed, then with your 13 years as the oldest daughter you will be there for your mother and your sisters. So go with God's blessings into the New Year with good health. Many birthday wishes and kisses. Stay healthy and brave in this difficult time. God will bless you all. Don't forget your dear brother Dieter in your prayers. We won't give up the belief that God will return him to us. And don't forget your father who thinks of you daily with sorrowful heart.

You, Atilein, Bärbel, many kisses and many greetings to you all. I'll always be yours and never forget you.

Your Papsi.

In Prison April 27, 1946

My Dear Dieter – my Son,

It's been 2 years since you have left me. You wanted to come visit me during your vacation and ended up in the hands of the enemy and I have not heard from you since. However I still believe that you are alive and will return.

Last night as so often you were in my dreams again. You have grown – yes soon you will be 18 years old, a young man. It is indescribable how I have been worried about you and tormented these last two years. Anneliese and I have sent many ardent prayers for you to God. I myself have been a prisoner for one year and with it I must also bear the sorrows about you and all of us.

When you return, and in the event that I shall not see you again, Anneliese will tell you of the injustice and pain they have inflicted on me. I will carry it through to the last consequence, if only you will all remain alive. Remain my well-behaved boy, not only toward me but Anneliese who also loves you as I do and who is and will remain your motherly friend.

Learn a trade as your schooling is now over. Work and nourish yourself with honesty and maintain goodness of heart, then you can always face up to your conscience.

I thank you my son for your mature understanding and loyalty which you've proven in difficult times when you stood by me and came with me. This same loyalty I will hold true to you as long as I live. It is hard to imagine how good it would be if we could all work and live together once more, even if it were in the lowest state of poverty. We have to believe in God's guidance even if it is difficult at times.

My thoughts are always with you no matter where you may be. I close you lovingly into my aching father's heart and will never forget you. Together with my beloved Annelie I will be with you. May God bless and keep you my dear boy and help you to survive. Don't forget me, pray for me my dear, dear Dieter.

I am sending you many affectionate greetings and kisses somewhere into the unknown and remain your devoted Papa.[3]

Chapter Seven

Betrayed and Banished as Refugees

It was in the fall, around September of 1945. Rudolf appeared at our door in St Gilgen, Austria. Mother assumed he had come to see Ilse. However, his plans were of a more treacherous nature. Our mother wondered why he had to make so many trips into Salzburg. He was clever and took this opportunity to go to the courthouse, where he made it his business to secure the appropriate legal documents to have us evicted from our own home. It seems we had no legal rights, no longer entitled to the ninety-nine-year lease on Austrian soil. The fact that our father had been with the SS were all factors that assisted in making him the new owner. We had three days to leave our home, with only a few belongings.

It is hard to perceive that this would have been accomplished without the exchange of any collateral. How could a former concentration camp prisoner, who had lost his entire fortune during the war, simply walk in and appropriate our property? My family's understanding was, since Rudy's only assets were the accumulated dental gold which he had smuggled out of the concentration camp, that this would have persuaded the authorities to let Rudy take over our home and force us to leave. Ours was not a unique fate after the war. Thousands upon thousands of other Germans, especially those from Eastern Europe, were driven from their land, and thousands were killed or died of disease and starvation.

Today, Antje has vivid memories of the cloth bags containing dental gold which were hidden in the closet in Ilse's room at our house in St Gilgen. My sisters were playing hide-and-seek, or maybe just snooping around, when they came across the gold, but they of course had no idea about its dreadful origin.

Ilse stayed on and a month later she married Rudy, on 29 October. He had the audacity to send a wedding photo signed: 'in memory of our beautiful wedding on the Wolfgangsee'. It took place in our home surrounded by all our belongings. Furniture, dishes etc.

It must have been a terrible disappointment and hurt our mother deeply, especially the betrayal by Ilse, whom she always trusted – and to think this was how she was repaid for her kindness and friendship.

When my sister Antje and I visited Austria, and looked up the house in St Gilgen in 1970, much to our horror, Rudolf was still living there. I remember standing at the bottom of the old rock stairs, looking up at a heavy set man whose body language alone gave off a presence of complete self-assurance and insolence. Almost immediately I recognized the face of uncle Rudy, as I used to call him years ago, when he gave me candy as a child. It was a cold reception. We were not allowed into the house, but we could see our family's furnishings still inside through the open door.

It was a shock, and unbelievable, especially remembering how he had treated our mother. What a strange, uncomfortable encounter, and to think that this wretched thief and opportunist was fortunate enough to have survived a concentration camp when so many innocent people met their fate in the gas chamber.

He told us that Ilse had died of leukemia in the 1950s. We went searching through the old cemetery that day, it seemed for a long time. I really wanted to find her grave, and it was only by peculiar chance that I came across her headstone, overgrown and covered up with ivy. Even then it seemed she was still reaching out to me.

So here was just another setback for our mother, having to leave all her belongings and the house that was so dear to her. The last tangible connection to my father was finally taken from her.

We were only allowed to take three to four suitcases, which contained some clothing and important personal papers. We were loaded onto trucks headed to Salzburg, and from there onto crowded freight trains, like cattle, to the city of Bonn. There were no toilet facilities, only large pails; there was hysteria and crying babies; the stench was terrible and all so humiliating for my mother.

She and my oldest sister Brigitte took turns staying awake, holding on to my carriage so it wouldn't roll out of the open freight car.

That night we stopped in the town of Eschwege where we were put up in a high school auditorium. We slept on straw bags and dirty blankets, and we were given some hot food and drinks. For three weeks this train rolled from town to village, but no one wanted us, the 'DPs' (displaced persons), to settle in their community.

Our fate had already been decided: our mother just happened to overhear that we were to be sent back to East Germany the next morning, since we had originally come from Oranienburg, now occupied by the Russians. Again, they recognized the family name and our mother had no recourse, or so they thought.

There was not much time, and when we made another stop to let people on and off, mother had to act quickly. She gathered us up and we got off the train. She talked with a young man who was also going to be sent back to Berlin. Our mother asked him to help her and together they plotted to catch a train back to southern Bavaria, which was under American occupation. She wanted to remain close to the Austrian border as she hoped to regain our house, or at least some of our furnishings and other belongings. She also realized that being sent to the Russian Zone would have been our downfall.

Mother had been left with very little money; we had only the clothes on our backs. In those days the situation was fearful, the trains were overcrowded with displaced persons and there was much confusion and panic. People even traveled by standing on the running boards, hanging from the exterior of the cars, taking them to who knows where; to places that no longer existed.

While mother and her young friend went to see about a train to Bavaria, she told Brigitte to watch the suitcases and stay with Antje and me, still in the carriage. Antje decided to walk off and Brigitte ran to catch up with her. When she returned, amazingly I was still there but two of our suitcases had been taken. Brigitte searched the crowd only to see people pushing, shoving and stepping over each other. Gone were our birth certificates and other important documents.

With the young man's help and our mother's persistence, we made the train, which would take us to Bavaria, to Berchtesgaden. It's hard to believe we even made the right train and actually stayed together safely.

We came to the town of Piding, to the barracks of the refugee camp. That's what we had become – homeless refugees. Our only personal belongings were now just two suitcases; we still had each other, but like all the other thousands of displaced persons after the war, we became lost individuals within the vast crowds of people.

The conditions were very poor: hundreds of people sleeping on small cots that were stacked three tiers high. Our mother tried to give us some privacy; she hung blankets on the sides of our bunks. It was very dirty and dusty with wooden plank floors. There was not much food … and where were we to go from here? This decision was soon made for our mother.

Since the camp at Piding was terribly overcrowded, a number of people had to be sent elsewhere. Therefore, we went to Berchtesgaden, to the camp 'Duerreck' on the Obersalzberg mountain, where Hitler's former house, the Berghof, was located.

It was late October when we arrived on the mountain. The Obersalzberg was already covered with thick layers of snow but it was very beautiful. We were placed in the barracks that previously housed Hitler's troops and guards. When we arrived there, moldy Kommiss bread was found that had been left behind by the SS. In 1944 this camp had been occupied by a command of over 2,000 SS men who closely guarded Hitler's Obersalzberg. Not far from the camp sat the Berghof, Hitler's private home, which for obvious reasons had been set on fire by the SS in May 1945, and the remains were destroyed by American and British forces.

The barracks consisted of many large rooms. Our mother managed to acquire one small room separated from the others, formerly a sentry station adjoining the main barracks. It had two cots and one single wood-burning stove. Finally we had some privacy and were not crowded in with all the others.

There was a kitchen facility that had been used for the troops. In the morning everyone went to get their rations, which in the beginning consisted of whatever had been left behind by the SS men. They made bread soup from the stale, moldy Kommis bread, which had been there for more than a year. Kommis bread is a firm, dark rye bread, made to keep for long periods of time, ideal for the men in the field. Many times the soup was spoiled and inedible, and we had to throw away the only nourishment there was, but usually it was eaten regardless.

Eventually we did receive better rations, supplied by the occupying American forces. Another problem was that the camp was situated high on the mountain, and in the wintertime the narrow, winding road leading to the top was not accessible, making it impossible to receive deliveries or even have contact with the world below. Once a week we acquired one pat of butter. Brigitte admired a pretty, middle-aged lady who never ate hers, but saved it and sparingly used it on her face as a moisturizing cream. My sister was in awe of her beauty and how she maintained her dignity, wondering who she might have been before she became a poor refugee.

Our mother could not afford such luxuries; she was doing everything within her power to keep the three of us from starving.

The winters in the Bavarian Alps are severe, with extremely cold temperatures. In the deep snow, lacking the proper warm clothing and shoes, my mother and Brigitte went looking for twigs and branches to heat the stove. What was found was usually too wet and wouldn't burn. They went at night, so as not to be seen, without any light for guidance, and tore out floor boards and walls of empty barracks with their bare hands; anything that made firewood for a little warmth.

The living conditions were terribly bad, making it very unhealthy with lice and disease. All this contributed to Brigitte's illness. When she was examined by a doctor she was diagnosed as having the forerunner to TB. The only positive thing that came out of that was that the doctor prescribed extra special portions of milk, butter and bread. It was enough to feed all of us, but only for a short time until the supply was exhausted.

The nights were freezing cold. We slept cuddled together in order to stay warm. It was an ultimate test of survival and we were not able to enjoy the beautiful mountains and countryside. Our mother knew that eventually we would have to give in, meaning the mountain and elements could get the best of us. The people who ran the camp really had no control over the situation. Mother knew something had to be done or we would all perish.

The people at the camp were refugees from all over Germany. It was a gathering place of various dialects and no one seemed to know what to do with all these 'lost' people. One day, our mother planned to build a sled with one of the other male refugees. They designed and assembled two sleds and, since we were snowed in with very little food at this point, it seemed to be the only solution for my mother to get us off the mountain. They were made with primitive tools and anything which was available that had been left by the SS forces, but most of all with mother's strong will for our survival. It is amazing how she and her friend accomplished this project under such destitute circumstances.

The materials came from the boards of empty barracks and metal pieces from old bed frames. Mother endured these unpredictable changes in her life with incredible spirit. She and the other refugee were very proud of their achievement, especially when the final trial run on the sleds turned out to be very successful, an event that was a fun diversion from the harsh realities as refugees. The sleds were surprisingly durable and lasted for quite a few years. Heidi's grandfather couldn't have done any better!

When her sled was ready, our mother left Antje and me with Brigitte while she rode down the mountain to the town of Berchtesgaden. She looked up the 'Wohnungsamt', a housing bureau which in those days helped the endless stream of refugees locate places to live. It was almost impossible then to find an empty available apartment; or even a single room. If you were among the fortunate it could almost be considered a miracle.

Mother made several harrowing trips down that mountain on the little home-made sled, climbing back up on her return, fighting the biting cold, wind and snow all the way. The altitude of the camp Duerreck on the Obersalzberg was 3,300ft, making it a steep, long and difficult ascent. Looking back, one has to wonder how she managed, but it shows her incredible courage and determination and the fight that was still left in her; the motherly instinct, the knowing she must do something drastic to protect us and to change what appeared to be a grim destiny. She was a good, caring mother and wanted us out of the camp and away from those barracks.

She was among the fortunate few, and finally found two small rooms in the house on Hindenburg Allee # 1. The friend who helped build the sleds gave us his. It seemed to be our mother's caring nature; she was friendly and drawn to people and someone would always take a liking to her, ready to help her out of compassion.

We stacked our few belongings on one sled and they put me onto the other one. And so we left the barracks and began our journey down the mountain, which only a few short months before had been Hitler's hideaway. Through feet of fresh snow we trekked the many miles into town.

I feel that these barracks, which were once part of Hitler's mountain domain, soon robbed what was left of my mother's spirit. It was almost as though Hitler was still lingering within the walls, reaching out and touching the intruders with his evil.

The emotional impact endured by mother would soon manifest itself in tragic circumstances.

Chapter Eight

Berchtesgaden

Berchtesgaden is the place where I have my earliest and most vivid memories. To my four-year-old eyes these rooms that we'd acquired, in what to me was a grand old house, were paradise compared to where we had been on the Obersalzberg.

The history of the World War II and the Berchtesgaden of my childhood are closely entwined with Hitler himself. He fell in love with this area in the summer of 1923 when he visited Anton Drexler on the Obersalzberg, who was there recuperating in a sanitarium. He was Hitler's friend and one of the early collaborators of the Nazi Party. For many years thereafter Hitler found himself drawn back to this region by the beauty of its magnificent, tall, snow-capped mountains and peaceful green meadows in the valleys. He visited the area regularly.

In the beginning, Hitler shared the 'Sonnenhaeusl' on the Lockstein with his friend Dietrich Eckard, also one of the founders of the Nazi Party and writer for the well-known newspaper *Voelkischer Beobachter*. He then lived for some time in a small cabin on the Obersalzberg called the 'Kampfhaeusl', and it was here he worked on the second volume of *Mein Kampf*. My later foster father, local artist and photographer Michael Lochner, took the famous old postcard picture of this little cabin, which Hitler occupied on the Obersalzberg, long ago.

Hitler was looking for a permanent home in Berchtesgaden, and sometime between 1925–8 he leased the mountain chalet 'Haus Wachenfeld'. He purchased Wachenfeld for 40,000 gold marks in June 1933. In January of that same year, Hitler had been voted in as the Reich Chancellor. After extensive and lavish renovation his mountain estate was renamed the 'Berghof', situated at the foot of the Hohe Goell Mountain at 3,281ft.

Once Hitler was on the Obersalzberg, he transformed the serene alpine resort into his own 'Administrative Community'. Hitler personally only owned the bordering territory surrounding his Berghof. The NSDAP seized all existing properties and homes on the Obersalzberg.

Rudolf Hess initiated the negotiations with current property owners and then Martin Bormann, called the 'God of the Obersalzberg', carried out Hitler's every wish. Some people left their homes willingly, but those who refused the offers of the Nazi Party were pressured and forced with conniving ruthlessness, and were threatened with incarceration in Dachau Concentration Camp.

By 1937 all the original property owners had evacuated their homes on the Obersalzberg. Most of these lovely homes, which had been in a family's possession for hundreds of years, were destroyed. In their place were built the more lavish homes of select Nazi officers within Hitler's close inner circle, among them Bormann, Hess, Goering and Speer, as well as numerous SS barracks, garages and buildings that housed the staff. The 'Platterhof', once a small pension established by Moritz Meier in 1877, was rebuilt into a hotel playground for Hitler's henchmen, and after the war was again refurbished by the Americans who renamed it the Hotel General Walker. They used it as a favorite place for rest and recuperation for their troops until 1995.

Buildings went up everywhere following the plans for Hitler's mountain community. Hitler and Borman started building the 'Kehlsteinhaus' in 1936, but it was actually Borman's project, as he wanted to present Hitler with this amazing building on his fiftieth birthday. It was also called the Tea House and named the Eagle's Nest by the French ambassador, Francois Poncet in 1938; it was therefore also known as the Eagle's Nest by American troops. It sits perched high above Berchtesgaden at 6,017ft, built by a workforce of 3,000 men, some of whom were Italians sent by Mussolini.

Two years later in 1938, after many difficulties relating to the terrain and severe weather conditions, and with a cost of 30 million Reichsmark, they completed construction. At the Eagle's Nest Hitler hosted and entertained many foreign dignitaries, while he held military meetings and diplomatic conferences in the large conference hall of the Berghof. This magnificent room had a great picture window, which at the press of a button could be rolled up and down. It held the breathtaking eastern panorama toward Salzburg, Hitler's Austrian homeland.

Hitler's ill health always drew him back to the Obersalzberg, but in 1943 and 1944 he spent a great deal of his time at the Berghof. On 14 July 1944, however, Hitler left the Obersalzberg for the last time, never to return.

Berchtesgaden holds many myths and legends of the surrounding mountains. But the part it played in the Second World War will leave a far greater mark, especially on the lives of those people who were there to see their beautiful mountain resort turned into Hitler's own alpine fortress. The people who lived in this area called it 'the day of anger over the Obersalzberg', when on a sunny spring day on 25 April 1945, the serene mountain was turned into 'a mountain of death'. The British RAF, with their Lancasters and Mosquitos, flew in formation along with the Mustangs of the American 8th Air Force, and dropped tons of bombs on the Obersalzberg. The Eagle's Nest, being well camouflaged, remained untouched and it still stands there today. This dynamic mission left thirty-one reported local civilian casualties, but the alert drove most into the extensive tunnel system and they escaped the attack. Bad Reichenhall was bombed that day with 200 people killed, and Herman Goering's house was also destroyed; he was under the house hiding in the bunker when the attack occurred and was then escorted by the SS to the safety of his palace in the Salzburg area of Austria.

In 1952 the last remains of Hitler's Berghof were leveled, but the Obersalzberg will forever live with its memory. Today, the last physical remains of the crumbling, catacomb-like remnants of the original Berghof, as well as other old structures, have been completely removed. A brand new Obersalzberg Documentation Center has been constructed as a Historical Museum. If the mountains could only speak, what tales they would tell!

Berchtesgaden is one of the most picturesque, quaint old towns in the Bavarian Alps. Few people lived there at the time we did, but it is now a great year-round tourist attraction. It has been Bavarian domain since 1810, ruled by the church and, sporadically, the Austrian monarchy of Salzburg. The first settlers came in the year 400 BC, and the oldest cathedral dates back to the 1100s. The palace and museum were established in the 1200s. The market place in the center of the town, with its old fountain built of marble in the year 1677, has special memories for me of the times I walked around there with my mother. The fresh mountain air was visible on the healthy faces of women wearing their traditional 'Dirndls' and the rugged men in their 'Lederhosen'. Colorful fresco paintings decorated the old buildings and hardly any cars or traffic were present to clutter the narrow streets and alleyways. What a wonderful storybook atmosphere it was in those years. Its salt mines are famous and today the Obersalzberg and Hitler's Eagle's Nest will always be reminders of the role they played within the Third Reich.

The Berchtesgaden as I once knew it, in a time and place so long ago, now remains only in my memory, and is where I often find myself reliving my childhood; dreaming of that beautiful area which was such an important part of my past. It will forever hold the most special place in my heart.

Even though we were left with only two suitcases of personal belongings, the two small rooms my mother was able to find for us in Berchtesgaden were home. We didn't miss the lonely cold barracks we had left behind on the Obersalzberg mountain.

It was an old, unique, several-story, multi-family house, on Hindenburg Allee, which has long since been replaced with a parking lot. The color was faded where once it had been a deep gold. There was a decorative iron fence around the property and I cherished jumping off the wall from the front stoop that led into the building, which at that time seemed incredibly high. Across the street was a lush green park lined with trees, benches and our favorite fountain, guarded by a monumental bronze statue of Prince Luitpold of Bavaria. I recall that aromatic scent of colorful fallen leaves, scattered in large heaps throughout this park in the autumn, creating soft beds for us to jump into.

I remember playing endlessly in the wild, overgrown garden around the house, and from the back was a great view down toward the railway station (the Bahnhof). In front of the house stood my favorite large walnut tree. I liked that distinct aroma of the nuts and remember how they stained my fingers as I cracked open their green prickly shells with rocks.

We ended up with two small rooms on the second floor. There was a balcony off our living room, which hung precariously off the building. It was not safe and we were instructed not to go out there, but I remember that on occasion we would. There were some very old furnishings that had been left behind and our mother acquired a few used items. I recall the red, Victorian-style sofa trimmed with ornate, dark-wood carvings around the edges – definitely left over from another era. A bureau and an eating table stood in front of it, which I don't remember being used frequently for this purpose, as there never seemed to be much food. A large potbelly stove was located at one end of the living area, and my sisters would toast bread on it, when it was available. Off this room was a small pantry. I remember being locked in there once. It was dark and dusty and the small brown weevils in the flour bags made my skin crawl. I was terribly afraid. I don't know who locked me in there or why, I only remember crying and begging to be let out.

In the other room stood a large old wooden wardrobe and three metal bed-steads with lumpy old mattresses. Under one of the beds we kept a white chamber pot made of china. On the dresser I recall the washbowl and pitcher, hand-painted with rose-colored flowers.

Out in the hallway was a very small chamber, and inside an old-fashioned flushing toilet. When I pulled on the long chain connected to a water tank, which was situated near the ceiling, the noise from the rushing water could be heard throughout the house. This was the entirety of our bathroom facilities. I always tried to avoid that room as the darkness inside was home to ugly spiders lurking in the corners … and I just knew they were waiting for me.

A hall window next to the lavatory looked down onto the street and the limbs of the magnificent walnut tree, with its long, oval, dark-green leaves, which always seemed to be affectionately reaching for me. I loved that tree.

One thing that stands out in my mind here, is the recollection of that familiar bottle which was labeled with a skull and cross bones. It was some kind of strong medication to eradicate head lice, which we had apparently been plagued with at the camp. My mother didn't want me to touch the bottle, but I never quite comprehended what the mystery behind the frightening label was all about.

Several families lived in the house. Frau Sichert lived downstairs with her husband and son, Franzl. Franzl was a few years older than Brigitte and she had her first schoolgirl crush on him. She was only fifteen and he didn't pay much attention to her but, out of kindness one day, he complimented her pretty black hair. She froze and could barely get a word out.

Franz (Franzl) Sichert would soon follow a highly successful career as an international chef and hotel manager in places as far removed from Berchtesgaden as Bombay, India. In 1962 he signed a twenty-seven-year lease and ran the restaurant of the famous Kehlsteinhaus (the Eagle's Nest) in Berchtesgaden until 1989.

Franzl's mother, at that time, roasted her own coffee beans in her oven and the heavenly aroma would linger throughout the entire house. They were fond of me and sometimes Frau Sichert invited me into their apartment to show me the large trays of raw white beans, which she roasted into fragrant, rich brown beans. Sometimes she let me help her grind them in the small coffee mill. She'd make fun of my little turned-up nose and would tell me it was reaching for the heavens. They knew of our desperate situation and felt badly for us.

On the opposite side, on the ground floor, lived Herr and Frau Willie Kempf. He was a nice-looking man who always wore a long leather coat, left over from the war years. His wife had reddish blond hair, very chic, and Antje admired her cork wedge shoes. They had a little girl with whom I sometimes played. Willie was an insanely jealous man; he and his wife were always quarreling and they eventually divorced. He ended up taking his own life.

The landlords lived on the first floor, older people named Staubwasser, but my best friend was Anneliese Pfingstl. We called her 'Puppi' (doll) and she lived right below us. Her parents were interesting and very kind people.

Her father used to read us the story *Die Schluchtensusl*, the legend of the Berchtesgaden area and the mysterious 'Schluchtensusl', a friendly spirit who lived in the forest at the foot of the 'Watzmann' mountain. He would read with great emphasis on how she was never seen by human eyes but was always there to help man, with her friends, the woodland animals. A wonderful, eerie folk tale; we could never get enough of it. Her parents had their own business, a small curio shop (kiosk) with photo developing. To this day Anneliese still runs this same business in Berchtesgaden, which was passed on to her by her parents.

There was never a lack of food for them; they were very well off even during the lean postwar years – unlike our predicament. Frau Pfingstl was a pretty woman; she looked as if she'd been in show business with her red lipstick, curly blond hair and her stockings rolled down around her ankles ... quite a contrast to the local, traditional dress. I found it very chic and always rolled my socks down past my ankles just like Frau Pfingstl.

Sometimes she chased Herr Pfingstl, who was a quiet sort, with a wooden spoon around their apartment. It seems it was all in fun, but we could hear the commotion from downstairs. Puppi was their only child and usually got whatever she wanted. Sometimes we traded little trinkets, which we sent from our bed-room window down to her balcony in a basket on a rope. If she liked what we sent her she would return the basket filled with cookies and candy, or sometimes even food. I'm sure she did not realize then, that what she sent us in that basket was often the only thing we had to eat.

Behind their beds they had stored bottles of liquor. One day, Puppi and I found the 'Eier Liqueur', a rich thick egg liqueur. It was sweet and tasty and I'm sure we'd had a little too much before they found us. We also found and ate what looked to us like little squares of chocolate, which turned out to be a laxative. Somehow I've chosen to forget what happened after that episode!

Often Antje, Puppi and I played in the park, and I remember one day Puppi falling into the old fountain. She will always remain my best friend. The adven-tures that filled our young lives, and the experiences our families shared in those postwar years on Hindenburg Allee, are memories that have created a very special, enduring bond between us.

It was the time of inflation; Germany's economy had completely collapsed. Our father had started savings books for us three children. They contained a total of 380 Reichsmark, which was of no value when mother went to cash the books in. We could have used the money as wallpaper; it was completely worthless. I can remember thinking how pretty the paper money was, but didn't comprehend why we couldn't buy things with it. I used it as play money. The government gave 'Kopfgeld', meaning every person received 40 marks. This was the equal amount of currency, which laid the foundation for everyone, based on a new-found economy.

Mother had always worked, even if only part time, out of the home. She was an intelligent lady who was very capable at typing and secretarial work. She searched, but no jobs were available, giving her no choice but to apply for welfare. We received 85 marks per month; our rent was paid, but not our utilities. Mother's dream was still to go back to our house in Austria, which seemed out of the question, but she hoped maybe to salvage some of our family belongings.

The few valuables mother still had left at this point in time, she traded for food. Among the items were her favorite earrings, the white gold teardrops with the aquamarine stones, which my father had given to her for her thirty-ninth birthday when she was five months pregnant with me. She kept the small wooden box, however, which was of no real value; only a precious keepsake reminding her of my father. I recall it sat on the dresser in the bedroom on Hindenburg Allee. Today, with the key lost long ago and the flowers faded, the box is one of my prized possessions, as is the photo of my mother wearing the earrings.

The Americans were in Berchtesgaden and had occupied all the large hotels. The old Hotel Berchtesgadner Hof, a favorite landmark of mine, was located just up the street from our house. The Americans were good to the German people and gave care packages to many that were starving. They were also responsible for the free 'hot lunch program' in the public schools. We were in the same poor predicament as most people and couldn't survive for a whole month on the amount of money allotted us.

It was about March 1947 that our mother received her amnesty (denazification) for her inactive membership in the Nazi Party. This is also when we started noticing changes in our mother's behavior. She wasn't well; she didn't seem quite right, but in a physical sense.

On the first of the month she would spend all the money and buy all sorts of unnecessary things. There would be those few glorious days when we had real food to eat and could enjoy the warmth of a fire in the hearth. She would give me a raw beaten egg with sugar, which was a special treat. I loved the slices of plain, dark bread with cold milk and she baked the wonderful 'Streusel Kuchen', this same coffee cake which she had baked for the concentration camp prisoners, who only a few years earlier had worked on the construction of the sun room at our house in Oranienburg. I fondly remember her delicious potato soup seasoned with marjoram. These are all things she prepared that I will never forget, and their flavors and aromas will always take me back to those two rooms on Hindenburg Allee.

But these groceries only lasted a short time and by the end of the first week we seldom even had a loaf of bread. Brigitte suggested we make a list and menu that would last us through to the end of the month, and would enable us to have at least one decent, satisfying meal a day. Our mother agreed to let Brigitte plan this for one month, but then she went back to her old ways. Brigitte was very responsible for a girl of her young age, but then she always was looking out for her younger sisters, just as Papa said she would be able to do.

Mother charged so many groceries at 'Meyerhofer's' on Maximilian Street, the small neighborhood grocer, that the owners finally cut off our credit. She would often send Antje and me to this store with a small notebook in which she kept track of her charges. I still have this little book; it dates back to 1948. Whenever Antje and I went to Meyerhofer's we usually shared a drink flavored like raspberries. I relished and savored this wonderful indulgence. I also remember standing in soup lines with Antje, where the sweet smell of hot pea soup lingered in the schoolyard, when they filled our metal canteens to the brim. I didn't know what it meant to be poor, but we gathered wood scraps from rubble piles left over from the bombings to burn in our stove. To a child of that postwar time it was a very normal way of existence.

There were people around us, however, even more impoverished than we were and mother always had a soft spot in her heart for them. I remember even when we were destitute with next to nothing ourselves, mother donated food and gave away some of our personal belongings to the needy. She befriended one person in particular, a poor sickly woman for whom she felt great sympathy. Antje recalls that some of these items our mother gave away and had loaded into our small wagon, belonged to her. I remember mother had us deliver these things to the woman. Antje, along with her friend Annemie Geiger and I made several of these deliveries, pulling the wagon down the streets to her house.

At that time, all over Berchtesgaden, one found beggars on almost every street corner; men who were ex-soldiers, many of them amputees, who panhandled for whatever small change they could get with the familiar 'alms for the poor'. This fascinated us as children. A lighter and rather humorous side of this sad situation was the time they found me and my friend Puppi sitting on a very lucrative street corner with one of my legs tucked underneath me holding out a cup, soliciting. I had pulled my skirt over my knee and hoped to gain people's sympathy by making the saddest face I possibly could, waiting for my own 'alms for the poor'! It seemed a very logical impersonation to make and was customary of life as we knew it. I believe our donations added up to a few pennies before Brigitte, aghast, caught us and discouraged us from continuing our venture. It was a four-year-old's answer to our dilemma … a sign of those times. It still brings a smile when Antje and I recall those days.

My sisters and I would walk into Berchtesgaden, always taking a short cut through the old cemetery. We loved looking at the old gravestones. Some had pictures of the deceased and others were of children. One man, Anton Adner, lived to be 117 years old. The recently deceased would lie in state, placed for public viewing in a round glassed-in building near the entrance to the cemetery. It was eerie and frightening, but all three of us were fascinated to see the newly displayed 'somebody' looking very peaceful behind those windows. I always expected them to sit up and talk to me.

Our mother became preoccupied with different facets of the occult and the supernatural. She was very interested in psychic readings and phenomenon. Frau Sichert and other people came in and they played the ouija board into the early hours of the morning. Glasses they touched would move involuntarily to spell words in answer to their questions. Once she'd asked about our brother Dieter and was told that when the church bells rang at Easter he'd return home … and so it was. A strange coincidence?

She was becoming more confused and always hoping to find answers about our father. She belonged to a fringe religious group called the Gral. Perhaps it was in relation to the 'Holy Grail'. She had me wear their medallion, a kind of a cross within a circle.

We walked through beautiful meadows of wildflowers and birch forests to Frau Burmeister's house, who was a somewhat strange, but intelligent old lady living in a large, traditional Victorian home. Inside I remember a winding wooden staircase where it was always dark and gloomy. She had numerous cats that I loved playing with while they had their seances in the spacious living room, communicating with the dead.

The Burmeisters were not very tidy people, and whenever they expected visitors or there was to be another seance, Frau Burmeister cleaned the house by throwing all sorts of clutter into large wall closets that occupied this room. On one such occasion, in the midst of their seance, the door to one of the closets flew open and there was a tremendous crash. Out spilled a huge pile of 'things' into the living room. Needless to say this ended their seance session for the day.

My mother was grasping at anything, hoping for some favorable prediction for the future. She still loved our father and the day she saw him in a newsreel at the movie theater she fell apart. She coerced the projectionist to snip her a small frame of the film by giving him her cigarette ration stamps. It was from father's trial in Poland and more than likely news of his sentence. She kept insisting that it wasn't really him, not wanting to face the reality of his fate.

Brigitte started cleaning for the people upstairs in exchange for food. She carried and beat their heavy oriental rugs, yet on one occasion they paid her with spoiled potato soup, treating her as though she should be grateful to receive anything at all. A rude awakening to the ugly side of human nature. She was very hurt.

Mother, amazingly, managed to pick up some of our furniture – the piano and some things that held sentimental value – from our house in Austria. Somehow she located a truck, and when the American guards at the border asked if she had papers or permission to move these things across the border she admitted no, but remarkably got through using the only thing she had left: her charm.

Besides the family piano, I remember one of the things in particular that she brought back with her, was the fragile beautiful 'Tee-Puppe'; a tea cozy. She stood about a foot high and looked like Marie Antoinette. Her face and hands were made of delicate bisque china and her full, padded hoop skirt covered a teapot to hold it warm. Another special treasure was our individual dishes consisting of a plate, cup and saucer. Mine was of yellow hand-painted bunnies. All remnants, almost a haunting, of a happier and more privileged time so long ago, when there were few worries of survival for my mother.

Christmas was ever so festive despite having no money in hand: A tree all lit up with real candles and sparklers, colorful candy and tinsel. I had to take a nap in the afternoon and on Christmas Eve the doors to our humble room were opened and there stood the tree in all its awe and splendour; an unforgettable feeling. My only gift was my favorite Victorian picture book *The Struwelpeter*. It was a dream come true for me and I memorized the stories by heart. This is the only Christmas memory I have with my mother. I treasure it and realize today the true riches we shared, throughout a time that was actually terribly sad and difficult, especially for her.

I also recall the old German custom of pouring lead on New Year's Eve. I watched my mother and a friend as they melted pieces of lead in a special spoon held over a candle. Once melted, they poured the liquid lead into cold water. The unique shapes that formed and hardened were believed to be a sign of what the New Year would bring. Mother and her friend poured what looked like a stork and I heard them talk of a coming baby. It was all very fascinating and mysterious and a fun custom that is still practiced today on New Year's Eve.

The sled my mother had built on the mountain, at the camp Duerreck, was of endless use that winter. We had some great runs down the long, steep road we named the 'Brenner'. Berchtesgaden really was a winter wonderland! One of the fondest of my childhood memories taught to me by my mother was her version of the traditional myth 'when the sky turns pink the angels are baking in heaven'. I passed this on to my own children, and to this day it's a special family fantasy from that wonderful world of make-believe that I think my mother existed in. I wrote this poem for my children:

The Angels are Baking

Childhood fantasies and Stories told
Were of Angels and Cherubs to behold,
These Angelic forms with extended wings
Forever back to my childhood brings,
These words still echo, so few to be found

In my memories of mother, short-lived yet abound.
Hence to my own children I have passed on this lore.
When the sun begins to set, painting pink skies above
That's the Angels baking in heaven with Love
This most magical of childhood dreams
Is as the world once was it seems.
If I could go back to yesteryear
It would be mother's whispers to hear,
'The Angels are baking in Heaven my dear.'

It was at this time, mid-1948, that the Americans and their allies felt the first impact of what would be known throughout the world as the start of the Cold War, when the Soviet Union staged the Berlin Blockade. The communists cut off all rail, road and water links with the city in an attempt to force the Allies to abandon their hold there, totally isolating West Berlin from the necessities of life.

Through the operation of the Berlin Airlift, over 2.3 million tons of food, supplies and fuel were received by Berlin. Americans, as well as the British, landed a plane every six minutes, twenty-four hours a day. The Soviets, realizing their defeat after eleven months of the operation and over 278,000 total flights, lifted the blockade in May 1949; the last flight took place on 30 September. This action created a lasting bond between the people of Berlin and their western allies.

Our mother had had premonitions of the severe Soviet dominance in Eastern Germany, the day she courageously took it upon herself to change our intended destination of East Berlin by boarding a train to southern Bavaria instead. Mother was strong, but she was ill, and becoming progressively worse.

One day mother took Brigitte to the dance studio of Eva Weigand in Bad Reichenhall. She wanted to do something special for Brigitte, and talked to the staunch and rigorous dance teacher who was the owner of the Ballet School. She was of the old school; of very strict, no-nonsense and disciplined ballet, who agreed to take my sister on as a student. She never asked for a fee.

It had been a long desire and much-wanted escape for Brigitte, and she even hitchhiked to her lessons. Bad Reichenhall was about twenty-five miles from Berchtesgaden; a beautiful health-resort town known for its natural mineral spas.

It was one evening in October 1949 when Brigitte returned from the dance school to find there was no one at home. She was panic-stricken when she saw the dark and empty rooms. Our mother had taken Antje and me and set out on a long, careless and difficult trek back to our house in Austria. The distance from Berchtesgaden to St Gilgen, Austria is approximately thirty-five miles by the roadways. We did not follow the road, though. Our mother took us through fields and forests. It is hard to say how many miles we actually traveled.

I have vivid memories. I recall a ring with a red stone, which my mother sold for a few marks to someone on a park bench across the street. She tried to get us on a bus, but evidently didn't have enough money. It was disappointing as I was looking forward to riding on a bus. We then took off on foot. I especially remember the nights were cold and we were very hungry. She walked with us randomly and confused, without any sense of direction, through the beautiful Bavarian countryside. She did realize she had to stay along the Austrian border.

We were on the road for two weeks, wearing only thin clothing, without provisions of food or shelter, sleeping under the stars. Antje remembers one particular cold night. We slept in a barn on the hay. I also remember this night and the comfort and security of the barn; I loved the animals and the scent of the hay and straw.

The next morning we sat on a wooden log bench in front of the farmhouse. Antje held a kitten on her lap, it warmed her body. The farmer's wife felt sorry for us and brought us warm milk and bread. But there were so many other nights that we were extremely cold and we were weak from hunger. I recall eating grasses and wildflowers that could still be found this time of year.

It being fall, I remember the smell of damp earth, walking across freshly harvested fields with partially dried hard stalks still left sticking out of the ground, making it especially difficult for me to walk through. Crows were flying over the fields, cawing in the eerie morning fog. My mother wrapped us into her heavy 'Loden Mantel' (coat) which was the only thing to keep us warm on those cold damp nights. We snuggled up to her soft warm body and at those times her closeness made me feel secure. I loved *meine Mutti*.

We stayed a few days at an Inner Mission shelter and each of us had a cot to sleep on. Our mother worked in the kitchen for our food. We continued on, and when we came to the river Salzach, which is the natural border between Germany and Austria, we were to cross over illegally. I recall the fear. We waited until nightfall and had to be very quiet not to arouse the guard's attention.

The people from the mission helped us to cross the river and a young man carried me across on his shoulders. Antje badly cut her toes on the rocks. The Salzach was cold, deep and rapid but with the moonlight to guide us we made it safely to the opposite shore without being noticed by the border patrol. I was afraid of being caught without identification papers etc. There was always that fear ingrained, if one didn't have the proper ID to show authorities, that we'd be arrested or they would take my mother away. It was something that went with that time and territory … a feeling which is hard to forget.

Exhausted and hungry after walking continuously for two weeks, we finally arrived at our former lovely, peaceful house in St Gilgen. Rudy and Ilse were present, but it was not a welcome reception. I recall the grotesque dental skull that Rudy kept upstairs in his dental office. The remains of someone from the Sachsenhausen Concentration Camp? I remember the warm glow of the kerosene lamps and the smell from the oil, and Ilse's presence, to which I was naturally drawn as I always had been. I recall how safe and wonderful it felt to be back at this house we all loved so much. Even then this place created an incredible sense of belonging. As for me, this is the one place that represents my parents and the family I was born into, but only belonged to for a short time.

Brigitte had been frantic and had called the authorities. They suspected something terrible had happened to us. In Berchtesgaden we were declared dead, and in the local newspaper an article read, 'Woman with 2 Children Drowned in the Salzach'. Brigitte had suspected our mother's urge was to go back to Austria. Rudy also notified the authorities since we were not wanted there and, as he had done once before, he had to get rid of us. They came with an ambulance to take us back to Berchtesgaden. It seemed great fun, and also warm and safe at the time to ride in that vehicle, especially after what we had endured those two weeks on the road. I don't know what thoughts were in our mother's mind, but she was now robbed of the only dream that remained.

It is a very dramatic indication of how very ill and confused our mother already was at this point. Again, our guardian angels had been watching over us. Antje will never forget the looks on her classmates' faces when she showed up in her classroom in Berchtesgaden.

Brigitte had previously notified the youth authorities of our mother's condition and strange behavior. I remember once she had locked herself with us in the bedroom, pushing our piano in front of the door. People that had gathered on the other side were shouting for her to open the door. Antje and I were terribly afraid. They finally broke through the door. Mother had become very paranoid and distrusted everyone. She feared they meant us harm and I was too young to realize the truth; as a result I also lived in fear – all these circumstances creating hidden insecurities.

When my sister Brigitte tried to tell Herr Mai, who was the pale-faced, tall and very thin youth counselor, of our mother's condition he told her, 'It's just a typical adolescent problem. I'm very aware of the differences between young people and their parents. It happens all the time at your age, nothing unusual to worry about. Be a nice girl and go home.'

So she went home where things had gone from bad to worse, and now it seemed there was no one who cared or would listen; no one we could turn to for help.

I remember I had started school at this time and was very excited. I was enrolled in the Marktschule in town. I had my own slate with frame and a small red sponge that hung, dangling from a long cord, and the hard wooden desks in the classroom had old-fashioned inkwells. I liked school, but I was there for only a few days when my mother would no longer let me out of the house, afraid something would happen to me.

Brigitte continued to take me to school, having to quickly dress me in the mornings and literally sneak me out of the house, or else make excuses that we were only going into town. My mother soon caught on and I heard her talking about 'criminals and communists' who would try to take me from her. I was afraid, but didn't understand how much she must have been suffering in her mind at that time. No one did.

Dieter, my oldest brother, came home to us shortly before our mother was taken away. I recall the day my brother returned home from Siberia like it was yesterday. It was a beautiful spring day and I had been playing in the garden on Hindenburg Allee, when I was called to come inside.

There stood a tall, very emaciated young man with big brown eyes and thick black hair. They told me he was my brother Dieter. He was 22 years old; a sad sight in a terrible condition. They had released him from prison in rags and in a shocking unkempt state of being. Insecure, but finally out of harm's way, he was clutching a small wooden suitcase, which had been infested with lice and bedbugs. This small suitcase with the 'black spots' seemed fascinating when he told us it was the remains of dead vermin, which used to attack his blanket at night. He sat me on his lap but I was shy and didn't know how to react because he was a stranger to me. Brigitte and Antje were very glad to see their brother. He had left us as a young boy and came home a grown man, to find his mother mentally ill and the rest of us soon to be separated and scattered to different parts of the country.

There was no place for him to stay with us in the two small rooms and he had to find a new home elsewhere. In spite of all this, he was grateful to have been sent home. Sadly, we've never had a real chance to get to know one another, but there seems to be a strong, silent bond between us, sensed through unspoken words.

The Americans who cared for these returning POWs first disinfected him of the lice and bed bugs, gave him a physical and supplied new underwear, socks and a clean outfit to wear back in society. They also sent him on a six-week rest & recuperation for POWs, where he received a special diet and care to rehabilitate him.

It was fortunate for us that we had ended up in the Western Sector of divided Germany and had the Americans as our occupying forces. The care for my brother was only one of the humanitarian efforts provided to help these POWs get back on their feet with dignity. This was unlike East Germany, the Russian Occupational Zone, that suffered terrible suppression under Joseph Stalin. It was found in a shocking economic condition after the Berlin Wall came down in 1989.

After Dieter came home, he took me for an outing one afternoon on the back of his bicycle. I hung on tightly around my big brother's waist and had a great time thinking it was a motorcycle, not realizing he struggled hard peddling up and down the many hills through the countryside. We laughed about this later; he remembered as he stopped to catch his breath, from sheer exhaustion, that I begged him, couldn't he go any faster? This reminded him of the past, and the days when I was a baby and he used to push me around in the wicker carriage, when we still lived as a family together in Oranienburg.

Dieter then met Steffie, a wonderful girl whose family came from Yugoslavia, and they married a few years later. Brigitte left us to live with the Hutterers in Bad Reichenhall. Their oldest daughter was Alberta, my sister's friend from ballet school. Antje and I were left alone with our mother.

This is a time in my life I will never forget, as they are the last memories of my mother. I recall playing for hours with my mother's collection of old buttons which were kept in an old tin box and were of various sizes and colors. Studying the pictures in my favorite *Struwelpeter* book also occupied a great deal of my time. Most of all I remember being so hungry that I was looking for crumbs on the table, but of course I could never find any. I remember lying in bed sleeping for long periods of time, or when awake staring blankly at the pink flowers in the wallpaper, deliriously hallucinating that I saw little faces in the flowers that appeared to be talking to me. Above all I fantasized about something to eat, but soon it seemed even that was inconsequential.

It had been several weeks when Brigitte finally came home and found me lying in bed, lethargic and almost paralyzed. As Brigitte relates this episode on tape it takes me clearly back to that day, and as I hear her voice catch in her throat I sense the tears welling up in her eyes as she says: 'You had been there for days without any food or drink, skin and bone with your ribs showing. You were very ill, suffering from malnutrition and dehydration. Light as a feather I picked you up out of that bed and carried you away.' I too feel the tears welling, as I hear her telling this episode.

She left with me, pleading with neighbors to help Antje, who remained behind helpless and alone with our mother. We hitchhiked on the back of a truck to the family Hutterer in Bad Reichenhall. I will never forget that day when my big sister carried me away to a safer haven, away from my mother and those two rooms on Hindenburg Allee.

Today, even after all these years, I still feel that void, as any child would who is taken and left without a mother. The happiest time in my adult life was reliving my childhood through my own children. I vowed that theirs would be a home-life filled with love, security and the comfort of a close-knit family unit. Since I never talked of my own childhood, they probably don't realize how wonderful it is to hear them tell me, 'You're the best Mom a kid could ever have asked for!'

Later, after Antje and I were both adults, I learned and began to understand what terrible experiences she must have gone through, when she was left behind with our mother. The knowledge left me with a sense of helplessness and further deepened my feelings of guilt, to think that I was spared while my sister had to remain at Hindenburg Allee, to suffer through that terrible ordeal alone.

The day Brigitte took me away and brought me with her to Bad Reichenhall, I had no way of knowing that I would never see *meine Mutti* again.

Chapter Nine

Leaving 'The Other Child' Behind

I vaguely recall the first days in my new home in Bad Reichenhall, following Brigitte's rescue and escape with me from our rooms on Hindenburg Allee in Berchtesgaden. I do remember a narrow room where I laid in a large crib-type bed, watching people coming in and out through the white-painted side railings. When the hazy, half-conscious dream state finally passed, I found myself sitting up, uncomfortable and afraid because I had wet the bed. I was crying and calling for *meine Mutti*. Where was I and where was my mother?

Frau Hutterer, who we called 'Christl Tante' (aunt), lovingly nursed me back to health with much patience and compassion by spoon-feeding me pieces of white bread soaked in warm milk. As a result she and her husband became my first foster parents. They also had been refugees who came from Hungary. She was a pretty, dark-haired lady and they were both very kind people. They were poor and didn't have much themselves, but shared what they did have. Christl Tante was a gifted seamstress who made the slippers and costumes for the ballet school. I was glad to be with Brigitte; it was a better life, but I missed my mother and also Antje.

The younger daughter Helga was my age. Alberta, Brigitte, Helga and I slept in one room and the parents in the other. All four of us went to the ballet school. They were good to Brigitte and me and we were never without food. Baths were taken once a week in a large metal tub in the kitchen. Sometimes, when Brigitte had an extra 50 Pfennigs, she took me to the public bathhouse with her. There were private rooms where we each had a large bathtub and we relished soaking in lots of hot water. I remember it felt more like a steam room and how it seemed like such a luxury to have hot, running water and to have my sister scrub my back and wash my hair.

Life was better, but Brigitte came to the hurtful realization that we were only foster children and didn't really belong. Christl Tante slipped quietly into our room one night, assuming that Brigitte and I were asleep, bringing some sugar cubes, but only for her own children. This was one of many times when Brigitte sensed the desperate need for our own parents, and her tears finally gave in to sleep.

The ballet school was our second home. Eva Weigand was especially fond of us and took us under her protective wing. She had the students at the school collect clothing and shoes for my sister and me. They called me Barby, but my nickname was 'Bambi'.

Publicity photos taken of Brigitte and me in our ballerina dresses were posted on a bulletin board at the dance studio. The caption under my photo read:

Barby Liebehenschel

6 years old. Very talented. Completely undernourished. Height and weight of a 4 year old.

Food and clothing donated by the Ballet school. Exposed to TB. Father deceased, mother mentally ill. There are 3 children – on welfare. Needed most of all are warm clothing.

Under Brigitte's picture was written:

Brigitte Liebehenschel

16¾ years old. Very pretty and very talented. Oldest sister of Barby Liebehenschel. Completely undernourished and exposed to TB. Supported by the dance school. Needed are warm clothing, primarily winter shoes.

Brigitte and I looked up and visited Eva Weigand in 1972. She tearfully gave us the original photos which she had then glued onto pages with her typewritten caption. She had saved them all those years. Today they are both my very special keepsakes, although the writing has faded on the paper which has become yellowed and fragile over the past fifty years.

I excelled in dance, but especially gymnastics. The lack of nutrition had stunted my growth, but my body could twist like a pretzel.

We girls had a lot of freedom and Helga and I would cherish following and spying on the older girls. They had a friend whose family owned a movie theater. We'd often follow them there, and as they went in the front entrance we would climb into the back room window from an alley where we then chose the best seats in the balcony section. I loved the movies, and some were American and I had a collection of programs that were handed out with each film. A favorite was a musical with Gene Kelly; the song was *Long Ago and Far Away*. I idolized the beautiful Rita Hayworth with her long red hair. The only thing I really comprehended was the music and the dancing.

We picked (stole) green apples and ate them until we were nearly sick. Lilacs and chestnut trees grew all around our area in abundance, lining the streets. The blossoms in the spring were unforgettable. The lilacs there grew so tall that the father of one of the little ballet students fell off a tall ladder, breaking his neck as he was cutting some blossoms for her mother.

We performed elaborate stage shows, and once someone from a newspaper praised my talents and the production. He wrote a very favorable critique on the leading role I played as a 'Haus Geist' (ghost). It was about an old spirit, and I had an extensive dialog part, even spoken in the Bavarian dialect. The play was a satire of that particular era. I still have pages of the written script and am amazed that I learned all those lines at such a young age, with the emphasis on the Bavarian dialect.

It was a great performance but my favorite was that of the little 'Hausgeist'. As you see these children on the stage you will find them in real life, without any inhibitions, especially not Barby Liebehenschel who played the part of the 'Hausgeist'.

Alfred Baresel of the *Sudost-Kurier*

I remember waiting with excitement and anticipation wondering if my mother was coming to see the program. When I asked, no one would answer my question. I searched the audience from the stage during my performance, hoping she was out there somewhere watching me, but to my great disappointment my mother never came. No one told me the real reason and I never divulged to anyone how devastated her absence made me feel.

We performed in many small towns, loading, unloading and traveling around in what were some pretty antique trucks that had seen their better days. They were wonderfully talented productions with beautifully designed costumes for which Eva Weigand was well known. She was like a tough drill sergeant with a heart of gold and really got things accomplished. It was all so exciting and I loved being under those lights on the stage. With a live orchestra, completely unafraid, I came alive with the audience.

One could say I was stage struck, and had I been given the opportunity to develop my talents further, I could have felt very at home in a life's career in show business, as both of Hutterer's daughters went on to achieve. I believe Helga has worked behind the camera, but Alberta became a seasoned performer of stage, screen and television. Still acting today, she is known as Barbara Schrott, the widow of famous German film star, Karl-Heinz Schrott.

The house we lived in was next to a tennis court and sometimes I would earn a few pfennigs retrieving their tennis balls. One of the couples who lived in our building operated a live 'Bauern Theater' (little country theater usually performed in the traditional Bavarian dress), and they also staged marionette shows. The acting and the plays such as *Faust* fascinated me. Many times after the performances they had me present the bouquets of flowers to the stars on the stage.

The Maiers were a childless couple and were very kind to me. One St Nickolaus day (always 6 December) they told me to polish my shoes and set them outside my door. The legend is that when children are good, St Nickolaus fills their shoes with fruits, nuts and candy. The next day in my polished old shoes I found an orange, a tangerine, nuts and some bon-bons. These few simple gifts in my worn-out shoes brought me unbelievable happiness. When my own children were small I carried on this tradition. My American version was their Santa Stockings filled with numerous tiny gifts wrapped in colorful paper.

One day Helga and I found some old cigarette butts. We took them home to our room and smoked them in front of the open window, not realizing the wealthy, meddling neighbor across the courtyard was watching, and soon told on us. Nobody was really very upset; I think our experiments amused them.

At the end of our street was a large deserted old house I liked to visit. The building was in a terribly rundown condition and looked haunted and lonely.

At one time long ago it had been a happy beautiful villa. We weren't supposed to trespass, but something magical kept calling me to the fascinating overgrown wild garden. It was as if I belonged there. I felt it was my secret garden. There were ruins of an old fountain, half-full of stagnant water, and swimming in there were wiggly little red worms that looked like pictures I'd seen of sea horses.

I'd find wonderful things to occupy my time and this was one of my favorite places to explore. I naturally adored this freedom that I had living with the Hutterer family. It's a wonder I didn't get into more trouble. My guardian angels must have been watching over me again!

I don't remember having a real doll of my own, but I used to take wooden matchboxes and line them with cotton, placing 1 Pfennig (1 penny) Gummi Bears inside. They were my dolls sleeping in their own matchbox beds. Gummi Bears originated in Germany and now children all over the world enjoy them, but not in quite the same way that I did over fifty years ago.

Brigitte and Alberta took a job smuggling coffee for the black market across the Austrian border. They thought that if they made only a few trips they would have some Christmas money. They had to pick up 5 or 10lb sacks of unroasted coffee beans at a tiny grocery store across the Austrian border. They then walked back at night into Bavaria and dropped off their loot at a small house in the forest.

During their very first trip they were caught by the border guards. The German Shepherd dogs detected their scent. They were never paid the 10 marks promised to them, but it was exciting and they were grateful not to have to spend Christmas locked up behind bars.

It was also at this time that I recall Rudy coming from Austria to visit with Brigitte and me. To me he was the rather 'round' jolly man who always brought me a special bag of candy. The dealings were actually with Brigitte, whose help he needed to finalize details concerning his imminent ownership of our home in St Gilgen, Austria, of which he had taken possession.

Meanwhile, Antje had been left helplessly behind with our mother. The fact that Brigitte chose to take only me, leaving Antje alone with our sick mother, became apparent later in Brigitte's life. It came back to haunt her with feelings of terrible guilt and regret.

The time Antje spent alone with our mother was an unforgettable traumatic experience for her. Aside from near starvation, there was the terrible psychological stress, accompanied by panic and terror. Annemie Geiger, Antje's girlfriend from school, would bring an extra sandwich for her every day, but Antje's young emotions endured so much. Our mother heard 'voices' that told her Antje should not go to school because 'they' would kill her. But since Antje wanted to go to school, she decided to tell our mother that she also heard voices, which told her she should definitely be going to school. Our mother then agreed that Antje should listen to her own voices and do what they asked of her.

At that time an entire family had been brutally murdered in our area and there were horrible pictures posted of them everywhere. Our mother's frightening talk and these gruesome pictures magnified the terrible fear which followed Antje into the night. She would lie in her bed in a cold sweat, unable to sleep. The room was pitch dark – there was no electricity – and the bedroom door wouldn't lock, not since they had broken down the door after our mother had locked us all in there. These fears remained for years into adulthood.

Anneliese paid a visit around this time, while Antje and Mother were still living in the house on Hindenburg Allee. In Father's last letter to Anneliese he had asked her to keep looking for us children, since he had lost all communication and didn't know of our state of being. He wrote: 'It seems peculiar that there has been no news or trace of the girls. Please keep searching and help them where you can.'

When Anneliese arrived at Hindenburg Allee she immediately realized mother was ill. The place was untidy, but primarily it was all very sad. She helped Antje hem up a dress and even did some ironing. Mother and Anneliese talked about my father and seemed to get along very well that day. When my mother found out that Anneliese had lost everything during the war, she gave her one of her own embroidered tablecloths which she had salvaged somehow. Anneliese still has this tablecloth today. She was very taken with our mother's compassion for her. It must have been a very moving experience for both women.

Finally, the families in the house alerted the authorities about our mother's condition and the neglectful circumstances in the apartment, the fact that there was no food or electricity and she was not caring for herself or my sister. Several families in the building signed affidavits, acknowledging her state of mind, and declaring themselves witnesses to the disturbing circumstances.

The authorities came while Antje was at school and took my mother away in an ambulance … but not without a struggle. She was taken to Haar in Munich, a mental institution, where she was to remain for the next sixteen years of her life.

My lasting impression of my mother will always be how soft and comforting she felt; I would often sit on her lap and we would hug and cuddle. I would kiss her with my nose like an eskimo. She always returned my affections that I showed and craved. She would say to me *Du bist ein schmuse kaetzchen* (You are as cuddly as a kitten).

Had all this occurred only a few years earlier, my mother would have been a victim of Hitler's euthanasia program. This was the extermination of mentally defective, 'feeble-minded' and crippled people. He found them dangerous for the welfare of the country and simply had them eliminated, as they did not fit into his plan for a 'pure race'.

Now we were orphans and officially became wards of the state, placed under the jurisdiction of the district court of Berchtesgaden. Antje was placed into foster care with the family of Michael and Elizabeth Lochner, owners of the 'Haus Bergluft' (mountain air) in the small serene vicinity of Strub, only a few miles from the town of Berchtesgaden. She too was terribly undernourished and

1 Arthur Wilhelm
Liebehenschel, 'The
Kommandant', in 1943.
My favourite photo of
father which I kept hidden
for many years. *(Author's
collection)*

2 My parents' engagement, 1927. *(Author's collection)*

3 Father in 1928 in the
'Reichswehr'. His rank was
'Sanitaetsoberfeldwebel', non-
commissioned Sergeant-Major.
(Author's collection)

4 My mother Gertrude Baum in 1921
at age 18. *(Author's collection)*

5 My brother Dieter at age 15 in his
Luftwaffe uniform. He was drafted as
'Flackhelfer' and sent into combat after
school as part of the anti-aircraft auxiliary
fighters. *(Author's collection)*

6 Mother with Dieter, Antje and
Brigitte in front of our house in Austria,
1942. *(Author's collection)*

7 Brigitte and Antje surrounded by flowers
given for my birth. *(Author's collection)*

8 Father in Berchtesgaden, 1940, recuperating from a serious heart ailment. *(Author's collection)*

9 My birth-house in Oranienburg, 1943. Father is in the doorway, Mother is with a friend and my sisters. *(Author's collection)*

10 A happy 7-month-old Bärbel in Oranienburg. *(Author's collection)*

11 Oranienburg, 1943. Our nanny Ilse with Brigitte, Antje and Bärbel. *(Author's collection)*

12 'The other children' as our father referred to us in his Journals. Antje and Brigitte holding me, wearing her BDM uniform (Hitler's Federation of German Girls) It was September 1943. *(Author's collection)*

13 Anneliese Huettemann, 1942. This photo was often mentioned by my father in his Journals, which he wrote while imprisoned by the Americans at Dachau following the war. *(Author's collection)*

14 My father and Anneliese while they lived at Auschwitz in January 1944. *(Author's collection)*

15 My mother in 1942, wearing the earrings my father had given her for her 39th birthday. *(Author's collection)*

16 Excerpt from German newspaper *Welt Bild*, 1960. The caption reads: SS-Lieutenant Colonel Liebehenschel had to give up his post at Auschwitz because he was in love with a girl who was found guilty of 'Race defilement'. He was the most 'humane' Kommandant of the camp. During his time there were no executions against the Black Wall. *(Author's collection)*

SS-Sturmbannführer Liebehenschel mußte seinen Posten in Auschwitz niederlegen, weil er ein Mädchen liebte, das „Rassenschande" getrieben hatte. Er war der „humanste" Kommandant des Lagers. Während seiner Zeit gab es keine Erschießungen an der schwarzen Wand.

im Häftlingskrankenbau und in den Schreibstuben als Schreiber eingesetzte Häftlinge mit den Radiogeräten ihrer Peiniger heimlich London und Moskau hörten, dabei erfuhren, daß die Alliierten von Ost und West immer näher auf das Herz Deutschlands zumarschierten, während sich in den Baracken bereits ein unterdrückter Jubel wegen der nun bald bevorstehenden Befreiung breitmachte, empfing Baer einen Befehl des Reichssicherheitshauptamtes. Er legte diesen Befehl weisungsgemäß in seinen Stahlschrank — bereit, ihn auf eine Anweisung hin zu öffnen.

Diese Anweisung kam für Auschwitz an einem Januartag des Jahres 1945, als bereits der Geschützdonner der heranrückenden Front wie ein andauerndes Grollen die gewohnten Geräusche des Lagers zu übertönen begann. Während bereits die Panzerspitzen der sowjetischen Armee langsam von Krakau her entlang der Kleinbahnlinie in Richtung auf Auschwitz vorstießen, rüstete sich die SS-Mannschaft des KZ-Lagers unter Baers Befehl, die letzte, abschließende Anordnung des SS-Hauptamtes für Auschwitz auszuführen. In seinem Zimmer öffnete Baer befehlsgemäß die „geheime Komandosache" und erfuhr durch sie Himmlers „Räumungsplan" für Auschwitz. Bei einer Kälte von über 30 Grad, bei hohem Schnee, begann das Ende des KZ-Lagers. Dieses Ende bedeutete zugleich den Tod einer großen Anzahl von Häftlingen. Alle Insassen der Baracken — alle jene, die bis zu dieser Minute den Gaskammern und Krematorien entgangen waren, in den Baracken bereits auf die Befreiung gewartet hatten, wurden auf dem Appellplatz zusammengetrieben. Unter dem persönlichen Kommando von Baer unterzog die SS-Mannschaft die noch lebende „Belegschaft" des Vernich-

17 Berchtesgaden, 1949. Antje, Bärbel and a friend, Puppi. My socks are rolled down around my ankles like Frau Pfingstl's. *(Author's collection)*

18 The first meeting with our half-brother Hans-Dieter at Haus Bergluft. *(Author's collection)*

19 Antje and Bärbel in the Lochner garden. *(Author's collection)*

20 Brigitte's report card from February 1945 while living in Austria. *(Author's collection)*

21 My big sister Brigitte was always there to protect and guide me, acting as a surrogate mother during much of my childhood. *(Author's collection)*

Mutter, Bärbel, Christl, Onkel Fritz Dinkelmeier, Hanna, Tante Hanna D. (at von Hanna) Großvater Merz, Onkel Karl, Großmutter Merz, Tante Emma, Ursula St...

22 Bärbel *(front left)* with family members of minister Paul Krauss. *(Author's collection)*

23 Rudy and Ilse in 1945 as the new owners of our home in Austria. This is after they had us evicted, making my mother, sisters and me homeless refugees. *(Author's collection)*

24 Rudy wrote to Brigitte on the back of the (above) photo 'In memory always of our beautiful wedding at the Wolfgangsee'. *(Author's collection)*

Liebehenschel
Arthur
25.11.01

Besoldungsstelle der Waffen-SS — Dachau, den 29. März 1943
Dachau

212/133

S 1/B/F.43/Bo/Ja.
An
die Standortkasse
in D a c h a u

Kassenanweisung

für die Auszahlung einer Beihilfe (Notstandsbeihilfe)

Verbuchungsstelle Kapitel 21 Titel 7 a

für das Rechnungsjahr 19 42

Haushaltsüberwachungsliste 19 42 lfd. Nr. 1716

Dem verheirateten = ledigen xxverwitweten

SS-Obersturmbannführer Arthur Liebehenschel, geb.25.11.01

sind in der Zeit vom 15. Februar bis 1. März 1943

durch die Geburt des 4. Kindes Bärbel

vermeidbare, nach den Grundsätzen für die Gewährung von Beihilfen bei Krankheiten usw.
beihilfefähige Aufwendungen im Gesamtbetrag von 325,-- RM erwachsen.

Beihilfe wird auf RM 260,--

Worten: "Zweihundertsechzig Reichsmark "

gesetzt. Überweisungsanschrift: Städt.,Sparkasse Oranienburg
Kto.:-2469-

Dieser Betrag ist auszuzahlen und wie oben angegeben zu buchen. Blu. 900 58

Betrag erhalten   Sachlich richtig und festgestellt

19   Der Leiter der Besoldungsstelle der
                                Waffen-SS

Unterschrift des Empfängers   SS-Obersturmbannführer

25 Document showing the subsidy paid for the birth of Arthur's fourth child Bärbel.
(Author's collection)

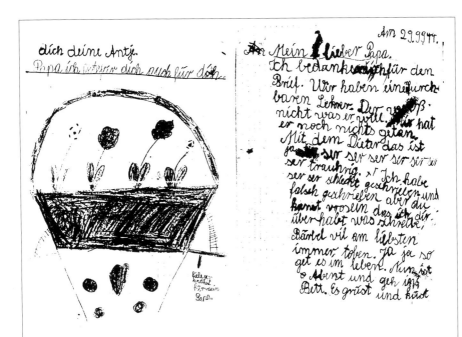

Austria
September 29, 1944

My Dear Papa,

I thank you for your letter.
We have a terrible teacher. He doesn't know what he wants. So
far he hasn't done anything to me.

About Dieter, it is so very very very very very sad.

My writing is very very bad, with many mistakes, but
you should be happy I'm writing to you at all.

All Barbel wants to do is "romp". Ja, ja such is life.
It is now night and I'll now go to bed.

Greetings and Kisses,

From your, Antje

Papa I pray for you
Great health for my Papa

(Antje was 7 years old. Our brother Dieter had just been
captured by the Russians. Our father was in Italy at this time)

26 Antje's letter sent to Papa in Italy. *(Author's collection)*

27 Bärbel aged 6, as a ballet student at the Eva Weigand School in Bad Reichenhall. *(Author's collection)*

28 Papa's postcard sent to us children from Italy in 1944. He had written my name under the picture of the small girl holding a pine branch. *(Author's collection)*

R. u. S.-Fragebogen (55)

(Von Frauen sinngemäß auszufüllen!)

Name und Vorname des ﬅ-Angehörigen, der für sich oder seine Braut oder Ehefrau den Fragebogen einreicht:

Liebehenschel, Arthur

Dienſtgrad: ﬅ-O.'Stubf. ﬅ-Nr. 39254

Sip. Nr.: _nicht bekannt_

Name (leſerlich ſchreiben): _Liebehenschel, Arthur_

in ﬅ ſeit _1. 2. 1932_ Dienſtgrad: _ﬅ-Oberſturmbannführer_ ﬅ-Einheit: _Waffen-ﬅ_

in SA von _____ bis _____, in HJ von _____ bis _____

Mitglieds-Nummer in Partei: _932 766_ ﬅ-Nr.: _39 254_

geb. am _25. 11. 01_ zu _Posen-Nord_ Kreis: _Posen_

Land: _Posen_ jetzt Alter: _42 Jahre_ Glaubensbekenntnis: _gottgl._

Jetziger Wohnſitz: _Katschwitz O.W._ Wohnung: _Hauptſtraße 33_

Beruf und Berufſtellung: _akt. ﬅ-Führer_

Wird öffentliche Unterſtützung in Anſpruch genommen? _nein_

Liegt Berufswechſel vor? _nein_

Außerberufliche Fertigkeiten und Berechtigungsſcheine (z. B. Führerſchein, Sportabzeichen, Sportauszeichnung):

Führerſchein Kl. IV

Staatsangehörigkeit: _Deutſches Reich_

Ehrenamtliche Tätigkeit: _Allgemeine ﬅ_

Dienſt im alten Heer: Truppe _____ von _____ bis _____

Freikorps .... _Posen u. Grenzſchutz_ von _Jan. 1919_ bis _Auguſt 1919_

Reichswehr .... _ﬅ 12 Jahre_ von _4. 10. 19_ bis _3. 10. 31_

Schutzpolizei .... von _____ bis _____

Neue Wehrmacht .... von _____ bis _____

Letzter Dienſtgrad: _Oberfeldwebel_

Frontkämpfer: _Grenzſchutz_ bis _a. a._ ; verwundet: _nein_

Orden und Ehrenabzeichen, einſchl. Rettungsmedaille: _K. V. K. II. u. I. Kl._

Perſonenſtand (ledig, verwitwet, geſchieden — ſeit wann): _geſch. ſeit 2. 12. 1943._

Welcher Konfeſſion iſt der Antragſteller? _gottgl._ die zukünftige Braut (Ehefrau)? _gottgl._
(Als Konfeſſion wird auch außer dem herkömmlichen jedes andere gottgläubige Bekenntnis angeſehen.)

Iſt neben der ſtandesamtlichen Trauung eine kirchliche Trauung vorgeſehen? Ja — nein.

Hat neben der ſtandesamtlichen Trauung eine kirchliche Trauung ſtattgefunden? Ja — nein.

Gegebenenfalls nach welcher konfeſſionellen Form? _____

Iſt Eheſtands-Darlehen beantragt worden? Ja — nein.

Bei welcher Behörde (genaue Anſchrift)? _____

Wann wurde der Antrag geſtellt? _____

Wurde das Eheſtands-Darlehen bewilligt? Ja — nein.

Soll das Eheſtands-Darlehen beantragt werden? Ja — nein.

Bei welcher Behörde (genaue Anſchrift)? _____

S8V K 7 ﬅ-Vordruckverlag W. F. Mayr, Miesbach (Bayer. Hochland) 439

29 The personal record of Arthur Liebehenschel. (*Author's collection*)

30 Arthur Liebehenschel. *(Auschwitz Camp Archives)*

(12)(a)		US.-ARMY				
WHERE ARRESTED (12)(b)		WAGRAIN - AUSTRIA			DATE (12)(c) 8.5.45	TIME

WHERE DETAINED

PW E 29 DACHAU BUNKER (13)

WANTED BY (LEAVE BLANK) (14)

OCCUPATION AT TIME OF ARREST

STATE SERVICE AND BRANCH OR WHETHER CIVILIAN	WAFFEN SS	(15)
DETAILS OF DIVISION, SHIP ETC., OR CIVILIAN EMPLOYMENT	BELONGING THO"HIGH COMMAND OF GERMAN SS AND POLICE"	(16)
DETAILS OF REGIMENT	STAFF OF DEPT.LAIBACH ITALY (17)	
DETAILS OF BATTALION AND COMPANY		(18)

RANK OBERSTURMBANNFÜHRER (LT.COL.) (19)

IDENTITY DOCUMENTS 19(a) KRS.SOLDBUCH NR.1 5
OFFICIAL NUMBER

DEPARTMENT OR PROVINCE STATIONED IN	COUNTRY STATIONED IN (20)	DATE STATIONED IN (21) 1944/45

TOWN STATIONED IN (BLOCK LETTERS) (22) GERMANY
VELBERT, TRIEST, LAIBACH

PREVIOUS OCCUPATIONS OR POSITIONS HELD, LOCATION AND DATE SINCE 1st JANUARY 1939

(15) OCCUPATION SERVICE AND BRANCH OR WHETHER CIVILIAN	SS		
(16) DETAILS OF DIVISION, SHIP, ETC., OR CIVILIAN EMPLOYMENT HAUPTAMT (CENTRAL AUTHORIM)	RANK OBERSTURMBANNFÜHRER		(19)
(17) REGIMENT	COUNTRY STATIONED IN GERMANY (20)	DATE 1939/43	(21)
(18) BATTALION AND COMPANY	TOWN STATIONED IN BERLIN (22)		

(15) OCCUPATION SERVICE AND BRANCH OR WHETHER CIVILIAN	SS		
(16) DETAILS OF DIVISION, SHIP, ETC., OR CIVILIAN EMPLOYMENT C.O. IN CONC.CAMP.	RANK OBERSTURMBANNFÜHRER		(19)
(17) REGIMENT AUSCHWITZ I	COUNTRY STATIONED IN POLAND (20)	DATE 1943/44	(21)
(18) BATTALION AND COMPANY	TOWN STATIONED IN AUSCHWITZ (22)		

(15) OCCUPATION SERVICE AND BRANCH OR WHETHER CIVILIAN	SS		
(16) DETAILS OF DIVISION SHIP, ETC., OR CIVILIAN EMPLOYMENT C.O. IN CONC.CAMP	RANK OBERSTURMBANNFÜHRER		(19)
(17) REGIMENT LUBLIN	COUNTRY STATIONED IN POLAND (20)	DATE 1944	(21)
(18) BATTALION AND COMPANY	TOWN STATIONED IN LUBLIN (22)		

SIGNATURE OF PRISONER (23) *[signature]*

FORM COMPLETED BY (24) LT.F.GELREN *[signature]* M.I.M.

THIS FORM TO BE COMPLETED IN TRIPLICATE AND DISTRIBUTED AS UNDER
ONE COPY TO CENTRAL REGISTRY OF WAR CRIMINALS & SECURITY SUSPECTS BY QUICKEST AVAILABLE MEANS.
ONE COPY TO ARMY GROUP COMMUNICATIONS ZONE OR NATIONAL ZONE HEADQUARTERS.
ONE COPY TO BE RETAINED BY THE OFFICER COMPLETING THE FORM.

31 The surrender in Wagrain, Austria. *(Author's collection)*

OFFICE OF U.S. CHIEF OF COUNSEL

APO 124A U.S. Army

7 October 1946

SUBJECT: Release of PW to Polish Government

TO : Commanding General, Headquarters Command
International Military Tribunal

Subsequent Proceedings Division approves the permanent release of LIEBEHENSCHEL, Arthur Wilhelm, to the Polish Government.

FOR BRIGADIER GENERAL TELFORD TAYLOR:

WALTER H. RAPP
Chief, Interrogation Branch
Subsequent Proceedings Division

Telephone- Justice—61195

32 The release of Arthur Liebehenschel to Poland. *(Author's collection)*

se No. 98-8   Ext. Req. By Poland   Dated See Requests

Name and Location	WCG	CROWCASS	G-2	OMGUS	TPM
DECKE, Hans					29 Apr 46
					28 Jun 46
GOETH(GOTH), Amon Leopold					29 Apr 46
					28 Jun 46
HOLZNER, Ludwig					30 Apr 46
					25 Feb 47
LIEBEHENSCHEL, Artur					23 Aug 46 / 25 Sep 46
				6 May 46	22 Nov 46
MANDL, Maria					11 Jul 46
				22 Apr46	4 Sep 46
MUSSFELD, Erich					25 Sep 46 / 28 Apr 47
				23 Apr46	30 May 47

e of WCG
e of G-2
e of CROW
e of USFA
e of Hist. Div.

33 Extradition from the American Zone. Amon Göth (highlighted) was the sadistic Kommandant featured in the film *Schindler's List*. *(Author's collection)*

Der Öffentliche Kläger
bei der Spruchkammer des Landkreises
Berchtesgaden—Bad Reichenhall

Auf Grund der Angaben in Ihrem Melde-
bogen fallen Sie in die Gruppe 4 der Mit-
läufer des Gesetzes zur Befreiung von Na-
tionalsozialismus und Militarismus vom 5. 3.
1946.
Da sich die Vergünstigungen der Verord-
nung vom 20. 2. 1947 zur Durchführung der
Weihnachts-Amnestie § 1 Ziffer 1,2 auf Sie
anwenden lassen, werden Sie hiermit auf
Grund der vorstehenden Verfügung

A M N E S T I E R T !

2 2. März 1947

(Datum)

D.. Öffentliche Kläger:
W. Frey

Vonderthaste Buchdruckerei u. Verlag Berchtesgaden. 3 47 5000.

DRUCKSACHE   Urgent German
Portopflichtige Dienstsache

Herrn / Frau / Fl./

Gertrud Liebehenschel

geb. 3.10.03

Berchtesgaden

Hindenburgallee 1

34 Our mother's denazification/amnesty. *(Author's collection)*

35 Father testifying at his trial in Krakow, Poland. This is the clipping from an original 1947 news reel film which my mother acquired from the projectionist at the movie theatre. She traded him her cigarette stamps. *(Author's collection)*

36 Arthur Liebehenschel was number one of 41 defendants at the 1947 Auschwitz Trial in Krakow. Arthur is at the forefront of the picture. *(Courtesy of The State Museum Auschwitz-Birkenau in Oświęcim)*

37 My father standing on trial in Poland. *(Auschwitz Camp Archives)*

38 The trial took place between 24 November to 22 December 1947. *(Courtesy of The State Museum Auschwitz-Birkenau in Oświęcim)*

39 The defendants. *(Courtesy of The State Museum Auschwitz-Birkenau in Oświęcim)*

40 The defendants. *(Courtesy of The State Museum Auschwitz-Birkenau in Oświęcim)*

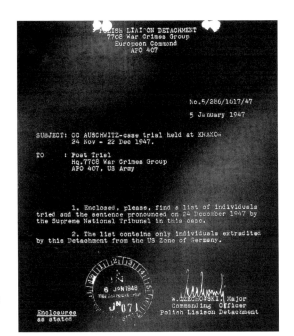

41 The list of individual sentences after the trial in Krakow. *(Author's collection)*

42 The list of individual sentences after the trial in Krakow. *(Author's collection)*

43 'The Little Orphan' in 1953, when I became
the foster child of Ursula and Earl Poune.
(Author's collection)

44 Ursula and Earl when they first took me in
as their foster child. *(Author's collection)*

45 My American ID photo with a new
name and identity in 1953. *(Author's
collection)*

46 Earl W. Poune, a Second World War pilot. First Lieutenant US Army Air Corps. My American Dad. *(Author's collection)*

47 Earl Poune standing second from the left with his flight crew in front of their B-17 bomber *No Sacktime*. *(Author's collection)*

48 Visiting the remaining ruins of Hitler's home, the Berghof, on the Obersalzberg in Berchtesgaden, 1998. (*Author's collection*)

49 Visiting the remaining ruins of Hitler's home, the Berghof, on the Obersalzberg in Berchtesgaden, 1998. (*Author's collection*)

50 The former Dachau camp in Munich, 1998. *(Author's collection)*

51 The prison block where father was held by the Americans and wrote his journals in 1946–7. *(Author's collection)*

52 Inside the prison block. *(Author's collection)*

53 Prison block at Dachau. *(Author's collection)*

54 The former 'Kommandantur' – the offices of the Kommandant within the original Auschwitz Camp I. *(Author's collection)*

55 Auschwitz-Birkenau II where my half-brother Hans-Dieter was born. It was also where the crematoriums and gas chambers were located. *(Author's collection)*

56 This 15-foot fence surrounds a marshy field where 300 wooden barracks once stood. *(Author's collection)*

57 The former Rudolph Hoess villa at Auschwitz. *(Author's collection)*

58 At the Auschwitz Camp Museum looking through documents/photos. *(Author's collection)*

59 Auschwitz survivor Dr Janusz Mlynarski reading letters from other survivors. *(Author's collection)*

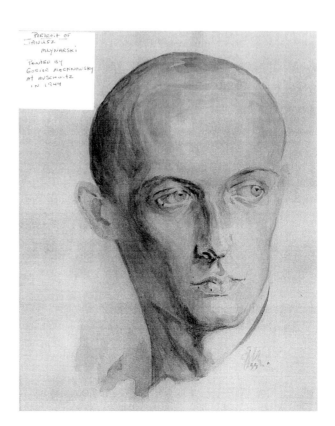

60 Portrait of Janusz Mlynarski painted by Gosior Macknowsky at Auschwitz in 1944. *(Author's collection)*

61 My meeting and interview with Dr Mlynarski, Auschwitz survivor # 355, in October 1998. He was a prisoner at the camp at the time my father was Kommandant. *(Author's collection)*

recalls her first breakfast at the Lochners was also of warm milk and bread; then finally a bath and clean clothes.

Michael Lochner's family had lived in the Berchtesgaden area for many years. They were among those who had been forced to sell and leave their home on the Obersalzberg when Hitler took possession of the area. In 1937 Martin Bormann and his associates 'negotiated' the sale of Michael's parents' lovely home, called the 'Baumgartmuehle', where he and his thirteen other siblings had been born. The NSDAP proceeded to remove the roof while the family still lived within the home and they were then forced to leave in the middle of winter. The 'Baumgartmuehle' was only a short distance from Hitler's Berghof. The Lochner home was destroyed by the NSDAP, as well as some forty others in the Obersalzberg vicinity.

The Lochners were old fashioned and very strict Lutherans. Antje was lonely and missed Brigitte and I and would sometimes walk or catch a ride to Bad Reichenhall, to come and see us at the Hutterers. I remember her large, dark, very sad eyes; they still have that sad unforgettable look today. Antje is the image of my father, although I've been told by my family that I also resemble father, 'especially in character, he was a very sensitive, considerate person'.

Brigitte then found out she had TB, spending eight lonely months in a sanitarium. Not many people came to visit her and after all that had already occurred in her young life, at age seventeen she wanted to die. She stood in front of an opened window in the cold of winter, letting the frigid draft blow in on her. I do remember going there to see her, and especially liked the box of chocolates on her nightstand which someone had given to her; she was happy to share them with me. I felt sorry that she had to be there and missed her; I felt very lost without her. She was my role model and I looked up to her; so pretty with her black hair. Later, I wore my hair black for many years.

She did recuperate, but was no longer able to continue the ballet. It was the end of showbusiness for both of us. At least for her it was the end of ballet, but she went on to do some other things in that field.

I had to leave the Hutterers and was placed into foster care at the Lochners with Antje. The state tried its best to keep the family together and it worked for a time.

Being with Antje made up for the loneliness I felt without my big sister, who hadn't just been a sister, but more often probably took the place of my mother. She'd always been there to protect me and gave me a sense of security.

'Haus Bergluft' was a beautiful Bavarian guesthouse, a 'Pension' where many summer or winter vacationers, usually the regulars, came every year. Each room was unique, named by color, and the wooden furniture was hand-painted by Herr Lochner, our foster father, who was a well-known landscape artist and photographer of that area.

The Lochners' living quarters were on the first floor; their only daughter Dorothea occupied one of the second-story guest rooms. Dorothea was a pretty natural blond. I always thought of her as quietly angelic, especially when she burned candles and incense in her room. Antje and I had an attic room. It was cozy up there with big puffy feather quilts on our beds to keep us warm in the cold of winter. There was only cold running water and we slept with our windows open for the exhilarating fresh mountain air, even when it snowed.

Antje would read me stories at night. My favorite book was *Die kleine Magd Karlson*, about a little girl and the trolls. Our father had given us the book. Sometimes she had a 'Bett Hupfer' – a candy treat at bedtime – for me. We were very close and were a comfort to one another. She combed my long hair every morning; sometimes she added a bow to a new fun style, but usually I wore thick long braids, as it was not proper to wear long hair 'down' or curled. I remember the tune of our special whistle, our own secret communication, to call to each other. Antje worked hard helping with the guests, many of whom befriended us.

The Lochners were strict, but we were treated well. We had to dress in the dowdy old-fashioned Bavarian style of high-top boots and wool stockings in the winter. These unattractive boots we had to wear would be considered high fashion today. On occasion, the Lochners received care packages for us from friends in America, and I was thrilled to have some pretty American dresses. I remember a 'Santa Claus' coloring book and how I adored the pictures of the jolly American Santa.

Antje was saving up her money and bought a pair of strappy black, patent leather sandals; chic and scandalous the way she would like to have dressed. Realizing the Lochners would disapprove of these risqué sandals, she talked our brother Dieter (who also lived in the area) into bringing them to her, under the pretense that he was giving them to her as a gift. From somewhere she got hold of some clear nail polish for her toes. We did a lot of walking in those days and the minute she left Haus Bergluft, off came the ugly boots – quickly cramming them into her bag – and out came the black sandals which she wore away from home every chance she had. I liked those sandals and thought she looked so very pretty.

We all ate together every evening in the family Stube (the sitting and dining room), always joining hands in prayer around the table, thanking God for our meals. Before we were excused from the table we had to each shake the hands of both Herr and Frau Lochner, while we did our curtsies, gratefully thanking them in this way after every meal. *Danke Schoen Fur Das Essen* (Thank you for the food – a most humbling practice).

I recall having to eat liver, which I detested (even to this day), and was left to sit by myself into the darkness until I finished – choking on every bite. My homework and penmanship was of the utmost importance. It had to be perfect. If I didn't keep my letters exactly between the lines it had to be redone, no matter how late it was.

The evenings were spent around the table near the tile 'Kachel' stove. Herr Lochner would play his Zither and we'd play games, read, knit, or at Christmas time we made the Bavarian straw star ornaments; wonderful creative things to occupy our time without TV or radio, almost as it was in the book *Heidi*.

We were taught to treat adults with respect. Actually, I don't recall having to be taught to be respectful; it was something that was understood by the unspoken rules (or fear) of our elders. It was more so for us, since we lived with strangers. I can't ever remember a hug or a kiss or even the word LOVE. Everything was very straight-laced and many things we learned, despite seeming severe, instilled social manners and respect that I feel fortunate to have been exposed to. Looking back today, it was a continuation of the subservient upbringing the men of the Third Reich had experienced during their childhood in the early 1900s. This was the unquestioned respect and obedience toward all adults and authority.

Liesel was the red-headed Bavarian lady who did the laundry. She had warmth that drew me to her and I looked forward to her coming every week. She took time to talk to me in a cheerful way, always with a big smile.

It was called the Wash Kitchen, the special room where she scrubbed the sheets with a brush, bent over a long wooden table. Large boiling kettles held the sheets and clothes, and I watched her toil with the big bars of laundry soap and wash boards. Later in the day the sheets and clothes were on the clothes line blowing in the wind. Her thick hair was in a braid around her head and the perspiration always ran down her weathered face. Liesel was just another stranger, but a kind, friendly soul who brought some sunshine into my life.

There were Americans living in what used to be private homes located near Haus Bergluft. Antje and I adored the darling little girl named Cherie who sometimes came over to play with us in the Lochner garden. There was also a red-headed and freckle-faced American boy named Billy. He was my age and I had a crush on him. Liesel never missed a chance to tease me about Billy, who later reminded me of Tom Sawyer when I read the book.

The Lochners' garden was naturally beautiful and had the largest sunflowers I've ever seen. Dahlias and Asters grew abundantly and the window boxes were thriving with colorful 'Impatients'. All proof of Frau Lochners amazing green thumb. Herr Lochner made *The Sunflowers* one of his most famous paintings, which I was thankful to purchase in 1970. There were green lawns and benches on which the guests could relax and enjoy the garden, and pine trees to cool off under.

The guests went on many hikes up the numerous mountain trails. Some went mountain climbing and would stay overnight in the alpine huts, and sometimes Herr Lochner, Dorothea and even Antje would go along. I missed her when she wasn't there, somehow always afraid to be left alone and worried she might not return.

I remember one incident in particular when Antje left on one of those overnight trips. It was the day I had been grounded and sent to my room. I knew I was in some sort of trouble when Dorothea informed me that her mother, Tante Elizabeth, wanted to see me in the Stube. (There was another larger Stube for the guests on the opposite side of the house.) Tante Elizabeth spent most of her time knitting or reading in the cozy room and the door was shut, as always, when I knocked apprehensively. My heart was beating fearfully as I heard her call *Ja, komm herein*. As I entered the room, I was overwhelmed by the heavy fragrance of old English lavender, which she always wore. It was pleasant but almost hypnotizing. Tante Elizabeth was sitting in her chair wearing her traditional dark green Dirndl dress, her hair wound in a thick braid around her head. Her speech, however, was without a Bavarian dialect; it articulated an intellectual upper class German that was spoken along the Rhine region in her city of Cologne. Her light blue eyes and the dimple in her chin added to the gentle features of this middle-aged woman. But that day she looked stern and let me know she was very upset that I had once again lost my knitting needles required for a class project at school. This was actually part of the girls' curriculum which taught us how to knit socks. My tearful explanation fell on deaf ears; the fact was that the metal knitting needles, which I had already lost several times before, once again had slipped out through a hole in my old hand-me-down carrying case.

She said she was very disappointed in me. I was upset with myself that I had displeased her, but it seemed no one ever listened. It was just another issue proving that whether it was right or wrong, we as foster children had to obey.

Punished for having lost the knitting needles, I climbed the stairs to the attic where Antje and I shared a room. From the small dormer window I whistled to Antje, who was leaving for the overnight camping trip. She turned and waved when she heard our secret call. I watched her walk away, down the long gravel lane, calling after her until she disappeared. I begged her not to leave me, but was left feeling alone and afraid. Then, in my quiet room, I wondered what it would be like to have been able to live with my own parents and why couldn't we be with our mother? That night I cried myself to sleep, once again.

I continued to lose those needles through the same gap in the old carrying case, but I never again told anyone, only my best friend Annemarie Hoffreiter who lived next door, where her family ran a small store. Annemarie knew I was afraid of the consequences and replaced several sets of knitting needles for me until we finished our sock project and went on to embroidery. I don't think she ever realized the importance of her caring deed.

Herr Lochner was well known around town and always wore his leather shorts (Lederhose). On occasion he invited me into his artist's studio where no one was ever allowed. One day I knocked on his door and he looked surprised to find me standing there with my hands behind my back. I had rehearsed this little routine, and after having finally got up enough nerve I brought forth the stem of pear I'd been eating. I had frayed its end and it looked like a small paint brush. I handed it to him saying, 'A paintbrush for an artist'. He smiled and nodded his head as he always would when he approved of something, and I was elated when he asked me in.

I loved the scent of the paints, the special paper and canvases. He showed me the paintings which he was working on, propped onto large easels, and also the many lovely postcards of the area that he'd photographed. He gave me some of the Berchtesgaden area, which I still cherish today. The ones I found especially pretty were those taken of Dorothea as a young girl, with long blond braids, gathering bouquets in a field of wildflowers. I felt very special to receive such attention and be allowed into his enchanting world of the artist. To this day, whenever I eat a pear I think of Onkel Michael and the 'paint brush', and will never forget the wonderful scent of his studio and the special moments we shared.

One of his photos in particular was his personal historical contribution to the Berchtesgaden area. He snapped a very extraordinary photograph of little Dorothea when she was just a toddler. She had walked away from her mother and made her way through a large crowd of people who had come to see Hitler. She was picked up and held by one of his men while Hitler, bending over her and taking her hands, greeted this beautiful blond and blue-eyed child with delight. This picture really portrays the image Hitler liked to convey to the people; that of a kind man who cared a great deal for Germany's youth.

Christmas time in the mountains was always very special and on Christmas Eve we walked many miles in the snow to the Lutheran Cathedral in Berchtesgaden. The bells could be heard ringing for miles. Even today I love that sound. The services were very festive and there always was a large tree with real candles; and the choir singing those never forgotten hymns. On the way back home the moon followed us and glistened off the freshly fallen snow. We left footprints with each step and I can still hear the 'crunch' under our feet, as the snow stuck to our soles in thick layers.

Simple gifts were of the traditional plate with fruits, nuts and cookies. This year I received a flute. It was of dark wood and one of my proudest possessions; I was even able to take lessons and learned how to play. I still have this flute today.

My fascination of cherubs and angels came from living in this beautiful Berchtesgaden region. Churches and chapels had lovely baroque angelic paintings and gilded statues. I used to go into every chapel along the roads in the country-side to look at the pictures on their walls and ceilings … but also something more powerful drew me in. I believe I picked up my guardian angel somewhere along the way.

My love for nature was also due to the beautiful Berchtesgaden area – the place where you find Enzian and Edelweiss and real violets and cyclamen (the Alpine rose) in the forests, in the moss hidden under ferns. In the meadows we strung wildflowers – 'Gaensebluemchen' – to make wreaths to wear in our hair, left alone to our dreams in the world of childhood innocence.

Aschauer Weiher was the pond where we went swimming. We would have to walk what seemed like a great distance through forests to get there. On the way we picked wild strawberries and blueberries. We worked up such a hunger from swimming and playing that the dry pieces of dark bread that we brought along tasted like cake to me.

Annemie Geiger was Antje's friend who brought her extra sandwiches to school when Antje was still living with our mother. Annemie's parents owned the large, lovely old Hotel Geiger in Berchtesgaden. We walked there often to play dress up, as Annemie had trunks full of lovely old clothes in her fascinating attic. At that time it was a great meeting place for many of her young friends.

In those days Annemie's cousin often brought along a friend; the boy's name was Wolf Rüdiger Hess, son of Rudolf Hess, Reich Deputy and once a member of Hitler's close inner circle. Wolf Rüdiger attended school in the Berchtesgaden region.

It was a memorable time in our childhood, and playing dress-up together in that wonderful old hotel was one of our favorite things to do. Today this extraordinary landmark stands vacant, awaiting a new owner. The interior, which is in need of major renovation, more than likely still holds the echoes of children's laughter, and if you wandered throughout the empty hallways the haunting voices of distinguished guests may still linger. The exterior looks as it did in our childhood, a grand hotel nestled in the clouds of the Bavarian Alps.

Even though we were without our parents, we were blessed with the meaningful things of childhood; growing up in this beautiful region and having each other.

About this time Anneliese came to Berchtesgaden with Hans-Dieter to visit Antje and me at Lochners. It seemed very strange to me to be introduced to a 'Frau Liebehenschel'. I took a liking to Hans-Dieter at once and somehow felt a bond with this brother. I didn't understand then and I really didn't process or comprehend the whole concept of why he was a half-brother, especially since I had never known my father. That day we played and had great fun together in the Lochner garden. I would only meet with him on two other occasions, those being my visits to Europe in 1970 and 1972.

Hans-Dieter and I talked for the last time when he called me for my birthday on 15 February 1990. He passed away three weeks later on 6 March. I didn't tell him of the difficulties I was facing at the time; that my twenty-eight-year marriage was at an end. My whole life at that time was shattered, all so bleak and devastating. He had asked me that day: 'Do you think we will ever see each other again?' Everyone was leaving me. He was only forty-five.

When Antje visited Hans-Dieter in the hospital weeks before his death he asked her, 'Do you think we have to pay for our father's mistakes?'

It was in 1975 when I lived in northern California that Hans-Dieter had wanted to come for a visit. It was the time of trouble in my marriage; I was ill and we were not doing well financially. My reply to him, without wanting to tell the true facts, was that it was just not possible for us at that time to have any visitors. I don't think he ever understood or forgave me for this rejection. He went away too soon and I have always felt badly because he felt he wasn't part of us. I can empathize with him, however, because I too have lived with those feelings of loneliness and lack of belonging; I wish I had been able to make him see how much he was loved and needed.

After Brigitte's release from the sanitarium she went to work in modeling for a fashion designer in the large Bad Reichenhall resort hotels. He soon moved to Munich and she went with him to work in his salon, showing his original designs, beautiful evening gowns and also his hats. She was named 'Miss Flamingo' and they wrote an article about her in a major newspaper; but it was the wrong timing, as people still had no money to spend on high fashions. The aftermath of war had left Germany and the other European countries still struggling with a poor economy.

While she was in Munich, Brigitte met, fell in love and actually became engaged to a handsome actor named Peter Garten. The relationship ended but she never spoke of him to me in later years, and just recently, as I was looking through a small family photo album (pictures my father had taken of our house in St Gilgen in 1942), a picture which had been hidden secretly behind others, fell out. It was a haunting likeness of a very handsome man in a tuxedo. Antje told me it was Peter Garten.

The other reason Brigitte moved to Munich was to be near our mother.

It was 1950 and the first time Brigitte went to visit mother at the Haar Institution was heart-rending. She had taken fresh fruit and waited for mother anxiously in the visiting room. Mother didn't recognize her own daughter at first, but then began crying and hugging her with joy. She was laughing happily and seemed quite normal. They talked about Antje and me. Then all of a sudden she changed and another personality took over. This part of her personality was overcome with paranoia, where she thought people were after her, wanting to kill her.

On her next visit Brigitte received a pass, giving her permission to take our mother out of the institution for the afternoon. They went to a small coffee shop where my mother enjoyed her unsurpassed favorite, which was cake and coffee. She was kept on strong medication and begged Brigitte to make them stop the painful shock treatments. She was terrified of this barbaric treatment and apparently she was not showing any improvement. There really seemed no hope for her condition and finally the shock treatments were discontinued.

This letter was from our mother written from the institution at Haar in Munich.

May 11, 1951
My dear Brigitte-Gitscha!
My dear Bärbel-Ulrike [Babuschkalein]

Today May 11, I received your dear package. The last 2 weeks I kept hoping and visualizing but didn't think of it today, so even greater was the joy and surprise. The egg went straight to the tummy, 2 pieces of chocolate and 5 bites of the cake, as 5 is the number of love.

Now I sit here very happily and think of you both with Love, great Love you two, and wanted to write to you right away.

The photograph brought me such happiness. Just the other day I thought, if I only had a few pictures, and then they arrived. I thank you dear Brigitte for your so loving thoughtfulness.

And you Babuschkalein, [her nickname for me] I thank you with great tender love for your dear note. 'So as the heartfelt wishes they shall insist on Happiness.' For your dear Mammie yes, then it should soon be fulfilled. [I'd written her that I wanted her to come home to us.]

I think of you both so often. Tell me Brigitte, what do you need? Evidently you've been in the hospital as long as I have been here. When I return home you'll quickly get well. That I know for certain. I know my Brigitte, but everything has to have its beginning, but also its end. And so it has to be the same, here with me.

You can't believe how good the cake was, something different for a change. You know how much I like cake and then every so often a cup of coffee. I miss it very much.

When I come home I'll write to you right away Brigitte! I hope you'll have this letter in your hands for the Pentecost Holiday Brigitte! My dear Babuschkalein you still love your Mammie as before and Mammie loves her Babuschkalein, just as affectionately and deeply as always. Such a pretty dress you are wearing in the photograph. Who gave that to you?

Now I will close and send many wishes to you both with Love,

Your Mutti

Brigitte was not earning much money and lived on one loaf of bread a week with milk from a milk bar. She was putting away 5 marks weekly to buy me a doll carriage for Christmas. My own doll carriage had always been my dream. It was of white wicker and almost the size of a real baby carriage. Brigitte took a train to Berchtesgaden and then walked the carriage the rest of the miles all the way up to Strub, Haus Bergluft, where Antje and I were still living.

She was treated very badly by the Lochners. They looked down on her for being a model and her involvement in show business. They never offered her any refreshments after the long walk; she was not even invited to sit down. They passed unfair judgement on her, thinking of her as being immoral.

I was deliriously happy with the wonderful and generous gift, and was not aware of what was transpiring between the Lochners and Brigitte.

Brigitte only stayed fifteen minutes; she was terribly disappointed and cried all the way home on the train. In 1972, when we had a family reunion in Germany, we all stayed at the Pension Haus Bergluft for a week and had a wonderful time reminiscing. Frau Lochner apologized to Brigitte about that day so long ago, when she had treated her unfairly.

From the modeling job Brigitte joined an Ice Revue dancing on the perimeter of the stage, her body painted gold. The second night their performance was in Fürth and the company went bankrupt and folded, owing everyone, including the performers. Left stranded without any money, Brigitte had no choice but to remain in Fürth. She roomed with an older couple who let her sleep in their kitchen on a cot.

Brigitte soon went to work at Grundig Electronics, gluing fabric on radio chassis for 95 pfennigs an hour. Shortly thereafter she was promoted 'upstairs' to do office work. She also took a side job as a reporter, even though she had no experience. She was sent to nightclubs and reported on their entertainment events. She met another reporter who was familiar with the name Liebehenschel; he had read about our father.

Meanwhile, Antje was sent to Wolfenbüttel in northern Germany, to go to work as an apprentice for a lady who owned a gift shop. It was also the time I was sent to another foster family – a family in the town of Landshut named Krauss.

Antje and I had been baptized at the Lutheran Church in Berchtesgaden when we lived together at the Lochners. Minister Paul Krauss had previously been the Lutheran minister in Berchtesgaden, where he and his family had lived for many years. They had lost their own little girl named Bärbel, who lies buried in the cemetery we frequently visited in Berchtesgaden. The families Lochner and Krauss were good friends. After the Krauss family moved to Landshut they returned often in the summers to spend their vacations at Haus Bergluft, and it was here that I became acquainted with my 'Uncle Paul' and 'Aunt Friedl'. After the baptism I learned that they were going to be my new foster parents.

The following letter was sent by Minister Paul Krauss to Antje and I for our baptism, shortly before I was to be sent to Landshut.

Landshut, February 22, 1952
Dear Antje, Dear Bärbel,

Day after tomorrow is the celebration of your Holy Baptism of which the family Lochner has written to us. This day should not pass without a blessed wish from us as you dear Bärbel will soon be part of our parsonage.

Dear Children! Throughout your childhood you've had to pass the test of many hard trials. What you've had to endure in your youth most people never experience throughout their whole lifetime.

To lose your father under such terrible circumstances, is alone enough to make one despondent of one's love of human nature and its Christianity, and on top of that, as a result, your mother also had to suffer so terribly. This is all so severe … but dear children, the God whom you will accept as your God on Sunday is merciful. In the end he has all that is good awaiting us. We want to make ourselves available to him and try to compensate for the loss of your home and parents.

Dear Bärbel, when you come to us this spring we want you to feel at home and know that you will be as dear to us as our own child. You know of the small grave in the Berchtesgaden cemetery, there lies buried and sleeps our own 'Bärbel'. Do you know it is as though God is giving us back our Bärbel, through you. We are happily looking forward to your coming, especially Christl and Hanne.

May you both know that on your day of baptism you will be in our prayers. God Bless You!

Our heartfelt greetings for the Lochners and you both on your Blessed Day.

> Your Landshut Foster Parents
> Paul and Friedl Krauss
> and Christl and Hanne

Before I left to live in Landshut I wrote this verse in Antje's autograph book of poems on 4 March 1952:

In Memory
Man shall be Noble
Helpful and Kind
Dedicated to you by your
Sister Bärbel
[I was 9 years old]

Much later during my research I was completely amazed to discover that this same verse appeared written in my father's journals and was one of his favorites, it had been passed on to him by his mother, my grandmother.

So Antje and I were separated, and I was alone for the first time. Dorothea and her fiancée Fritz drove me to the family Krauss in Herr Lochner's classic old 'Hanomag' sedan, which was never driven, only parked in their garage. I can still hear Dorothea's words ringing in my mind: *Fritzchen bist du schon Muede?* (Fritzchen, are you tired yet?). We drove to Landshut on small country roads, which took us several hours. Sitting in the spacious back seat next to my old suitcase, which held the contents of my entire belongings, I quietly wondered what my new home would be like … a terribly lonely and frightening feeling.

I remember being afraid about leaving Antje and my familiar surroundings; those fears I had from the past, of being once again taken from my family, had now finally came to pass. How many more times would I be uprooted and how many more of these trips would I have to take? I was broken-hearted and cried secretly at night for my sisters and mother, and for a father I never knew.

I had no idea in advance that they were planning on sending me to Landshut. I don't recall the letter Onkel Paul sent to us for the baptism. 'Children are to be seen but not heard' was the way we were brought up. In our case, children without parents in an adult world, we had no rights … but then we never did have any say about these things as it was all decided by others; strangers who fortunately did seem to have our best interests in mind.

A walled medieval castle sits overlooking the quaint historic old town of Landshut on the river Isar where Heinrich Himmler, the former SS Reichsführer, attended high school. I lived with the Krausses who had two daughters, and whose spacious house was adjoining the old church. They were good people. One of my all-time favorite old movies is *The Bishop's Wife*. The rectory and cathedral in the film always remind me of this foster home and the church in Landshut.

In their garden they grew all sorts of fruits and vegetables and I was allowed to help myself to the currants, gooseberries and loganberries. Minister Krauss (Onkel Paul) was a very tall man and I recall sitting in the old church on the hard wooden pews, listening intently with great emotion, to his powerful Sunday sermons. Up in the pulpit, wearing his long black robe with a white starched collar, he portrayed strength and decency. On the cold winter days when I sometimes stayed behind at the house and did not go to the church services with them, I surprised them by placing their house slippers by the fire on the hearth, so they would be warm and cozy when they returned. The best part was their radiant smiles of approval and the feeling that maybe I was loved just a little. On cold winter nights they filled heavy green beer bottles with hot water, securing the clasps which were then placed under the covers at the foot of the bed, keeping me snug and warm.

Sometimes Onkel Paul took me for walks with him along the river Isar where willow trees lined the path; he held my small hand in his large hands, which made me feel very protected. He told me stories and explained things of nature, the stars and the universe.

On Sunday afternoons we all climbed into their Volkswagen Beetle car for outings into the country. How I loved those times. I remember playing in potato fields, corn and wheat fields where between the rows of crops grew wild, red poppies and blue corn flowers. I collected large June bugs and fireflies in jars. Most of the time we stayed until late into evening, but it was never long enough for me.

Christl and Hanne were their daughters. Christl was the oldest and very pretty with long, black hair. Tante Friedl was kind and gentle. She always wore her hair pulled back into a bun. She sewed Christl beautiful dresses which she wore to the many dances and social functions she attended. I remember how I loved to see her all dressed up in taffeta gowns, with silk flowers at her waist and very full mid-length skirts, which was the fashion in the early 1950s. I dreamed how maybe someday I could wear pretty dresses like hers and go dancing.

Hanne, the youngest daughter, had an outgoing, enthusiastic personality and I recall her friendly smile. She bought me my first bottle of original Coca-Cola.

I was without a warm winter coat that year and badly needed some new shoes, as my old hand-me-down shoes were several sizes too large. Brigitte had requested that I might come and stay with her for a few days, and I was happily sent to Fürth for a visit. She was rooming with a Frau Lesemann at that time.

Brigitte took me shopping and I was very excited. She bought me a faux-fur dark blue coat – I called it my teddy-coat – and a new pair of shoes; she was still looking after her 'baby sister' as she always called me. I was so happy and proud of my new shoes and recall they were of a light camel-colored leather with squared-off toes. I wore them immediately after she bought them for me, and we continued on to a restaurant for lunch. I went into the ladies lounge and in front of a large mirror I danced around elated, keeping an adoring eye on my shoes, until someone came in. I was very embarrassed.

My new 'fur' coat was one of, if not the only thing I ever had to wear that was new and not a hand-me-down. Brigitte showed her love in so many ways, even when she had next to nothing herself. I loved my oldest sister so very much. She always felt responsible for me after our mother became ill, even though I had been placed with various foster parents.

After my visit I wrote a letter to Brigitte:

Dear Brigitte!
You wanted to know how it went when Tante Friedl picked me up. Ulf and I were playing when suddenly the doorbell rang. I went to answer and it was Tante Friedl. Quickly I dressed, showed everyone the new things I had received and said my goodbyes. Then we left. Just imagine I was given a 'Zehnerl' [10 Penny coin] by Frau Lesemann! Please write soon and often. I will then also write very often.

Your Bärbel

The Krauss family had a housekeeper and a cook. Even then I loved watching the activity in the kitchen. Everything was homemade. I especially liked the potato dumplings that had little toasted bread cubes in the center. It was a complicated, lengthy process, but the end result was worth it! They ate very well, but I didn't appreciate delicacies such as tongue or brain.

Just as it was customary at the Lochners in Berchtesgaden, here at the Krauss's we also joined hands around the dinner table saying our blessings before each meal. But here I was not expected to thank them for my meals. The evening light meal was of sandwiches and I too would be served a small glass of beer. No one drank water and beer was a common Bavarian beverage for all ages. In today's society that would not be looked upon as a proper practice for a religious family, but in this reality it was a most innocent and wholesome way to grow up.

Minister Krauss had a twin brother, Onkel Karl, and their mother lived with Onkel Karl and his family. When their mother passed away in his house we went there to stay a few days. I was chosen to sleep in her room, in her bed where she had died. It had an antique wood-carved headboard with a large featherbed that was trimmed with Swiss lace. An old grandfather clock ticked loudly and struck every fifteen minutes as I lay paralyzed, too afraid to move all night. I saw a vision of her ghost standing in the room in her long white lace nightgown. I don't think I imagined it nor was I dreaming!

Again I had been placed with a good family, but I was always aware I was only the foster child. Something was missing … I needed to belong and to be really loved. I was basically a happy child, but lonely without my family, and not really understanding my loneliness.

One letter I wrote to Brigitte said: 'I am so happy and looking forward to Christmas because I am allowed to come spend it with you. That will be so fine.'

Tante Friedl added to this letter: 'Bärbel is very happy that she can spend Christmas with you. Now the question is if Bärbel will be here for Christmas Eve? Sincerely, The Krauss'.

Consequently, it was this year, through my sister Brigitte and her fiancée Heinz, that I was invited to spend a memorable Christmas with them at the home of Heinz's sister Ursula, and her American husband Earl Poune. This event would eventually determine my future, as Ursula and Earl became my adoptive parents.

After I left the family Krauss, Christl and Hanne became sisters once again to a new baby girl. They named her Ulrike.

Christl's husband, Roman Herzog, was elected President of Germany for a five-year term on 23 May 1994. Sadly Christl passed away on 19 June 2000.

Chapter Ten

Journals of a Prisoner

Excerpts From: 'Letters to my Wife Annelie'
From: Books # 3 & 4
By: Arthur Liebehenschel

These following excerpts are from a series of heart-rending letters written by my father to his beloved Anneliese, in the form of journals. They provided me with touching insights into a soul in torment. The depth of emotion in his writing shows a passionate, loving man, devoted to the highest principles. This segment of my research takes me back to postwar Munich in 1946, to Dachau, which had once been a concentration camp, now used by Americans as a detention camp, where my father is imprisoned as their Prisoner of War.

Here, Father actually worked as a trustee in the administrative offices of the Dachau camp, and was given quite a bit of freedom. He seemed well-liked by the Americans and his cell was no longer locked. He worked long hours, but back in his cell in quiet solitude, he became absorbed in writing his journals. He convinced his prison guards to let him have paper and pencil; sometimes he only had a stub to write with. This privilege was allowed only on weekends, since during the week his letters and supplies were taken away. Father had sewn the fragile pages together with gray thread, apparently taken from his blanket off his cot in the cell, then bound them together into four separate journals. Anneliese received these journals – but only books 3 and 4; after my father's death, books 1 and 2 were presumably lost.

Around 1994 Anneliese turned the letters over to my sister Antje. Since it is nearly impossible for me to decipher Father's beautifully handwritten old-German script, Antje spent her evenings after work, painstakingly copying my father's words from the aged, yellowed pages, into a small black-and-red bound notebook, her fingers cramping with the effort.

As I translated the German into English I actually felt myself living and experiencing his pain and loneliness as he wrote these letters in his cold cell. I felt him pulling me into the past … draining my emotions and physical strength … almost as though I had crossed over and was transferred into this other dimension in time. I could only work on a few sentences at a time before I had to lie down from complete mental and physical exhaustion.

These were obviously intimate letters to Anneliese and their son Hans-Dieter, but as I re-read these letters I looked for evidence that my father loved me, that he missed me and thought of me, but he barely mentions 'The Other Children', least of all me, whom he didn't know at all. Had he forgotten I ever existed? The thought leaves me with a hollow feeling. And yet, even though the letters left me inwardly shaken, for the first time I sensed the heart and soul of this stranger who was my Papa.

My excitement and need to search was, however, not always shared by my family. For most of my family the subject was still too painful and uncomfortable and I found it increasingly difficult to convey my intentions across the many miles. My frustrations mounted, as the answers I was looking for continued to elude me. I felt very alone in my quest. My sister Antje expressed her concerns about publishing father's journals in a letter written to me in July 1994, and I wanted to explain my reasons for doing so. I wrote:

Dear Antje,

Today I received your letter, which left me very sad. I don't think you understand what I am trying to do or how important it is. I didn't start out with the thought of using Papa's letters but as I evolved further into translating the pages, I found myself actually living with him through his captivity, not only in spirit but I could almost feel his physical and emotional pain. I then knew that his letters belonged in the book and I would some day, want to have it published because it is a piece of history we need to share with the rest of the world. Antje, I really feel that Papa would want me to use his letters and I wonder if it was mere coincidence that they came to us at this precise moment? It is his declarations of love which show his true soul. ...Through Papa's portrayal of her [Anneliese] and their great love for one another, he brought Anneliese into a whole new light for me. I hope this won't create any problems between us. Can you understand what I'm trying to say? I am doing this for all of us, it may be the most important accomplishment of my life. I have come to feel very close to all of you through my writing ... I have only you and need you to believe in me! I will now continue with my writing ... there is a drive within me that I can't explain, but I'm beginning to realize the source!

Love, Bärbel

I don't believe at that point in time, Antje fully understood the importance of what compelled me to delve so deeply into our past, but these last few years she and her husband have been a tremendous help to me and I could not have done it without them. I also believe today that Anneliese would be pleased about my book and the use of Papa's Journals.

Nicknames father used in his letters:
For Anneliese: *Annelielein, Luschilein, Luschi*
Our Father: *Hansilein, Hansi*
Hans-Dieter: *Hadilein, Hachilein, Hadi*

January 15, 1946

My beloved Annelielein, with grateful heart to God I begin this notebook.

I'm healthy and content and happy that I can at least chat with you. These lines are actually only to hold the inner connection, which in any case makes our souls inseparable and I'm always with you my beloved wife. I see you very alive before me, past the barrier of the gates, barbed wire and high walls, although for almost a year the eye has not seen beyond into the vast wide-open spaces. What is my Hachilein doing? Oh I long for you both, you, and my boy. When will I see you again? I wait patiently because I believe this. Now I give you many kisses. Indeed come soon Luschilein, come to your very lonely …

Hansilein

January 19, 1946

It has been 24 weeks now that you my beloved have been away from me. What may you be doing today? You have been my greatest gift. . . . What more could I ask for? That my good deeds at Auschwitz be known, other than the acknowledgement on my behalf from the people I took care of. Wasn't it at this time that our Hachilein came into being in this very town [Auschwitz]? Is it not a gift from God of which we will be forever reminded? And so I keep thinking that justice will win.

Oh, one thing I can tell you about. Do you know where I now have your picture? I now have a bed (since yesterday) which has another bunk above very close, to which I have fastened your picture to the underside only for me to see. Now when I lie in bed I can look into your eyes. You are above and by me all night and so I talk to you and everything comes alive in your facial image.

Good night with many kisses. I hold you tight in my arms and press you close to my heart and remain yours completely,

Your Hansilein

January 27, 1946

Do you remember, Luschilein, the young Polish man at Auschwitz, who escaped from the camp, only to return three days later saying he did not want to make trouble for me? All he wanted was to see his mother once again whom he loved more than anything … then he returned. I understand precisely what he felt and let no harm come to him. The reason I mention that here is that I would do the same, if I could see you once more, I would voluntarily return because I am not afraid and have no reason to flee from my fate.

Many kisses, Hansi

January 29, 1946

My Annelie, I actually shouldn't be writing to you again, as I don't know how much longer I will have paper. But I must, I must come to you. Out of 9 months captivity I have been under investigative arrest for 160 days … why? I was the only concentration camp Kommandant in Germany who stood up for his prisoners

100% and through my actions saved hundreds of lives, only to be tricked and punished by my superiors like a criminal. It is known not just from me but proof from the prisoners who as witnesses testified for me of their own free will.

I think back to August 25th of last year [1945]. It was my first day of interrogation and I had already been cross-examined twice by the American officer. I was one of 40 people who had to face a commission of former prisoners of all nations. They had to confirm who I was. Yes, and they did. Most of them just nodded to me sympathetically and verified that I was a decent person. They then came to my cell and grasped my hands with compassion and then wrote their reports.

It was Germans, Poles and Jews that knew me from Auschwitz. Then as the American officer questioned me again with the reports in his hand [8 to 10], he said to me, 'it's really something, how you treated them, even a Jew spoke in your defense to save your life. Nothing will happen to you, you can rest assured'.

That was on the first day and so it went.

Luschilein, come soon to your,
Hansi

February 2, 1946

A new month is beginning, and if one reads this it seems time is passing quickly, as in these words 'How the time rushes so swiftly, wasn't it yesterday I shared my joy and sorrow with you … wonderful was the time, yes heavenly it was!' Yes and it was and I always think of your advice to always remember our good times together.

Certainly I was a Nazi, of which one side did so many wretched things, and because of this I too have to suffer the consequences even though I never did any wrong and with a clear conscience can always say that at all times with decency and heart, treated all people well. Even if the outcome was often harmful to me. At least in my conscience I know that I always lived and acted out my life decently.

It is justified for them to say 'Those of you who took part have many innocent people on your conscience.'

Hansi

February 8, 1946

Three-quarters of a year I've already been in captivity. Such is the fate of man in a time of so much guilt and sin. God has passed a hard criminal sentence on our people. He took millions on the battlefields and under the ruins of our cities, millions more left crippled and turned into refugees to carry on the guilt of the German people. No not its people but its wrong leadership, so I ask myself daily if there isn't still some things that I should tell you? Yes to tell but to write about is difficult.

I know you will raise our Hadilein into a decent man who shall carry my name proudly in this world, I am with you in my thoughts and am grateful.

Your Hansi

February 10, 1946
Sunday Afternoon:
An overcast dreary day as all others, even when the sun is shining outside. No sun comes into our cell for which the wounded soul so yearns. Sometimes a calm comes over me and in my heart there are the wonderful sunshiny golden images performing such magic within my soul. And with these images I pass the many hours of my sad existence. As of now all postal zones are open but we still can't receive mail and are not allowed to write.

> If you go to a foreign place, I shall quietly follow and quietly a hand leads you.
> That hand is mine.
> If you wake in darkness of night
> I reach for your heart and realize it is mine.

It's a wonderful gift to have found you ... I lay my hand on my heart on which I inscribe the name you so often called me,

Hansi

March 3, 1946
Sunday:
Where might Dieter be? And the other children? We can't even help and will just have to ask God to protect them. So much suffering and worry and then to be behind bars and barbed wire.

Hansi

April 19, 1946
Good Friday:
Mine Forever, My Beloved Annelielein,
Today is Good Friday, the day of the death of our Savior and also my Good Friday. Today I was informed, that as a result of my Auschwitz and Lublin activity, I will be extradited to Poland. I don't know why and wasn't told. The Polish Officers said only that there weren't good reports of me in Auschwitz. I told him that was impossible, the case can only be the opposite! Especially the Poles experienced my good treatment and decency. Not only here the former prisoners but also in Auschwitz, how often did they tell you almost daily when they recognized you that because of my decency and good heart they wished me a life of 100 years. I did nothing special but was a man with a heart who made life bearable for the entrusted poor people and shaped their lives where I could. I did not inflict any harm, this God knows and also my conscience.

I don't want to complain about my fate. Neither am I afraid of my innocent death; that is not the most difficult. It was more difficult that my beloved son Dieter at 15 years of age, still a child, had to go to his death because of my disciplinary relocation to Lublin ... Disciplinary Relocation, because I did good things and stood by my most beloved person ... What does life mean when so many thousands and millions of people in the world, from all sides, had to perish through the fury and hatred of war. I would gladly and easily go if it wasn't for you, Hadi and the other children who still need me.

As long as you carry my name you can truly be proud. It is pure. If it wasn't I would have told you on this difficult Good Friday. My boy was born out of our God willed great love and carries with our flesh and blood my name into the world. Whatever the world may label me with, may he remain as pure as this name. I tell you once more before God I have done no evil. Why do I keep repeating it? You and many others know it.

Send my wishes to Brigitte, Antje and Bärbel and I wish them all well, tell them of my sorrows. I send my heart that belongs to you, it calls to you … Auf Wiedersehn …

Always, Your Hansilein

June 2, 1946

It's Sunday, swallows are chirping and the sun is shining again after cold, rainy days.

An American officer who was in Auschwitz as a Pole while I was there expressed his thanks in beneficial words in the presence of the camp commander Dr. Dortheimer. I mention his name explicitly as I want to adhere what a honorable and good person he is. He thanked me for the good treatment I gave to him and his father who was also at Auschwitz. I hold your hands and kiss you my brave little wife.

Always your, Hansilein

June 29, 1946

Forever Over-All Beloved Luschi!

We never knew what detours we'd have to travel during our separation! When I am with you again we will start a new life from the 'Inside Out'. On the outside I probably appear much older from the spiritual sorrow, but my heart and soul stayed young. But outside appearance is only superficial. Our love is only concerned with our inner life, and that will be nice if we are allowed to go on living.

Hansilein

July 28, 1946

We have now, since July 13, been released from the military defense status and turned over to the civilians. How much longer? Yesterday again they brought a former prisoner who verified that I only did good. How many is it now that always say the same?

Just now we had a mighty storm with thunder, lightning and a cloud burst. God Almighty is expressing himself with clear speech. One only needs to see, hear and understand. How small in comparison is man with all his supposed power.

I've been thinking so much of Dieter, especially now when the first POWs are coming back from Russia. If God would only give him back to us.

Another week has passed and can be deducted from my captivity. Now this notebook is full. How many more pages will I write under these conditions? It's become a little piece of work, my thoughts that I always send but only to you, during this long separation.

With God I start the new week and close this notebook with our favorite saying, 'The Lord will guide us.'

Your Hansilein

August 4, 1946
Dachau:

> Begin with God, with God we End
> That is the Best of life's long Trend

My Dear Beloved Annelielein, with this motto, I start the new journal, and begin another week. It's Sunday afternoon and if the sun is shining for you, you're taking Hachilein for a walk.

When I started the first journal last September over one year ago, I thought I had to rush to fill the pages. This is the fourth journal and I write in it only once a week and still we're not back together. But believing in God we know things are going, as they should.

There is some happy news in my cellblock today. I'm so excited I can hardly write … someone here spoke with my former driver, Lang, who was in the Russian prison camp with our Dieter for some time; they worked together in a factory in the Ural region, building tanks. Lang was also taken prisoner at Lublin along with Dieter. Dieter is alive!!! This news comes to my cell all the way from the Ural. It will probably be difficult to contact Lang for some time as he was injured and sent home to Hungary by the 'Amis'. I'm overjoyed, God has answered our prayers. Only yesterday I was saying to a comrade that I could feel Dieter is still alive. Now I know that God means for us to live on. Maybe he is among the prisoners released through the American Red Cross and is on his way home. It was another miracle. With this joy and thankfulness in my heart I'd like to close for today.

Stay healthy, pray for our Dieter, for me, for our life.

Your Hansilein

August 21, 1946
My Over-All Beloved Annelie!

Today I have been here one whole year because of my involvement in Auschwitz, and because of my two short months of duty in Lublin they want to send me to Poland. I don't know why? You know Luschilein, that I already suffered innocently, within the Nazi Government because I looked out for the oppressed and this affected my career. I did not commit any crimes but was a member of the SS and as such I am treated. I was different because I especially believed its members had to consist of those who had the best of the basic human qualities. With these principles I have lived and tried my best to bestow compassion onto my fellow man … in the meantime, in the eyes of some people I have become someone other than myself. But that I have to perish so miserably because of this I can't grasp and cannot believe that this is what God wants after he has led me through so much turmoil.

Forever, Your Hansilein

On 24 August 1946 my father was taken to Nuremberg to testify in the Oswald Pohl case; Pohl having been his superior. His case was one of twelve separate US military proceedings, which took place from 1946 to 1949. My father arrived at the prison section of the old fortress building called the Palace of Justice. Under the authority of the International Military Tribunal, presiding over the war crimes trials, extensive documented interrogations were to be used against the major Nazi war criminals. The records taken here from witnesses were used in the following prosecutions of more than 185 officials or citizens of the Third Reich.

These proceedings were held in the town of Nuremberg, the southern section that was the US Zone of occupied Germany. Nuremberg was an ancient Gothic city, where most of the Nazi Party Rallies took place and where great stadiums and auditoriums had been built with the thought in mind that it would eventually serve as the capital of the Nazi Party. It had been left as a pile of rubble, heavily bombed during the war. Major reconstruction of the landmark known as the Palace of Justice took place to accommodate the infamous war trials of Nuremberg.

Appointed by Justice Robert H. Jackson, the US prosecutor at the International Military Tribunal was Brigadier General Telford Taylor, as his deputy for subsequent trials. Later, General Joseph T. McNarney, the commander of headquarters US Forces European Theater, appointed General Taylor as Chief of Counsel for War Crimes in 1946.

Among the twenty-one high-ranking defendants whose trials convened in January 1946 was Ernst Kaltenbrunner, Chief of Security Police, who came to my family in Austria after the war with the intention of taking refuge with us. Wilhelm Keitel, Chief of the Armed Forces, was once our neighbor in Oranienburg. While imprisoned he confided to G.M. Gilbert, the American psychologist, that he felt betrayed by Hitler, telling him: 'If he did not deceive us by deliberate lies, then he did it by deliberately keeping us in the dark and letting us fight under a false impression!' Oswald Pohl's sentence was handed down months later.

On 18 September, after waiting and agonizing for almost four weeks, my father was finally called to testify and was picked up and escorted from his cell to the interrogation room # 163. He was led past the cellblocks of these once-important officers of the Reich, who without their magnificent uniforms, looked gaunt and insignificant in their black prison fatigues. I wonder what he was thinking as he quietly walked between the guards down the long, empty corridors. Was the adrenaline pumping with vigor making his weak heart muscle race with fear? Could the pounding in his chest be heard throughout the halls of the old Palace of Justice?

My father, although he would be returned to the Dachau camp, was still at the Nuremberg prison when the sentences of the notorious war criminals were declared, on 1 October 1946.

Those defendants who received death sentences were hanged at the gallows and their bodies were cremated at the Dachau camp. For this purpose the crematorium was once again reactivated there and their ashes then scattered into the River Isar. The banks along this river would become my playground just a few years later.

My father's testimony at Nuremberg finally determined his extradition to Poland, which was approved by General Telford Taylor on 7 October 1946.

Father continued writing in his journals at the Nuremberg prison.

September 1, 1946
Sunday, Nuremberg:
Beloved Luschilein,
One week has gone by and I still don't know why I'm here but it doesn't matter. I see all things with a clear, calm conscience.

Life here is very different. In Dachau I had quite a bit of freedom and here it's all taken away. There I had been an entrusted worker for ten weeks. Yes, it felt good to work and I threw myself into it and was busy and they knew what they had in me. The name 'Liebehenschel' was called all day and could be heard throughout. And now I'm here again in solitary confinement. 'Again' is saying too much as I haven't really been in solitary, not even in Dachau, only the first hard hours a year ago. That evidently is customary here with everyone. But what does it matter as I don't like these people anyway … always again more disappointments even here. Few and seldom times can one find the well-known German loyalty. Maybe that's why this loneliness is easier for me than for others, and more undisturbed can my thoughts be of you. Do you want to know how I live this life?

At 6:45 I get up, wash, straighten the bed, and then the cell, then breakfast and then the waiting if they will pick me up for the hearing. In between time I am with God and you and all my loved ones. There are also books and I read. About noon comes our lunch, then continuation of the already described, then at 16:00 hours we take a half hour walk in the yard under strict supervision (no talking). Between 17:00 and 18:00 hours it's dinner and at 21:00 hours back into the tank. Every two days they shave us and once a week we can bathe. This is what my life is like here. The most terrible thing is waiting and not receiving mail … often I weep …

How is Hachilein? Just a few more days and he'll be two years old. My heart is aching because I can't see him and he doesn't know his father. And our big Dieter, how is he coping and enduring his imprisonment? Tomorrow he'll be 18 years old and captured over two years ago. Our poor boy. May God give him strength and health and may he return to us with strong spirit. I am thankful that we were allowed to find out that he lives…

Hansilein

September 3, 1946
Nuremberg:
Dearest Luschi!
Quickly a few lines to you. Besides my dreams of you there's also someone else I dreamed of. I'd like you to know it was 'Ossie'. He was not a purebred but he had a darling dog soul. What exactly does it mean 'PURE OF RACE'? This was the much preached insanity, but to be soulful and loyal that is pure and worthy. So it has been from the beginning of time and man can't change it, not even with brutal force.

So Ossie was in my dreams, it was nice but much much nicer when you are in my dreams and so much nicer when you will be with me again and I with you.

Good night, Always
Your Hansilein

September 4, 1946
Nuremberg:
My Dear Dear Annelielein!
Until now nobody has been able to declare any allegations or cause. No one has brought suit, not one person.

As an intervention there's a group of former prisoners of mine that are officers today in American service. They gave their testimony for me. Then I suppose this was the cause for the alleviation and I was allowed to work in the administration and my cell was no longer locked.

With my belief in justice I, of free will, surrendered to the Americans after the first day of the fall. I had nothing to hide, did not need to hide and have anyone search for me. At that time confessions were not only few but actually unheard of.

How often did civilians come to my cell and tell me they knew of me. They wanted to look out for me and see that nothing would happen to me. They would always bring cigarettes.

The first camp Doctor was a former prisoner (a Jew) from Birkenau, he knew of me. He likewise, respectively spoke on my behalf. From him I received smokes every day. He would bring them with my heart medication. He was touching. So it has been until today. Sometimes cigarettes would come to my cell with a note saying, 'as a small recognition for the good treatment'.

Luschilein, I'm not doing this to glorify myself, you know me. I didn't call these witnesses to make excuses, they came alone.

Again night time is upon us and I send my heart and soul.

Good night! Forever your Hansi

September 8, 1946
Nuremberg:
Fifteen long days have passed here now at Nuremberg and I still know nothing and haven't been called for the hearings … It is presumably not an altogether great human sin to fall back into doubt every now and then.

What does it say in Psalm 109: 'They have rewarded me evil for good, and hatred for my love.' This is how my life was, you know that and I don't want to start about that again. When I can reach for the Journal in my great loneliness and need for the soul, I have actually had much freedom within.

They have taken it all and can take everything, you, your picture, your heart, but never your soul. My thoughts are always with you every minute. At any rate, this too shall pass.

I yearn for you so much,

Hansi

September 22, 1946
Sunday, Nuremberg:
My Beloved Annelielein!

Again a Sunday, the fifth in the Nuremberg Prison. On September 18 I was called the first time to the hearings. They wanted to know the whole course of my life. It appeared important and maybe they want to use it against me, that I represented Gluecks from the beginning of 1942 until November 1943. Certainly as I stated only in his absence, of unimportant matters, a duration of one to three days and this very seldom, as Gluecks hardly ever took leave … but often enough if they wanted to find a reason. There as in Auschwitz I did not take the way of evil doing. Maybe the higher up gentlemen such as Pohl, will try to throw off blame as much as possible to save their precious lives. That is what this man has done all his life and vile and brutal enough is he to do it, even now, after hiding out for a whole year, to try and save his skin and not bother himself with 'his dear comrades'.

But Luschilein, whatever will be, I can go everywhere, whether it be Berlin or Auschwitz it can be with a clear conscience, even if they are making it so difficult and I'm having my doubts of the human and democratic justice … now on to you…

Forever Faithful
Your Hansilein

September 29, 1946
Nuremberg:
My Beloved Wife – My All!

The sixth Sunday in a solitary cell, in Nuremberg Prison. Yesterday we moved from cell # 94 to cell # 361 in a different wing. I only see half as much of the heavens as before. It is 2.5m by 3m and I see through a broken windowpane. Otherwise nothing has changed for the better or worse. Always the severe but otherwise decent treatment. I don't know my own voice anymore, my talk with God and you only happens with the heart and soul, and it really can't be any other way.

In my other cell (2.5m by 6m), I had a view of the heavens and when I lay on my cot in the evenings I could see several little stars. Exactly at 22:00 hours a very bright one would appear and I always thought, since it probably showed up sooner elsewhere in this whole vast heaven, that this was seen by both of us and was a sighting that made a mutual bond. It seems however that this little piece of heaven has no stars and I am searching so yearningly. Nothing eventful happened this past week.

I handed in a petition to the American High Command of the Occupational Zone. How they will respond or where, I don't know. But I had to do it. It was like an order from God. I will hold this petition herein that you can see that I don't let everything just go by me, especially since so much injustice has been done.

Pray for Dieter and for me. I take you into my arms and kiss you.

From your lonely, yet strong remaining,

Hansilein

October 6, 1946

Nuremberg:

My Dear Luschilein, My Faithful One,

They are searching to find something. I have not found out anything about my petition, everything is very slow here. This too shall happen, as it should.

It just sounded 4:00pm … Sunday afternoon, coffee time. What may you be doing? Fall is here; it is very cold in the cell. I've thrown blankets around me, my fingers are stiff as I write. There is a terrible draft through the door continuously day and night. In my window there is still a large piece of glass missing. The stone floor makes icy legs all the way up to the mid section but it isn't worth complaining about. I've had misery throughout my life and learned not to complain.

From a child on I have had hard times and always had to go where there was more hard times and misery to perform my duties, and because of this I understood and had compassion for other people and was a person who lived 'from the inside out'. I gave my heart and soul to help them. And this time I will survive with your help, my loyal wife.

I firmly believe this. My riches are your strong faith, your faithfulness and your love. With this we will master everything, as will our children, our Hadilein.

I hold you ever so near my heart,

Your Hansilein

October 10, 1946

Nuremberg:

My Beloved Annelielein!

Last evening your letter from 9/28 arrived and in it was Hachilein's picture. The surprise and joy was indescribable. The tears flowed and I couldn't look enough. Such a big, darling boy – my son, our flesh and blood. You've brought much happiness into my difficult and lonely days. This is how Dieter looked when he was small. He resembles his Papi but also his mother. Right away I glued his picture on a piece of heavy paper along with yours and Dieter's. Now you are around me day and night. It is so infinitely painful that our Hachilein will be two years old this coming Sunday and doesn't know his Papi and isn't even allowed to see him. That is very hard for me but thank God that he doesn't understand it yet.

Even in the large Penitentiaries, the criminals sentenced are given visiting rights from time to time. This I can't understand of the Americans who usually have so much heart but it can't be changed, power is above right so we'll have to endure this time also.

When will it be over?

Forever I remain your Hansilein

October 15, 1946
Dachau:

Luschilein, today I returned with a PKW from Nuremberg to Dachau and am now back at my old job. After hard and lonely hours it is good to again have some freedom, and after doing nothing in solitary, to again be able to work!! My hopes are now I don't have to go to Poland, although it would be nice to arrive at peace once and for all.

I remain with many kisses, Your Hansilein

October 20, 1946
Dachau:

My Beloved Annelielein!

It's Sunday again. I can't tell you how often my thoughts are with you. These pages will once tell you so much, although I can't put everything down on paper that moves me, throughout our lives of separated souls. Your spiritual strength is so powerful, that we are one.

Have you heard anything from Dieter? It will probably take a while. Where may the other children be?

Greetings for all and you my beloved Huschilein, I kiss you and am always

Your Hansilein

October 27, 1946
Sunday, Dachau:

My Dear Luschilein, these weeks are hurrying by in a rage as if they were driven, so this terrible time will finally come to an end. It makes a difference that I can work from early morning until late, as work has always been the best comfort in such situations, for this I am thankful.

Day before yesterday I talked to the man in charge of the camp, Dr. Dortheimer, about my extradition to Poland. He told me that first of all the proposal was answered with 'NO' and something else was considered that he couldn't talk about as yet. So that's where the situation stands and what can we do?

If only I could take some of the hardship from our Dieter. I'm hoping that maybe as a young person he will endure better and easier than I can. If he'll just stay in good health.

And so my thoughts are always with you. Nothing else interests me. The sun keeps on shining over justice and injustice and after every winter spring follows again. And so another winter of imprisonment stands before the door with much uncertainty and another Christmas! Do you know how much Christmas with you would mean to me?

Forever Your Hansilein

November 10, 1946
Dachau:
My beloved Wife, My Annelielein!
November is my birthday month, grey days, with Christmas premonitions in the air. Last year at this time I wagered to believe that by this Christmas I would be with you all. Man thinks but God does the directing, and rightly so … no one can know the hurdles that we have to overcome. The nicest thing would be to be free and with the people I love, even if times were difficult.

Yesterday we had our first snowfall this year and once again it is winter. I don't see much of the white splendor through the bars on my window. White roof tops and the barbed wire was transformed into a white thick cord and hid the barbs on this Sunday morning. Another stressful week has passed.

On 11/7, I went through a short hearing headed by a Major of the Polish Army. He explained through the interrogation that I would go to Poland for negotiations, when I asked what the allegations were he couldn't answer me. Even though he had the documents from the hearings, which had only good reports, he couldn't tell me why I was to be extradited. I was told the Americans had not yet made a decision on my extradition to Poland and not to worry as the documentation was proof that I ran the camp and its people with decent and humane leadership.

I am with you and with my beloved Hachilein on this November Sunday, with pre-Christmas mood, with childlike believing heart.

Forever Your Hansilein

November 17, 1946
Dachau:
My beloved Annelielein,
I am thankful to be able to write to you again this Sunday. The papers say the west is starving, that is my worry. A Polish officer (my good witness) who was a former prisoner of mine came to see me again. He said he had done everything to stop the extradition. If I had to go, he said he'd go with me to speak on my behalf. His father, who I also helped, lives in Poland and always inquires about me. He too

was a prisoner at the camp and I made it possible under my command to have them both released. They knew of my effectiveness and stand behind me on many things.

My birthday and Advent holidays, normally such happy times, are saddened and dark as they probably are also for you but they too shall pass.

I dreamed of Hadilein today. I returned home to you and you sent him down the stairs toward me, I could hear your voice. Hachi kept saying 'My Papipa, my Papipa'. That was too good to be real. So with these Sunday thoughts I go into the new week. You my wife, my all, I take you into my arms as so often in happy or dim hours and kiss you all.

If only I could see you again, to once again hold your hands, to see your loving eyes, to hear you speak … what I would give…

Your Hansi[1]

-end of journals-

The following are excerpts of letters to Dr Dortheimer, who was the American camp commander at Dachau at the time my father was their POW. This was written the day after father was informed of his intended extradition to Poland.

April 20, 1946

Herrn Dr. Dortheimer:
I am hereby today including the letter that I wrote to you five months ago. I had decided at that time not to forward it as I didn't want to influence your decisions with my apologies and I trusted you. From the time I was first taken as a POW I put all of my faith in American Justice when you told me 'Nothing will happen to you, because it has been proven that you have a good soul.'

Knowing this gave me strength and I was able to wait patiently and with peaceful conscience and was able to make it through some of the most difficult times of my physical ailments. This I was able to do until now. I now realize this no longer holds true, when I was informed yesterday by the Polish Officer that I would be extradited to Poland. I can no longer believe in those words you spoke.

As I pass on this letter to you keep in mind it is not to influence any decisions or to ask anything of you. What I had asked of you then was asked with the faith and trust that I had in you at that point in time. I am not a criminal and have never hurt anyone and therefore do not have to ask for forgiveness.

That I must however suffer the collective consequences is very clear to me. I agree to my given signature, which you need for my extradition, merely as a personal favor to you, not as a sign of guilt.

Take my words for what they are, nothing more because I am not a criminal Herr Dr. Dortheimer.

With High Regards,
Arthur Liebehenschel

The following are portions of the letter mentioned by my father but were never sent to Dr Dortheimer on 10 December 1945. This very special, valuable piece of documentation came in my father's own handwriting. He pours out his heart with fragile emotions while his words are haunting.

Liebehenschel Arthur
POW # 5058923
Dachau, December 10, 1945

To the Command of the P.O.W Camp
Interrogations Division
Dr. Dortheimer, Dachau

Honorable Herrn Doctor:
Forgive me if I take up your time with these pages. But from the first time I saw you my impression was that you were a man that I could approach as any human being if it became necessary. With this belief in mind I ask you to read these lines, just as I had done in the past as Kommandant when I was there for each prisoner who came to me or needed my help in a time of their hardship.

My physical condition (I suffer from severe heart damage) compels me to once again reiterate for the record, my case which is familiar to you through the written and verbal interrogations and the evidence brought forth by these statements. I hereby await judgment in my favor, which must come from a higher command.

I was transferred to Auschwitz on November 15, 1943 which had previously been run as one single camp by the Kommandant Rudolf Hoess. I took over Camp I which was a Labor Camp. Its prisoners worked in the armament factories and other businesses which engaged in economic trade and whose buildings and structures made it known as the best camp of Auschwitz.

But otherwise it was a dismal place which of course its motive would make evident. There was not much I could do to change the ugliness of its past not to mention the ugliness of Hoess' past … but I could make things better … and this I did starting from the moment of my arrival until my release on April 5, 1944. Keeping in mind I was thrust into this position of which I was only familiar through the administrative side. It is impossible to itemize all the incidents, which occurred after I was entrusted with the lives of these prisoners of Camp I. It was my full intention to improve the conditions. Please let me mention just a few of these.

First of all I wanted to win their trust and I had to erase from their souls the fear of the nightmare, this oppression which showed on their faces. For this reason I called together the Capos on the first days and told them I had come to help everyone and to make improvements and alleviate the hardships for the prisoners. This was made known to all the prisoners and also the fact that I would confront anyone found beating, mistreating or otherwise performing any type of chicanery. I asked for their help in this matter. Up until then, no Kommandant had spoken to them in 'such' a manner. I was told generally as a rule they were never spoken to at all.

To prove my point in light of this matter, I immediately put a stop to the previous customary punishments inflicted on prisoners and replaced them with penalties that would be filed against any SS member who would not follow through or carry out my orders. All SS men who had been camp 'Blockführer' were replaced with men I had personally chosen who were not just men but who had to have a heart and soul and who had to answer to me on a regular basis. I did the same with the Capos who were not particularly liked by the prisoners. I replaced the then Elder Capo, who was a criminal, with the political prisoner named Worl who had been incarcerated in concentration camps for many years. He was a quiet, decent man. I prohibited the political section to mingle with or enter the protective camp in order to prevent the elimination of prisoners at random, which was a well-known practice. I immediately replaced the first official of the political division, because he followed in the footsteps of the previous Kommandant and the prisoners feared him [Grabner]. He had quite a past record and through my pursuit was finally arrested.

I immediately released the prisoners from the crammed bunker of the Politische Abteilung, most of whom were there for no valid reason. They were released to be among their comrades within the camp. Jews as well as Poles came to me and tearfully declared that I had saved their lives.

I took time to talk with my prisoners and in this way found out what concerns I needed to tackle. It made no difference to me whether it was Germans or Foreigners, Jews or Christians, for me they were all human beings who needed my help. All mishandling and chicanery was ended instantly during my assignment at the concentration camp.

I personally inspected each kettle in the kitchen daily checking the ingredients used.

The group of young Jewish and Polish boys, who were sent as apprentices to a Masonry-Bricklayers school, received my special care. They as my own children grew close to my heart and I would give them extra attention whenever possible. [Special rations out of the SS kitchen.] I was often told that these boys felt very close to me and that was my greatest acknowledgment.

Early every morning I stood and watched them march to work. (I was told my predecessor was not seen for months.) I visited the work places of my prisoners, many of whom were ill I would place into the sick bay. How many of these people's lives alone must have been saved through this measure?

As one reads this it could be said that these were ordinarily expected deeds but these did not come from written orders, but the lives saved were the results of human compassion. These people were imprisoned merely because they were of a different faith or belonged to a different race.

With despair and misery all around, anyone with a heart and soul would be willing to help where possible. Every day I visited a 'Wohnblock' [living quarters] and spoke with individual prisoners and inquired about their conditions there and at home, and in this way had a closer connection to them. I experienced and saw through their spiritual agony, most of which resulted from the separation from their families. This was enough to make me even more determined and fanatic to help these poor people.

In my office at the prison camp I would take several hours every day and see approximately 30–50 prisoners with whom I would try to work out personal matters. In this way I was able to help some obtain their freedom and alleviated the hardship of others, some were able to contact their families and more mail was allowed without the approval of the Gestapo … Always again the heart rules, not the command.

The faces of my prisoners became more cheerful and their eyes radiant as they saw me, and no matter where I went within the camp there was a sense of breathing easy throughout.

Illnesses and deaths ceased and all existing ordinances were terminated, especially if I saw that they interfered with my goals to help the prisoners. It didn't matter to me that my superiors persecuted and punished me and treated me as a criminal as well. I could never have handled it any other way.

And as 'the' Kommandant of Auschwitz I saved many many prisoners, especially Poles and Jews who have thanked me for their health and have themselves told me and written to me their best wishes for a long life. I am this same Kommandant who with a heart ailment has already been imprisoned for 4 months, tormenting with the uncertainty of the fate of my family as that of my own fate.

Certainly I was a member of the Nazi Party but nevertheless have I not proven that my heart was that of a man who believes in democracy, who has always done good for mankind? Should my actions not speak for themselves and bear enough proof to be awarded denazification and amnesty?

Many former prisoners from Auschwitz, including Germans, many Poles and one Jew, (a former prisoner who saved my life with his statement and report to the officiating American Officer) were God sent to me and as fate would have it they all gave statements which verified the truth of what I had accomplished at Auschwitz. Had they not been able to substantiate my declaration then my statements would just have been empty excuses. It was very satisfying to hear you say 'As Kommandant of Auschwitz, Liebehenschel was *in Ordnung* [all right], had they all been like him there would be no concentration camp trials today.'

Of course a Camp Kommandant of this sort was naturally not wanted at the 'Top'. I had to be replaced with a 'real' Kommandant and so it was done. I had to leave the camp, which I had improved with so much love and turned it back over to Hoess, the previous Kommandant, who once again would carry on with his old methods of running the camp. He still had his beautiful home within the camp where he would once again live as before. He informed me he would also resume with the old procedures that had been founded by the Gestapo, which I had ceased.

After some time Hoess turned over Camp I to Richard Baer the adjutant of Oswald Pohl (the Erz Lump) who was much of the same in character and actions. His first goal was the building of a lavish house for himself complete with central heating, garage and all imagined amenities. His main responsibility was to go hunting. It was this man who publicly declared me an incapable idiot and that I was not able to perform my duty as a concentration camp Kommandant. What fate may my poor prisoners have suffered?

My wife was stopped everywhere by the prisoners who told her, 'If only our old Kommandant Liebehenschel could return'.

I had been transferred to Italy at this time, and my wife lost the housing eligibility (not a pretentious house) and had to move. It was my prisoners whom we had encouraged to help themselves to our vegetables from our garden at our house. These were then seized and confiscated by the new leadership. It was Polish citizens from the town of Auschwitz who helped my wife to move with horse drawn carts, after they found her alone where she had been literally set out on the street. She received no assistance from the SS. Many of the SS Officers were afraid the acting Kommandant would find out that they had any kind of contact with me. At the time of the evacuation of Auschwitz the SS men reserved rail cars, each of which accommodated two of their women first class, fully prepared for their comfort. My wife was restrained and not allowed to board the train. She was told I was no longer the Kommandant of Auschwitz and she was now part of the Auschwitz community and should find shelter there. In freezing cold temperatures she stood alone for hours within the train station, a nursing mother with her three-month-old baby. No one was there to look out for her, not until a Polish railroad employee found her a seat in the coach section.

It is these certain matters which I only mention as they show how viciously I was treated and that it was not my SS comrades but my prisoners who stood by my side. And after all these experiences it should not be too hard to understand that there is hardly a spark left for my 'companions'. I had my fill. After the above mentioned chicanery I was relieved of my duty on April 5, 1944 and was given a disciplinary relocation to Lublin after having recuperated from a reoccurring illness.

I found the camp at Lublin evacuated of its prisoners and they were awaiting the advancing Russians who invaded on July 21, 1944. Unknown to my superiors I was taken away on a business trip to Krakau on July 17, eluding the Russian invasion, foiling their obvious attempt of my annihilation, which had been the purpose for the chosen locale of my transfer.

Based on the facts of the suffering I had seen in the concentration camps, and the vile treatment I myself received because I stood by to help my prisoners, I did not want to remain in concentration camp duty. After several requests I was transferred to Stellungsbau in Italy, in August 1944. From there I became a POW held by the Americans on May 8, 1945.

I believe in the justice of the American Army through whose interrogations I have endured these last 4 months, even with my ailing heart, without complaint.

I don't want to anticipate and am not afraid to wait or hereby seem to complain but ask you to please examine my case and take into consideration the significance of the facts. As well as the given statements and written reports by my prisoners which verify my own testimony and ask you if this is not enough evidence to give me my freedom?

First of all, if you could turn me over to the occupying forces of the British Zone along with the given present evidence so I could at least be near my family who is presumed to be in Velbert, Rheinland.

It is of course understood that I would never again be involved in the military service or have anything to do with Nazism. I would only want to live and work for my wife and my family, it would really make no difference where or what the job would be. We no longer own anything but the clothes on our bodies.

May I ask of you honorable Doctor, to believe me and to help me so that I may return to my family, something that is unquestionably hard to fulfill at this time but could be possible if these exceptional cases were brought to justice.

I can not continue to exist in my present physical state. I don't want to die a 'slow death' and be put on the same level as those unworthy sadistic people who I myself detested at the concentration camp.

I ask not out of self-praise but proven facts substantiate my request.

Respectfully,
Arthur Liebehenschel[2]

On 17 November 1946 my father's journals stopped abruptly. It had been decided that he was to be extradited to Poland to stand trial. The Americans drove him as far as the border where he was turned over to Polish authorities. He would not be returned to the Americans, as he believed. It seems he was under the impression that he was only loaned as a witness for negotiations.

What my father didn't know was that as early as April 1946, Belgium and Czechoslovakia had also requested his extradition for alleged war crimes, although no extradition requests were submitted by these nations. Under the provisions of International Law at that time, prisoners accused of war crimes were to be tried by those countries where the alleged crimes were perpetrated. Even after a year of my father's arrest the Polish Government sought him for crimes perpetrated at Warsaw, Radom, Budzyn, Auschur, Birkenau and Blitzen concentration camps. He was not actually Kommandant of these camps but these camps were under the jurisdiction of Lublin.

The Commanding Officer of the British Liaison Detachment to the War Crimes Branch, has relinquished Great Britain's claim against Liebehenschel in connection with the trial of the Auschwitz Concentration Camp Case, with the provision if he is not convicted, or convicted and not sentenced to death, Great Britain will request his extradition for trial, for crimes committed at Auschwitz Concentration Camp.

May 6, 1946
C.B. Mickelwait, Colonel
Deputy Theater Judge Advocate

It was requested that my father be delivered to Colonel Marion Muskat, the duly authorized representative of Poland, at Regensburg.

The details of delivery may be arranged by contacting Colonel M. Muskat, Commanding Officer Polish War Crimes Liaison Detachment, War Crimes Group, APO 633, US Army. In this connection it is requested that such transportation as may be necessary to effect prompt delivery of Arthur Liebehenschel, be furnished by you.

August 23, 1946

C.E. Straight, Colonel

Deputy Theater Judge Advocate – For War Crimes[3]

The above correspondence was sent on 23 August 1946, but on 24 August my father was taken from Dachau to Nuremberg. His first day of interrogation was on 18 September but on 25 September 1946 he was already cleared for extradition to Poland by the International Military Tribunal, even though there were further interrogations, his last on 7 October 1946.

There were 19 other individuals extradited from the US Zone and tried in the Auschwitz Concentration Camp Case at Krakow Poland. Out of the 40 defendants, my father was number 1. It took place from 24 November to 22 December 1947. On the list of names a few were familiar. Amon Goeth was on this list; he was the Commander at Plaszow Labor Camp, whose evil character was portrayed in the film *Schindler's List*. Of the accused, 6 received prison terms and 12 death sentences.

Dr Hans Muench was the only one acquitted. He was at Auschwitz at the same time my father was the Kommandant. He had volunteered for military service, but had never been a member of the Nazi Party or the SS. His professional duties at Auschwitz were found at that time to have been purely ethical, and as a physician he did not take part in medical experiments. He sent a letter to my sister in 1982, after she had inquired if he had any knowledge of our father. She had seen Dr Muench, along with pictures and mention of our own father, on a German television documentary about the Auschwitz Concentration Camp.

He wrote to Antje:

It is with regret that there is not much that I can tell you about your father. I only know what one knew of him and what was said about him within the organization.

It was known for the most part that there was considerable corruption within the camp. Soon after his take-over with absolute integrity and incorruptibility he put things into order.

The discipline which he achieved, astonished everyone who had been under the regime of his predecessors, who were widely corrupt. He ran the camp by strict military standards. This, however, obviously was not brought up at the tribunal. His prosecutors were only interested that he, as the Kommandant, carried out his [Himmler's] instructions.

He used as his defense and appeal, that he as any soldier carried out his given orders.

I had no personal contact with him in prison, so regretfully am unable to answer your questions.

Dr. Hans Wilhelm Muench

February 11, 1982[4]

In March 2000, a suit filed against the 88-year-old former concentration camp doctor by the American Anti-Defamation League was dropped. No further investigation would take place, although Muench allegedly stated he did participate in human medical experiments with the camp doctor, Dr Mengele, at Auschwitz. Muench is now suffering from Alzheimer's disease.

There was no further communication from our father after he was extradited to Poland, only the last letter to Anneliese, which he was allowed to write from Krakow prison. It is especially sad and disturbing to think that in the end my father had no knowledge about his 'other children'; he was left wondering about our welfare or where we were, or if we had even survived the war.

Papa had also written a last farewell letter to us (Brigitte, Antje and me), which was unfortunately lost. But it was his moving journals which gave me a closer look into my father's soul. Antje and I treasure his eloquent writings, but wish our sister Brigitte could have been here with us to read through them.

Chapter Eleven

The Trial

During my research I acquired an enormous number of documents from Poland, revealing significant information, such as my father's own handwritten statements and given testimony, as well as testimonies from other witnesses. My father had indicated in his Journal writings that while at Dachau, he had received a hearing in which he faced a commission of former prisoners from all nations. These prisoners testified on his behalf, describing lenient policies, especially toward Jews. But when it came time to produce these testimonies at his trial, they had mysteriously disappeared. In my own research, I was unable to locate any records of these witnesses. Whatever words were spoken in my father's defense have been lost forever.

The actual Trial and Court Summary was located through Antje's efforts and came from the Fritz Bauer Holocaust Institute in Frankfurt. Then began my lengthy, harrowing job of poring through each page, translating the technical utterance that ultimately decided my father's verdict.

Excerpts from Statements given by Arthur Liebehenschel
Krakow Prison, Poland – Cell # 115 – 10/9/1947
Written To the Examining Court Magistrate

From pages 78 & 79:
To begin with I would like to emphasize that since I have been in custody for 16 months, at Dachau and Nuremberg by the Americans, it was repeatedly explained that nothing would happen to me, as there was evidence in my files, the facts stated by former prisoners who volunteered and came forth on the first day of my imprisonment. These true statements were recorded in August 1945, given in my behalf by Poles, Jews and former German prisoners of the camp Auschwitz, the witnesses were: Herbert Kloye, Hermann Karoly, Marian Bialowiejski, Captain Piotr Lisowski # 113345, ZugFührer-Fahrich Kazimierz, Wolf Zdzienicki # 119503, Fahnrich Wieslaw Piller # 350 and many others whose names I don't remember.

You yourself, honorable Judge, stated yesterday on May 8, 1947: 'unfortunately are no longer to be found in my files.' I myself saw these statements taken at the interrogation on 8/25/45 which were translated in my presence, from Polish into

English and then these depositions were read to the interrogating officer, head of the Dachau camp, Dr. Dortheimer.

The American officer then explained, that as a result, I had nothing to worry about, that especially the Jews gave favorable testimonies and one Jew in particular was responsible for giving life saving evidence. Even Dr. Dortheimer explained to me shortly before my extradition to Poland, that it was merely to testify against Hoess and bear witness to the fact that one could be put in charge of a concentration camp without violating the rights of humanity. My objection to Dr. Dortheimer, that Hoess and his comrades could give incriminating evidence against me, placed doubts on the indicating evidence from former prisoners, which alone would have been substantial. Even so the Polish officer who came to pick me up for the extradition on 11/22/46, explained to me and the Americans that I was to be a witness against Hoess and to settle the cases of various administrative matters concerning concentration camps in Poland; nothing would happen to me and I would be treated well.

Now after five and a half months in solitary custody in Poland, the situation seems to have changed after the incriminating testimony ... lies ... by Hoess, suddenly other written documents have appeared in my files, concerning the time during which I worked as chief of section D-I, documents which are to link me with matters to which I had no connection or knowledge. To prove that this is the case and the truth, I will hereby describe once again the duties of the Amtsgruppe D in the WVHA, in particular those of section D-I.

The Amtsgruppe D of the WVHA had the responsibility of all matters concerning the concentration camps, which were under their command. Particularly the camps in the German Reich and also several in the occupied countries; not included were the many SS camps. The highest superior was Reichsfuehrer-SS Himmler, next was chief of the WVHA, SS-Gruppenfuehrer and General of the Waffen-SS, Oswald Pohl and the chief of the Amtsgruppe-D, SS-Gruppenfuehrer and Lt.-General, Richard Gluecks. These three were the sole disciplinary authorities, administering all commands and orders concerning concentration camps; carrying out inspections which were delegated to Sturmbannfuehrer Maurer, Pohl's personal confidant, and also supervising all activity of the camp Kommandants.

Both Pohl and Maurer were cold, calculating men, responsible and guilty of numerous transactions which resulted in the suffering and death of prisoners and therefore making circumstances impossible for the camp's authority, who were responsible, and today must suffer the consequences.

For example, the inadequate working condition at the armament factories and also the crowded camps. Glueck's objection and intervention to this was replied with, 'the soldier at the front also has to perform his duty under primitive conditions and every day in Germany thousands of people are dying from bombing attacks.'

The Chiefs of section D-III and D-IV, together with Gluecks, tried to remedy this situation, taking into consideration there was a war going on. To bring this about they requisitioned such necessities as straw mattresses, padding, shoes, blankets, firewood, medical equipment and first-aid materials for the infirmaries, all which were of course also needed supplies for the troops and therefore appropriated and never delivered to the camps.

In Himmler's estimation these procurements would have been a drop in the bucket. In my opinion Pohl should have asked Himmler to intervene by putting a stop to this misappropriation, by refusing all further responsibilities of the camps … but this did not happen.

The reason I was considered Gluecks' representative, even though I never was, occurred because I had seniority in the Amtsgruppe. And so it is possible that in Gluecks' absence I signed documents, which Gluecks had already initiated, which facts and contents he never discussed. Gluecks generally seldom spoke of matters concerning the job. Often when he was asked about certain things his answer would be, 'That does not concern you, while on my business trip I have discussed this verbally with the Kommandants in question. Write to him the following … or send him the following…'

Not only did he handle me in this manner, but also the heads of Sections D-III and D-IV whenever he had to communicate with them. This, however, was not the case with Chief Maurer from Section D-II who became my successor. With him he discussed everything and through him learned everything, as Maurer spent days every week in the camps and was available to Pohl at all times. Therefore, he was actually Gluecks' representative. If there had not been witnesses to prove Maurer's authority, and that in reality he was Gluecks' acting representative, then surely I would have remained in Nuremberg to testify further against Pohl, which was not the case as I did not have enough knowledge about these matters.

From page 84:

I can only repeat, that not until I was at Auschwitz did I find out through the prisoners about the mass murders there, and I had no knowledge of such orders and commands. I was, however, familiar with the fact that executions were carried out in the Concentration Camps, by orders of the Reichsführer and the Chief of SD, but I had nothing to do with these. When I came across such orders through the paperwork, I could not and did not consent to these orders. I told Gluecks before I started my duty at Auschwitz that I could not carry out any executions and therefore asked not to be sent to Auschwitz. He virtually gave me his word of honor that I would have nothing to do with this and would not be given such assignments and commands and I wasn't and would not have carried them out.

From page 85:

I had no knowledge that Zyklon Gas was located at Dessau. Not once did I hear while I was at Auschwitz the name of the gas used by Hoess and I never saw it there. Not until I was at Nuremberg was I shown a photocopy of this with the label inscription.

From page 86:

I did have knowledge that Russian POWs were used in the concentration camps as forced laborers in the armament factories, but I was not aware that they were murdered in the camps. It is hereby worth mentioning: Regarding the meeting with the members of the Wehrmacht's High Command (OKW – POW detachment) about the use of Russian POWs in the armament factories in the Concentration Camps: Gluecks was on a business trip and I had to attend the meeting. I can't recall at what time this took place. The division Chief of the OKW was a First Lieutenant. I had a conference with Gluecks prior to this meeting and he told me I should try to reject this proposal as well as the plan to then accommodate these additional POWs in the already overcrowded camps, and also convince the representatives of the armed forces to refuse this matter. The result of the meeting was a unanimous rejection, concluding that aside from political reasons the concentration camps did not have adequate room and accommodations for these POWs. Herr Himmler, however, had other ideas and because of my unsuccessful negotiations with the armed forces he punished me with several days of strictest house detention, the highest disciplinary punishment for a Staff Officer. Some time later, as he achieved greater authority and power, he then reached this goal. I was always the 'Odd Soldier', the 'idiot' [trottel] who acted too much with the heart and unfortunately I am still a 'trottel' today.

From page 102:

What was my first impression of the camp? Unhappy, sad and frightened people, who finally after long encouragement began to open up to communication, as we shared and smoked an occasional cigarette together. I had won the trust of the prisoners, but the fear that I eliminated would however reappear every month as Hoess reappeared at Auschwitz. He let it be known it was to visit his family, but he would be seen everywhere throughout the camp. By orders from Berlin I had to have motor vehicles and horse and carriage available to him and ready at his disposal even though I had strictly prohibited all members of the Politische Abteilung to ever enter camp I. This came as the result of the earlier occurrences in Block II.

Hoess even had his personal informers placed throughout the camp to keep an eye on me. One such informer was a clerk on my own Staff, of whom I was fully aware. The Standortartzt [doctor] had been a colleague of Hoess for years and even after Hoess had left, the Dr was still his confidante. Although Dr Wirths would declare that he was relieved that Hoess was gone and he was able to once more perform his profession free and ethically, today I don't believe these words he spoke.

I often told him that I expected him and his colleagues to give every possible care to every ill person, even those for whom nothing more could be done. That was proven as there were no longer any epidemics. When there was the case of an outbreak of spotted fever I quarantined a whole Block in my camp for 3 to 4 weeks and kept them from their work detail, so as not to infect healthy prisoners at Birkenau and the others at the hospital section, going against the Doctor's suggestion.

And so I tried to help, which was acknowledged by all those who experienced this and because of this it is I, this same person, that they are trying to associate with the likes of Hoess and his annihilation of human lives. He is supposed to have said that he was the one to have commissioned these alleviations. He … ? I was never given such orders [to annihilate anyone] and never had anything to do with them. Had I had anything to do with this then someone would have come forth by now to testify to this fact. I have no knowledge whether Hoess, who returned monthly to Auschwitz for several days at a time, continued the atrocities on those occasions.

From page 107:

Following my hospital stay in Kattowitz, I was transferred to Lublin in May 1944. Reason given 'It was established that as Kommandant I was too soft and because I defended a woman (who is now my wife) who was arrested by the Gestapo for her association with Jews.

From page 108:

Hoess returned to Auschwitz and I had to once again turn Camp I over to him. Not only myself, but my adjutant and many of my subordinates were transferred. Many of Hoess's old colleagues were reinstated and everything I had initiated once again ceased. The transfers of myself and the others was a clear indication that my work performance and conduct as well that of my subordinates did not meet with their approval.

A never ending chain of vicious events and treatment followed. While ill at Kattowitz I requested Berlin to relieve me of further concentration camp duties. It came back with my orders for a transfer to Lublin. After my refusal, citing ill health, and Pohl's inference that I was unfit for duty as a Kommandant, I was threatened with arrest. I found out later that Pohl already had a warrant out for my arrest.

From page 109:

When I arrived at Lublin on May 19, 1944 I found the camp evacuated. 450 prisoners remained to disassemble the concentration camp barracks, which were to be utilized by the Stellungsbau. Another 450 prisoners were left in the armament factories; part of the camp was used as a military hospital, occupied by Russian POWs who were not under my command. Another section had been taken up by civilians working for the Wehrmacht in the Stellingsbau. These were all under the jurisdiction of the armed forces and the 'Sicherheits Police'. I as the Camp Kommandant no longer had any authority but it was under the command of the head of SS Police of the district.

From page 111:

The following September 1944 I went to Triest, Italy where I worked in the 'Baugruppe-East' until mid-February 1945 and then on to 'Baugruppe-Laibach' until the end of the war. In both cases I worked in the administrative offices, contrary to the false given statements by Hoess that I was in combat fighting against the Partisans. May 8, 1945 I voluntarily surrendered to the Americans and chose not to hide, as for example Pohl, Gluecks, Maurer, Hoess and many others.

From page 113:

I was never in solitary while I was imprisoned by the Americans. Since November 27, 1946 I have been in solitary prison in Kattowitz but have, however, received very decent treatment. Although I have been permitted to write to my wife I have had no news from her or my children for over 6 months. On September 24, 1947 I was admitted here to the Prison in Krakow.

From page 121:

It can only be Germans who now have found a new way to get rid of me and it seems, without a doubt, that Hoess is behind this, as I would not continue with his unscrupulous ways but also uncovered and reported many of the wrong doings, even if they were not acted upon (because more of the same scoundrels were within the system). And therefore the fact that I was sent to Lublin is a good example of what is often the classic case when one wants to conceal any wrong doing and there is a need for a cover-up. This territory had already been declared a zone for military operations. There was no need to send a high ranking officer, a Lt.-Colonel, to an already evacuated, deserted camp, in a region where I no longer had any authority. They knew precisely that the Russians were only 80 km away and the tanks were advancing. It so happened that I was not there at that time but unfortunately as a result my poor young son was lost to the Russians.

From page 124:

As I have already explained about said documents which were actually drawn up by Gluecks but appear to be signed with the initial 'L'. Is it possible that it could have been the signature of D-III Section Chief 'Lollig', who also signed with the initial 'L'?

From page 125:

Regarding Pohl: I often refused to follow his commands and dared to contradict his orders but I would act in a manner so they could not 'directly' find enough reason to bring suit against me. They however took every chance to ridicule and embarrass me, and since no other reason was found, only that I was too soft as a Kommandant for Auschwitz, they used my wife as the other motive. Through vicious lies and falsehoods trumped up by the Gestapo, she was accused of a relationship with a Jew. And so through their devious methods they arranged to do away with us. Taking these charges as evidence was enough reason for them to send me to my death in Lublin and brutally evict my wife and baby and throw them out on the street.

From page 129 & 130:

As the Russians were advancing and the invasion of Lublin was inevitable, the prisoners of the camps in Lublin, Warsaw, Radom, and Budczyn [Budczyn was already evacuated] were to be returned to Germany by orders of the acting SS Police who had jurisdiction over these camps. For the most part these orders came too late, as was the case with Lublin. I found out from the marching men passing through town that my representative in Lublin, Captain Melzer, was still awaiting his orders whether to 'march or remain' in Lublin, this was when the Russians had already invaded. Only then did he send the prisoners marching toward Germany, as there were no trains available. The SS Chief of Police at Radom, who was also responsible for Budczyn, had these prisoners leave their camps and walk on foot. The Chief of Budczyn camp was the only one who was able to acquire 60 rail cars and evacuate his whole camp consisting of ill prisoners. I was at Krakow when I was informed of the situation at Lublin and as a result was unable to return there.

Even though I was not responsible nor had the jurisdiction I took it upon myself while in Krakow to inquire about rail cars throughout the SS High Command. It was no longer about competency but about human lives and a week long march for these prisoners could not be justified. In that case they could well have been left in the camps.

I made some telephone calls and was told this was impossible and all requisitions for rail cars had to go through the 'Raeumungs Kommissar', and whoever should procure these trains without his approval would be punished by death. I did not know what kind of man this Kommissar was or where he stood but it made no difference to me. I had made my decision and decided to go to the 'Reichsbahn President' (I don't recall his name, something common like Walter?)

In light of and in the best interest of the numerous lives that were at stake here I told a necessary lie and introduced myself as a 'Special Courier and Officer to Himmler'. I explained to him I was sent to take all those prisoners marching on foot and immediately find adequate rail transportation for them, as it was very important and they were needed to work on special arms projects, even for the new secret weapon. I told him this order, that came from Himmler himself, was now his responsibility and his life was also on the line and he had until 22:00 hrs to carry it out, as this would be the time I would have to telegraph Himmler with the response.

The immediate resolution to this situation turned up ample rail cars and the locomotives needed. I believe it was 30 cars for Lublin, 60 for Radom and 60–70 for Warsaw. The prisoners had already walked a distance but were no longer at risk to walk through all of Poland. The ones in authority, the SS Police and Officers within the ranks of the Generals, were unable to accomplish this. For me it was not only determination but beside using my head I also used my heart. They wanted to know how I did it … I kept this to myself … because it was 'Selbstverstaendlich' [Natural – a matter of course]!

From page 133 & 134:
Regarding the Exchange of Prisoners between camps: I hereby want to express that I allowed only completely healthy prisoners to be sent to work in other camps.

I believe it was January or February 1944 that the administration of the Politische Abteilung readied the prisoners that were to be sent to Mauthausen Camp to work for the 'Steyr-Werke'. They had been placed in the requisitioned rail cars. Then, as would happen frequently, 'I' appeared unexpectedly for inspection and then ordered the prisoners to be returned to the camp. Why? Because people could not be transported by a train in such poor condition (defective cars without heaters). There were no others available they had been told … that remained to be seen.

Concerning this matter, telegraph messages to me from Pohl and Maurer read something like this: 'Severest punishment if orders are not carried out immediately, the case in question is considered sabotage of arms, etc.' My answer to this was that I could only carry out the order in question if there was no risk to human lives, which in this case would not have been possible.

I then dealt with the Reichsbahn-Director who was under the supervision of the Armed Forces Transport Kommissar. 8 days later I had a transport train which had in each of its cars an iron stove and boxes of coal and firewood. From the camp came added straw and excelsior and thermoses with hot tea. All prisoners had coats, blankets and enough supplies for 4 days which would actually only be a 2 day trip.

The departure and arrival went without any occurrences and all were healthy upon arrival at Mauthausen. They claimed never to have received such an orderly transport. This is how all my transports were carried out, there were not many but they were sent with decency. Others said it, 'Even when he does things the correct way it seems to be wrong in the eyes of his superiors.' It is unfortunate that these confirmations are not brought to the surface by all the witnesses who experienced this, especially my adjutant Zoller.

From pages 141 & 142:

And therefore with my statements and examples I have tried to show how things really were, even if my signature may be found on documents and speak against me. Reading the documents today that are signed or initialed by me, it stands to reason I would have had knowledge of what I was signing. But often, as in the military when working in the administration, one has authority to sign documents of which the contents need no explanation (as for promotions, punishment or even death sentences), or may not have much significance but they are signed with the trust and responsibility of your given duty.

May justice and truth prevail!

[Signed] Arthur Liebehenschel
Krakow Prison – Cell # 115
October 9, 1947[1]

Trial & Investigation of German War Criminals in Poland
Excerpts from: Witness Testimony
The Case of: Arthur Wilhelm Liebehenschel

Court Witness: Wladyslaw Fejkiel
Date Taken: August 26, 1947
Examining Judge: Jan Sehn/Krakow, Poland

My name is Wladyslaw Fejkiel/I am a 34 year old Doctor by profession/Roman Catholic/Nationality and Citizen of Poland/Residing in Krakau.

I spent the time from October 10, 1940 to January 1, 1945 in the Auschwitz Concentration Camp. I recall the change of command of the post of Kommandant. Rudolf Hoess took leave and in his place came Obersturmbannführer Arthur Liebehenschel. Like his predecessor he was not interested and did not concern himself with the hospital for the prisoners, which was under his command.

During his command there were no positive changes for the care of the prisoners, related to food provisions or medications. The sanitary conditions remained insufficient as they had been under Hoess. These shortages were remedied by a group of organized prisoners within the camp itself. This took place although the Auschwitz camp had available huge quantities of high-grade medication and highly modern precision instruments, which had been confiscated from the displaced and perished victims. Even under Liebehenschel's command these items were not made available to us for use by the camp hospital. That we as the prison doctors were able to help the sick can nevertheless only be attributed to being clever and to the [underground] 'organization'. Even during Liebehenschel's time, selections of sick prisoners from the prison hospital were carried out by the SS Camp Doctors [Dr. Rhode] at Auschwitz I. In the case of these ill prisoners it was a matter of their physical conditions having no prognosis for a quick recovery and their return to their workstations. There was even a rule where all sick prisoners whose prognosis of convalescence would take between 6 weeks to 3 months should be evacuated from the hospital. In this case the chosen ill were shipped out of the hospital to the gas chambers at Birkenau and there killed.

As far as I can remember, Liebehenschel left Auschwitz in May 1944. While he ran the camp, as I recall, two selections from the hospital took place, under his command. During each of these selections two hundred prisoners were chosen and killed in the gas chambers.

Liebehenschel did not change the official rationing for the prisoners laid down in 1942. As in the past these rations were not sufficient to sustain a healthy living entity, especially for those prisoners performing hard labor. For those individuals the assigned camp rations resulted in starvation.

The camp leadership under Liebehenschel continued to demand increasingly strenuous working conditions from the prisoners. Their work was steadily increased in the interest of production in the armament factories.

Liebehenschel had set forth a whole succession of ordinances which were supposed to have the appearance and prove leniency of the camp regime. He put an end to the duty of removal of caps at roll call in some special cases, for example during bad weather. He released the confined prisoners in Block 11 but most of them were transported elsewhere. Only those that we were able to hide in the hospital could be saved from the transports.

His leniencies were misleading, for example permitting to wear the hair at a longer length. He ordered that he be informed of those prisoners stricken with poor health as they would be considered first in the cases of those who were to be released from the camp. I do not know of a single case of those prisoners brought to his attention who were therefore released. These cases were brought to Liebehenschel's attention by Dr. Wirths [Standortarzt] while he was the Kommandant.

In my opinion both used one another in these matters and possessed a talent to deceive, which had nothing to do with the reality of Auschwitz. During Liebehenschel's post the concentration camp correctional reports were reinforced. These concerned reports to the RSHA about the number of prisoners. These reports had no influence on the number of prisoners released. The percentage remained at the same level as they were in Hoess's time.

-end Fejkiel-

Court Witness: Stanislaw Klodzinski
Date Taken: September 15, 1947
Examining Judge: Dr. Henryk Gawacki/Krakau, Poland

My name is Stanislaw Klodzinski/I am a 29 year old Roman Catholic/Nationality and citizen of Poland/Occupation: Medical Doctor in Krakau/No previous Convictions.

I was a Political Prisoner # 20019; I spent the entire time from Aug. 12, 1942 to Jan. 15, 1945 at the Auschwitz camp. I was held at the hospital in Block 20 first of all as caretaker and then engaged as a physician.

I remember distinctly and have determined that after Liebehenschel's take over of command two 'selections' for the 'gassing' of prisoners took place, that is to say both out of the hospital [Krankenhaus] as well as directly out of the camp. The prisoners were first taken to Block 10 and then from there selected and transported by LKWs to Birkenau. Systematic selections for the purpose of gassing prisoners was not carried out in this time period.

-end Klodzinski-

Court Witness: Adam Stapf
Date Taken: September 15, 1947
Presiding Circuit Judge: Henryk Gawacki/Krakau, Poland

My name is Adam Stapf/I am a 40 year old Roman Catholic/Nationality and Citizen of Poland/Occupation: Merchant/Residing in Poland/No previous Convictions.
I came from the prison in Tarnow and spent from August 28, 1940 to July 30, 1944 in the Auschwitz Camp as # 3704.
Liebehenschel, the successor of Hoess, can be considered as one who continued the action of annihilations although with the exception that Liebehenschel conducted these annihilations as an intelligent individual without brutal qualities or tactics, and in an inconspicuous and discreet manner.

Before Liebehenschel's take-over rumors disseminated that after the change of command [personnel] a more lenient camp regime would take over instead. In actuality it was only in some apparent respects that Liebehenschel brought about alleviances of the hardships in the camp. For example: Ending the removal of caps at roll call; ending beatings for menial crimes; even in cases where prisoners were caught stealing bread, he ordered that these prisoners be given additional double portions of bread. Liebehenschel prohibited the striking of prisoners. He converted the 'Loeschwasserbecken' into a pool by adding steps and a railing. It was even used by the prisoners for bathing. He gave his approval to the establishment of a 'Freudenhaus' [brothel] in Block 24, a place of recreation, which could be used by well-behaved prisoners.

Before the arrival of Liebehenschel, the SS men announced that in the coming future there would be no more executions and gassings without the orders from Berlin, as it was the Führer's opinion that every prisoner, as well as free citizens, were part of a potential work force for the cause of the Third Reich. Liebehenschel also ordered the release of the prisoners who had been incarcerated in the bunkers for many months.

He put an end to the informer network against prisoners. He officially prohibited these disclosures against the prisoners. This was a very evident and well-known practice and the informers were known throughout the camp.

In spite of all these ordinances there was no change within the system. Furthermore, the executions continued to take place in Block 11 but now only during the night; it was also during the night that the corpses of the murdered prisoners were removed; it was also during the night that the prisoners chosen to be gassed were taken to Birkenau. After some time, the latter was discontinued. Those patients diagnosed as recovered by the physicians were then listed as unfit to work; they were then given fresh prison uniforms and sent to Birkenau to one of two Blocks, a camp for recuperation from which they never returned.

The gassings in Birkenau were intensified especially in Liebehenschel's time, however it was his habit at those times the gassings took place to choose the opportunity to conveniently take leave. That meant it all happened without his knowledge, behind his back, when he was absent.

Liebehenschel as I had mentioned eliminated all informers, but in its place he built a strict conspiracy or espionage group, subordinates of the Politische Abteilung. Active informers known during Liebehenschel's time were Malorny and Olpinski. Joining Liebehenshel at Auschwitz came a group from Berlin who also conducted investigations outside of the camp. Their uniforms bore the SD insignia. They investigated every contact between the prisoners and SS members or prevented any such initial opportunity to occur.

Regarding this matter, Liebehenschel threatened punishment by death of all SS members who did not conduct themselves to absolute secrecy concerning the activities of Gustav Kuny, which I had mentioned earlier … [text incomplete]

-end Stapf-[2]

Franz Hofmann, who worked with my father at Auschwitz as the SS camp commander, testified later at the Frankfurt trial concerning the above statement given by witness Adam Stapf on 15 September 1947. Regarding my father 'conveniently taking leave' whenever 'selections' were made, Hofmann testified:

There were never any 'Selections' during Liebehenschel's absence, that is not the truth. There was, however, a selection from Block 2a that took place and 400 to 500 prisoners were chosen. After that Liebehenschel drove to Berlin, and as a result a meeting took place where he tried to prevent these gassings from occurring. He returned and said to me, 'Hofmann, these people are not going to the gas chamber'. During Liebehenschel's time the first selection was in January 1944 and the order came from Berlin. There was another attempt by Liebehenschel to try to delay the course of the exterminations. He took the occasion to report to Berlin, claiming the Ramp was in need of repair before any new transports could be directed to Auschwitz. The central office, however, disregarded this and the mass murder actions continued. To my knowledge, under Liebehenschel's command, the only actions carried out were those ordered by Berlin, contrary to the actions during the time Hoess was Kommandant.[3]

Testimony taken from the Accused: Arthur Liebehenschel
Date Taken: May 7 & 8, 1947
Presiding Examining Judge: Jan Sehn

The Amtsgruppe D had no influence over the incarceration or release of the prisoners or other matters in general. These decisions were made by the RSHA. During my function as Chief of Section D-I in Oranienburg, I had no knowledge of the prevailing circumstances within the camps. I especially did not know that in these camps masses of people were dying from starvation and that they lived under inhumane conditions, e.g. as in the case of Auschwitz where in horse barracks suitable to accommodate only 200 prisoners, 1,200 prisoners were forced to live. I did not know that the camps' leadership was responsible for mass executions; I did not know that the prisoners were made to wear uniforms that were unfit to protect them against the elements; and I was not aware that the death rates noted in the Kommandants' reports, reflected these conditions. I believed that these mortality rates were the result of epidemics, which were a common wartime occurrence. At that time I was also not aware that under the supervision of the 'Inspektion', masses of people were killed in the camps by gassing; that people in the camps were 'selected' and taken to be murdered or that in the camps regular executions were carried out… .

A few days before my arrival at Auschwitz on November 11, 1943, Hoess, Hartjenstein, Schwartz and I, were called into Oswald Pohl's office. Hoess was released from his post as Kommandant of the concentration camp Auschwitz and given the assignment of Chief of Amt-D I, whereby I was released as Chief of Amt-D I and made Kommandant of Auschwitz I. Hartjenstein was made Kommandant of Auschwitz II, and Schwartz became Kommandant of Auschwitz III. That is to say that at this conference, Pohl decided that the once single formed administrative organization of the concentration camp Auschwitz, would be divided into three sections. At this time as he delegated the Kommandants, he announced at the same time what were to be the regulations and collaborations between the three camps.

Pohl took this opportunity to thank Hoess for his efforts and brought up his successes and accomplishments. He assured us, the three new Kommandants, that if we would achieve one third of what were Hoess's prior accomplishments, that he would be satisfied.

I would like to emphasize that Hoess left with feelings of resentment, as he took leave of his command as Kommandant of Auschwitz, when I was put in charge to take his place. Frau Hoess, who continued to live at Auschwitz, especially resented me and influenced her husband, inciting ill feelings toward me.

Upon my arrival at my destination at Auschwitz I moved into a house on Bahnstrasse [ul. Kolejowa], as the Kommandant's residence continued to be occupied by Hoess and his family. That is to say, Hoess stayed on at Auschwitz until December 1943, and later frequently came for visits during my time there, as his family remained in the home until the end of my duty there. My family [Anneliese and Dieter] came to live with me a short time later, but we were evicted from our residence after my transfer to Lublin and then found an apartment in the town of Auschwitz.

I took over the responsibility as Kommandant of the entire Auschwitz Camp, as well as the assignment of Chief of the SS-Garrison. I stress that I was only officially responsible as I had seniority, as Hartjenstein and Schwartz took over camps II and III. My camp take over and function as Kommandant and as Garrison-Chief was announced in the Ordinance Nr. 50/43 on November 11, 1943 the copy of which is shown me here [Bd. 12, K. 59]…

I was also named honorary 'Amtskommisar' by the local head of government of Kattowitz for which I received no monetary compensation. I had administrative duties such as writing reports, distribution of ration cards, as well as the Garrison-Orders, among them # 2/44 – Pkt. 10, which stated the ordinance of non-placement of Jewish women prisoners for indoor employment, these jobs to be filled only with Aryan female prisoners, preferably Germans. Jewish prisoners to be placed in 'Aussenkommandos', for example into road construction. This proposal was then submitted to the Kommandant of Auschwitz II, who had jurisdiction over the women's camp.

My father spoke of apparent ill feelings between him and Frau Hedwig Hoess, wife of father's predecessor Rudolf Hoess. Stanislaw Dubiel, the Hoess's gardener, testified at the Auschwitz trial that Frau Hoess had an insatiable appetite for the seized property of the prisoners, such as fresh groceries, expensive silks, women's purses, shoes, suitcases; the Hoess children even wore the clothes of children murdered in the camp. She and the children had to leave the camp in the summer of 1944 after Richard Baer became the Kommandant, when my father was transferred to Lublin. She was unhappy having to leave her comfortable home at Auschwitz, but was accompanied with several railcars brimming with the personal effects taken from the prisoners. In the official camp ordinances written by my father, he refers to anyone taking these goods as felons. He must have been aware of her actions during his time at the camp.

The document shown me here, was signed by me on October 1, 1942, in Maurer's absence. I did not know at that time that the word 'Sonderbehandlung' denoted or was in reference to the murder of people. This meaning was first made clear to me after I started my duty at Auschwitz. I remember that in the case of deaths, that these documents which came from the 'Inspektion' [Berlin], as well as the concentration camps, bore the number '14', as in relation to the cause of death [natural or unnatural] those then were marked with further significant letters and numbers.

The document shown me here, dated October 21, 1942 was written by me. The document was directed to the Kommandants of the concentration camps whose supplementary signature was required. This correspondence was in reference to Soviet POWs. These matters were denoted with [14f7] for natural deaths, suicides and accidents [14f8], shot while escaping [14f9], injured during use of fire arms [14f10], executions [14f14]. These specific letters and numerals along with signatures, corresponded with the way documents were dispatched within the Inspection.

In reference to the correspondence between the Kommandants of Gross-Rosen Concentration Camp and the 'Einsatzkommandos' of the SIPO and the SD regarding the transport of approximately 180 Soviet POWs from the Stammlager to the Gross-Rosen Concentration Camp: It was stated very clearly that this was about the executions of Russian POWs. This I must say, however, was the only case of which I had any knowledge, and only after it had been dispatched and I had received a copy and then spoken on the telephone with the Kommandant of the Gross-Rosen Camp [Roedel] did I sign and confirm this as is shown here in evidence.

I will establish that I did not know of the mass murders of Russian POWs in the concentration camps which was with the knowledge of the 'Inspektion'. Furthermore, in this same correspondence regarding the unnatural deaths of Soviet Russian POWs, these cases of deaths were the results for example: shot while escaping, suicides, accidental work casualties, as well as other such related unnatural death cases, but it was not about mass executions.

Furthermore, while I worked in the Amt-D I, I did not know that the concentration camps under the regulation of the 'Amtsgruppe' were using poison gas in order to perform these mass murders.

Concerning the details of the documents to which I gave my approval, which was for the requisition of LKWs to be taken from the destination of the Auschwitz camp to the Dessau camp, where the company of Tesch and Stabenow was located (which has just been pointed out to me), which was the manufacturer of 'Zyklon'; regarding this I would like to make it clear that I was not aware that the chemical 'Zyklon' was procured at Dessau and acquired by the camp command of Auschwitz for the purpose of performing mass murders at that camp. [Document Bd. 12, K. 169 172] I will explain that such documents were prepared and compiled by a highly competent expert and after final verification I would give my signature without examining the text.

At the time I signed this document that depicted designated characteristics such as 'Material for Sonderbehandlung' [special treatment] and 'Material for Judenaussiedlung' [resettlement of Jews] I was under the impression these signified medications and healing remedies for use by the doctors for the prisoners. I believed that this meant that the prisoners were to receive special treatment for which there existed sections in each hospital; as for example in Dachau for lung diseases.

The text which is here shown me in evidence were orders signed by me. It was referring to the blood-stained and soiled clothing of the prisoners, in regard to the dispatch by the Kommandants of the personal items of the prisoners who had died of natural causes, as for example those shot during escape. It had no relation to the illegal and arbitrary executions in the camps, as at the time I signed this command I had no knowledge of such executions. I suspect the beneficiaries, that is the families who received these articles of the deceased prisoners, complained to the RSHA, that these items were stained with blood. It was an unusual matter to send these soiled articles to the families and must have intensified the shock and aftereffect of their deaths; therefore as a result I prohibited the dispatching of those articles as set forth in this decree.

To answer the question if the Crematoria in Birkenau were in use during my tour of duty, I cannot say. If they were in use at this time it would only have been to cremate the corpses, those who died as the result of an outbreak of a Typhus epidemic. If Jews were murdered and sent to the Gas Chambers, then this happened under the direction of Hoess who visited regularly during my entire stay at Auschwitz. The statement shown me here, given by Hoess [translation – Bd 21, K. 155] in which he alleges that after he left Auschwitz the murder of Jews continued at the camp and that I as his successor carried out these actions, is not the truth. This is the most powerful 'Hassrakete' [hate rocket] which Hoess has fired against me. With this he ended the campaign he had waged against me, as other means he had employed in the past were unable to accomplish the results.[4]

Court Summary

Archival photos taken of father prior to his surrender in May 1945, portray him as a healthy, handsome, medium-tall figure, compared to his frail appearance and stature at the trial, as a defendant accused of war crimes. A photo of father standing in the Krakow courtroom depicts him as a small, mere shadow of the man he once was.

My father was number one of forty defendants in the Auschwitz Concentration Camp Trial held in Krakow, Poland, who were accused of various offenses on the following counts:

1. Conspiracy to Wage Aggressive War
2. Crimes Against Peace [members of organizations e.g. the SS and Nazi Party were declared criminal by the court]
3. War Crimes
4. Crimes Against Humanity

Accused of the following offenses:

I. The accused having perpetrated crimes in the occupied territory of the Polish Republic after September 1, 1939 as members of the criminal organization the National German Workers Party [NSDAP] and whose goal it was to subjugate other countries with intention of organized Crimes against Peace, War Crimes and Crimes against Humanity, or that of the criminal organization of the SS or both.

II. The accused who were members of the board of the Administration and of the occupying forces of the Concentration Camp of Auschwitz; depicting the criminal organization and Hitler's program of subjugation; physical and psychological degradation to completely annihilate the conquered people and accomplishing this goal by terrorizing and taking advantage of the prisoners in the concentration camp Auschwitz, taking extreme measures by exploitation of forced labor; mass plundering of personal possessions and their corpses used for the purpose of the wartime economy of the Third Reich, that is to say through the following means:

a) The creation of camp conditions which caused the confined prisoners to lose their health and their lives.

b) Systematic starvation, forced hard labor, inhumane camp punishment, medical experiments on prisoners which caused illnesses, crippling or death. The use of deadly effective Phenol-injections and eventually death of prisoners by means of torture, executions, hanging, suffocation and gassing.

c) Immoral treatment of prisoners, humiliation of human dignity, arousal of lowest of human instinct for their fight for survival, killing of all sense of decency and making a mockery of the female sense of dignity.

d) Mass murders of the Soviet POWs in the camp which was contrary to the outline of the fourth Haager-Convention of 1907.

e) Overburdening of prisoners with forced labor, excessive workload for the purpose of capitalistic war aggression and the mass murders, which resulted from labor under these conditions.

f) Mass robbery of their possessions, clothing, shoes, tools, jewelry, money and other valuable objects taken from the individuals arriving at the camp, these supplies stored for the enrichment of the economy of the German Reich and its citizens.

g) Systematic plundering, the extraction of gold from the jaws and teeth of deceased and murdered prisoners, which was turned over to the German Reichsbank.

h) Cutting of the hair of females and their corpses and delivery to German Industry used as raw material, as was the use of ashes left from cremated bones of the victims, used as artificial manure.

III. That the accused Liebehenschel was acting deputy as Inspector of Concentration Camps in the office of the Reichsführer SS from beginning of 1940 to January 1942 and from February 1942 until November 1943, was acting deputy of the 'Amtsgruppe D' of the Wirtschafts-Verwaltungs-Hauptamtes of the SS in Berlin and Chief of Department D-I of the same which are within the framework of the criminal organization which through the leadership of the SS, handled the affairs of the concentration camps which through their actions followed orders and directives, committing crimes mentioned under the written counts, section Abs. II, who as part of the occupying powers were in charge of the Administrative Organization of the concentration camps.

IV. That all the accused who were within the said framework of the above mentioned Criminal Organization of the NSDAP or the SS and the German

Administration of the concentration camp of Auschwitz; realizing what the objectives would be regarding the prisoners, Polish Civilians, Jews and other nationalities when they as members were under authority of the National Socialist Party of the German Reich.

Court Verdict
According to the Statute and Laws of the Polish Republic, punishable for the crimes set forth in the previous decrees: Arthur Liebehenschel is found guilty on all 4 counts:

I. Conspiracy to Wage Aggressive War
II. Crimes Against Peace
III. War Crimes
IV. Crimes Against Humanity

The accused defendant number one, Arthur Liebehenschel, found guilty for his acting position as Inspector of Concentration Camps in 1940–1942 and his position as the Chief of Section 'DI' in the W.V.H.A. and his position as Kommandant of the Auschwitz Concentration Camp during the time of November 11, 1943 until May 8, 1944; in reference to the prisoners and Soviet POWs for which he personally, as well as his subordinate personnel, was responsible:

a. taking part in the mass and individual murders of the prisoners carried out through the Selections for the killing in Gas Chambers or through executions.
b. taking part in and thereby causing humiliation and bodily harm, causing punishment by beatings, emaciation of prisoners resulting from the insufficient diet, unfit clothing and lodging, gaining profit through prisoners' labor and through the central authority of the SS acquiring the personal possessions and extracted gold from the teeth of those prisoners brought into the camp to be murdered.

Court Sentence
December 22, 1947, according to said Decree of the penal code we the High People's Court of Poland sentence the accused Arthur Liebehenschel – TO DEATH.

The tribunal declared the members of authority in German concentration camps in Poland as a 'criminal group' rather than a 'criminal organization', but the court dismissed criminal charges of the accused as to their membership to the NSDAP, which would be a punishable offense only if the accused held active positions within the organization.

Given the detailed offenses, the High Peoples Court hereby declared the accused as guilty for having been part of this criminal group of the SS, who as the occupying power were in full authority over the administration of the Auschwitz camp. The court concluded and found my father innocent of the mistreatment of prisoners but the court turned down his plea of innocence regarding his refusal and disobedience to orders given by his superiors; the court however concurred that the prisoners were never mistreated by him, on the contrary they stated that he helped the prisoners thereby saving many lives, but considering the extent of the crimes and his high position held within the organization of the SS, the plea was denied.[5]

Father's defense that he ran the camp as properly and humanely as possible was not taken into consideration, although the court concluded that his fair treatment of prisoners and alleviation of hardships was found to be the truth. The fact remained that he was acting Inspector of Concentration Camps from 1940–42, Chief of Section D-I, and in the eyes of the prosecutors he, as the Kommandant, was the one person responsible for all that transpired during his six months of administrative duty at the Auschwitz I Concentration Camp, and he was thereby judged and sentenced.

The last letter and communication with Annelie:

December 21, 1947
Krakau, Poland
My Innermost Beloved Annelielein, My Wife!

Today is the 4th Sunday of Advent. The third Christmas of our separation. Torn apart is the soul and wounded the heart after all the torment, especially these last weeks.

Luschi, I can't describe what I've endured, especially at the hearings, and alone to hear of all the contemptible things Auschwitz stood for, and with these dreadful things they wanted to associate me because of my high position there. Many sordid tactics were tried and evidence given by Hoess and his likely companions … Germans … Luschi!! I felt shame and embarrassment when I thought of all these Germans.

As I promised you, even with all these accusations, I followed through to the end. Often I felt I could no longer go on with so much gross injustice, yet then you would appear next to me with pleading eyes always there and with God's help it continued.

Along with all the detestable things you must have heard good words about me over the radio and in the newspapers. Of almost 200 allegations nothing concrete or incriminating could be proven against me, for this the counsel for the defense brought forth a great number of Polish witnesses in front of the court who confirmed that overall and always I had done good and proved what I had always said and you also know.

They wanted to charge me with Gluecks' actions, just as they did with Auschwitz if it hadn't been for my witnesses.

I stood in front of the Highest Polish Criminal Court and I tell you, Huschilein, no matter what comes, I still believe in Justice. Tomorrow, 2 days before Christmas Eve, I will be sentenced. I will make a note of this at the end of this letter.

I see peace for all in these grave hours as our Lord wants, Annelielein! I am so grateful that I have you and at least am able to carry you in my heart and that I was able to struggle and fight for you, and with you and our great love, able to go against all the evil and viciousness and always took the straight road even if time and time again they tried to drag us through the dirt. Actually I don't need to tell you again what I did but in these dark hours let me repeat it once more: In my life I have always gone a decent path. I never had anything to do with the terrible portrayed crimes and my hands stayed clean. Luschilein my beloved wife, I place these hands into yours and go with you wherever my chosen path may take me.

You have always been with me and with me through this long captivity, and such bitter captivity it has been. Your beloved eyes always looked at me, calling, pleading and gave me the strength, the faith to God's just ways. The Lord and you stood by me through my miserable loneliness and so I was never alone in my cell. Over one year in solitary and yet enough of this little piece of heaven for me to bring my daily worries and suffering before God, something so beautiful which could not be taken away from me.

During the trials, which began 11/24 and will end tomorrow 12/22, I have received 5 letters from you [9/30, 10/16, 10/29, 11/8, 11/20] with great joy and found out that after lengthily waiting you too received mail from me.

I thank you for everything you've told me in your lines and I feel all. What you are to me, you know my 'All', my beloved wife. And your and my heart blood is Hadilein our son for whom, as for you, I have such great longing. How funny he must be now and I can't experience any of it. How that cuts into my heart daily. How I call for you both! Do you hear it Annelie? Yes, but you must hear me especially now in these dreadful hours.

After much pleading yesterday they returned to me the pictures of you, Dieter and Hadi. It makes me happy especially through these bitter hours, even if I have you all in my heart and no one can take that away, so now I sit in front of the pictures and write to you.

It's snowing and the sun is going down on this last pre-Christmas Sunday. What morale is in the hearts of man, the worries as we now bear them with no idea how to devote oneself to the magic of Christmas? What all will Hadilein tell you and how many questions, and how happy I am that he can take away some of your worries.

How pitiful I look on the outside but yet within myself I am so rich in spite of the bleeding soul, through you Huschi.

What may our Dieter be doing? Sometimes I believe he is not alive, but then ask God and his voice says, 'he lives'.

It seems so peculiar that there has been no news or trace of the girls. Thank you for your trouble, please keep searching and help where you can. When Dieter returns he may want to learn something and help your father, and through it you as he always wanted, if I wasn't able to. I am happy you still have your dear parents there for support. My warmest wishes for a healthy and happy 1948. And our little son, my Hadi, many loving kisses. Tell me everything about him and what he said at Christmas. I love him so much.

But you my beloved Huschilein, you stand above all, for you this struggle against these deceitful and corrupt people was worth it and so stay always on my side, especially now when so much slander is thrown at me. With strong faith of our never ending great love I close you tightly into my arms with innermost kisses and will forever be your Hansi, totally, forever Yours!

12/22/1947
My sentence has just been passed, 'DEATH' ... I Die Innocently for Germany ... [6]

The Censorship crossed out the word 'innocently' on the original letter. He was executed at 7:30 a.m. on 24 January 1948 in Krakow, Poland.

Chapter Twelve

A New Family,
A New Identity

The events leading up to my adoption began when my sister Brigitte, who then still lived in the town of Fürth, worked at Grundig Electronics. She received a surprise phone call from a Mrs Earl Poune who invited her to a dinner party. Her explanation was vague and Brigitte thought it strange as she had no idea who this person was who offered to pick her up at the bus stop in town. She didn't know where she was going, and as in a foreign intrigue film, she carried scissors in her small black bag for protection. A friend followed her on his motor scooter and watched from a distance to get a license number in case of foul play.

Germany was still considered a postwar country, left in almost total destruction, especially the town of Fürth-Nuremberg. A result of the poor conditions was a rising crime rate, escalating out of fear and desperation. It was not safe for a woman to walk the streets alone, especially at night.

Brigitte waited on a bench at the designated bus stop and finally a young man whom she had seen at Grundig came walking toward her. He was nice looking and seemed a very proper gentleman. He told her his name was Heinz and Mrs Poune was his sister, who subsequently pulled up in a large American car. They took Brigitte to their apartment in the American sector of Fürth, near Nuremberg. Heinz had been too shy to ask her out, so Ursula Poune had helped him set up this date. Ursula tried to remain discreet and not divulge the actual reason for the invitation.

Heinz and Ursula were German, and Ursula was married to Earl, an American working for the European Exchange System in the old Palace of Justice building in Nuremberg. This was the same building where the war trials had been held and where my father had waited in the prison section to be interrogated, just a few years before.

Earl had been a pilot during the war and had received his law degree at Oklahoma State University. He worked at the Palace of Justice in Nuremberg from 1952 until December 1956. He met Ursula after the war through mutual friends and it was love at first sight for him. On their third date he asked her to marry him. When Brigitte met them they had a darling baby boy named Dale.

It seems of strange coincidence that Earl had also been in the war, but fighting against the Germans. He had been a pilot first lieutenant in the Army Air Corps,

352nd Bombardment Squadron, flying the B-17 aircraft. He flew over forty-nine missions. He received the Distinguished Flying Cross for the successful mission of the bombing of the Prufening Aircraft Works at Regensburg on 25 February 1944. At that time my father, on the German side, was only a few hundred miles away at the Auschwitz Concentration Camp in Poland. Earl fought through countless enemy fighters and was cited for extraordinary skill and courage as he returned the squadron safely to his base in a crippled aircraft.

Another seemingly strange coincidence between Earl and my father, was the fact that they were both inflicted with the rare condition of an infection of their heart muscle.

Ursula had been in the Luftwaffe during the war. She had worked in the communications divisions operating Morse Code and it was at that time that she was regularly coerced and threatened into signing up to join the Nazi Party – nearly landing her in one of Hitler's labor camps. But she voiced her strong will and opinion, refusing to become a member of the Nazi Party. However, she says she never knew of the atrocities which had occurred during that time, and not until after the war did she hear about the systematic annihilations which took place in the concentration camps.

Today she is very proud that she was awarded a lifetime membership to the US Air Force by the Civil Defense after donating many hours of air watch spotting for unidentified or enemy aircraft in New York during 1957.

The dinner party was an exciting new experience for Brigitte. She was made to feel very welcome; it had been a long time since she had had any sense of family, and she had a delightful time. This was the first time she was introduced to rum and coke.

After the dinner party Brigitte began seeing Heinz regularly. He'd leave her at night with a hand kiss and after their fifth date he finally kissed her good night. This went on for some time until one day, a couple of months later, she asked if their relationship was going anywhere. He took her hand and asked her, 'When do you want to get married?' They became engaged.

That following Christmas, Ursula invited my sister Antje and me to come and spend the holidays with them at their apartment, along with Brigitte and Heinz, so we could all be together as a family. Antje came from Wolfenbüttel and I took the train from Landshut. We met at the depot in Nuremberg. To us children it was not unusual to see the remains of bombed-out buildings, still visible throughout this town which had been severely damaged during the war. After walking around lost for hours looking for the Pounes' apartment on Dr Frank Street in Fürth, we finally arrived at the new complexes built especially for Americans and their dependents.

When the door on the second story opened it was like a breath of sunshine, as we were greeted by the very attractive, well-dressed lady named Ursula. She invited us in with a warm smile and gave me the biggest hug I had had since my own mother had held me so long ago. None of the other people I'd been with had made me feel so completely wanted, loved and secure.

Earl was tall and handsome with dark wavy hair. He had a great sense of humor and constantly made me giggle. I myself adopted him as the father figure that had been missing in my life and felt very at home with both of them. I loved Dale, their baby boy, the minute I laid eyes on him. Blond, blue-eyed, with chubby little cheeks, he was a live doll to me.

Shortly upon our arrival Ursula and Earl took Antje and me to the American PX and bought us some new clothes. I cherished my poodle skirt and saddle shoes, but my favorite dress was of red velveteen with a gray bolero jacket with red trim and under the skirt a full, stiff petticoat. No one had ever treated us so well.

It was an unforgettable Christmas. The colored lights on the tree and the jolly American Santa Claus were all part of the magic.

I had a wonderful time and was fascinated with everything American. Peanut Butter was the ultimate new food as were Baby Ruth, Hershey bars and of course Wrigley's chewing gum. The use of bright colors, from labels on canned goods to the clothes people wore, had left a big impression on me. I also noticed this carried over into their friendly, cheerful personalities. These adults were not like my German care takers; on the contrary, life seemed so happy and carefree. It didn't take long for me to feel a true connection with these American people and their way of life.

After the holidays, Ursula and Earl put me on a train with the large rag doll they had bought for me and I returned to Landshut to my foster parents, the family Krauss. Dale waved bye-bye calling me 'Baba'. I cried all the way back to Landshut. I was no longer happy to be there and couldn't eat. All I could think of was to be back with the people that had made me feel so wanted.

It happened that at this time the Krausses were expecting another child and I was to go to an orphanage. They were also concerned about me and contacted Earl and Ursula who were really just starting their own lives together; and it was out of their love and compassion for me that I was taken as their foster child. They came to pick me up in their great American dark-blue Chevrolet, which had a visor in the front across the windshield. I can't remember when I'd been happier.

The day Ursula went to enroll me in the German school in Fürth, the children there called me names and ridiculed me because I was wearing American clothes. They were very cruel and at that point I felt that a part of me was already American. When they saw how upset and hurt I was that day, Earl and Ursula decided to place me into the Nuremberg American Elementary School.

On the first day of school I fearfully clutched my new pencil box, but soon felt at ease as the teachers and classmates were friendly and helpful. It was much more fun than the strict German educational system. I was proud of my new reader and the class applauded and cheered me on as I read *See Jane Run*. I learned the language very quickly and was extremely happy in my American environment, adapting without any problems. I was accepted as one of them and knew I belonged.

David Meyers was my heartthrob, the class clown who kissed me under the mistletoe in our classroom. He no doubt had the advantage, as I didn't understand why he held that green sprig over my head. It was a very memorable moment and

I liked this special custom, just like the exchanging of valentines on 14 February; all so new to me.

Susie Carmen was my best new American friend who taught me so many things that were completely strange to me. I'll always remember her explanation about Graham Crackers. She held one in her hand and said 'you break them in half through the middle right here, then you give one half to a "friend" to share'. She smiled as she handed me the half for a 'friend'. I took this very seriously and remember thinking how wonderful of Americans to think of such a great custom, making a little section in the cookie so friends can share. Susie Carmen and I lost track of one another over the years but just recently found each other again.

I had not been allowed to go to the movies since I had lived with my first foster parents – the times I used to climb in the back window of the theater in the town of Bad Reichenhall. When I went to live with the Pounes I looked forward to the Saturday morning matinees: Cowboys and Indians and the continued weekly serials like *Captain Midnight*.

When Dale was old enough to walk I took him with me. The Neighborhood Theater in the American Sector was close by and cost 25c plus 5c for candy bars and Juicy Fruit gum. Sometimes I was able to go in the evenings as well, with the adults, to see beautiful musicals made in those years. Americans also had their own radio broadcasts in Europe then and 'The Shadow' and 'The Whistler' were my favorite mysteries that I listened to regularly in front of my ivory-colored plastic dial radio.

I feel very fortunate to have been able to experience some of that wonderful entertainment, which a few short years later was replaced by the new media of TV and life would never be the same again.

I always got completely lost in the fantasy world of the comic strips in *The Stars and Stripes* newspaper which were in color in their special Sunday editions, and I collected the many exciting comic books which had been unheard of in Germany.

Even though I learned the language within a short time, sometimes I would still get words confused. Ursula sent me to the little store for 'potatoes'. Skipping rope all the way, I kept repeating 'potatoes, potatoes, potatoes', but by the time I got there I was no longer sure of the English word or what it was I should ask for, and came home with 'tomatoes'.

Consumed by the writing and research of my past I often had curious dreams, which intertwined past with present. The night of 13 November 1997 I had the most incredible dream of Dwight D. Eisenhower, who was the President when I first went to live with the Pounes. In my dream he looked as he did during his presidency in the 1950s. I sat across from him at a table located somewhere at an outdoor restaurant. I told him I wanted to share something with him and apologized if I became emotional, but explained that's how I was, especially when

I recalled the past. I related to him how I was taken as a foster child and then adopted by Ursula and Earl.

My story to him continued with the day they went to enroll me into the German school, when the children ridiculed me for wearing American clothes and the fact that I was very upset because at that time I felt like I already was an American; how I had an immense adoration for everything American, especially the Nuremberg American School which I attended, where my teachers and class-mates applauded as I learned to read English. I had this unbelievable sense of pride in the flag, bearing the red, white and blue Stars and Stripes, as I learned to recite the pledge of allegiance. I told him I always admired him as 'President Eisenhower' and remember the 'I like Ike' buttons. I asked him, 'Wasn't it those years that you were President?' Quietly he answered, 'I believe so'. He had tears in his eyes when I confessed I always loved his kind face which to me represented what America was, at that time. He smiled as I expressed how I often wondered why he had the German name Eisenhower?

Before he got up to leave I said, 'By the way, I've been doing some research on World War II for my book (I didn't tell him of my father). Have you heard of James Bacque? He wrote the controversial book *Other Losses*?' (This book did not always characterize Eisenhower in a favorable light.) He seemed nervous and uncom-fortable about the question, but said he had read it and it was interesting, with extraordinary documentation. He started to walk away, then stopped and looked back at me, waving goodbye, before suddenly disappearing into the crowd.

Meanwhile, Brigitte and Heinz were married and to them was born their only son Kye. Dieter, my oldest brother, married Steffie and they also lived in Fürth, where my brother still resides today. Steffie passed away a few years ago. They had a son and a daughter. Dieter and Heinz worked for the Americans as guards at the US Army Base in Nuremberg for some time.

Antje met and married Walter Behrens in Wolfenbüttel, who came from a large and well-known family. He had his own business and finally she too found secu-rity and a family to belong to. Antje has three sons.

Earl's assignment in Europe was coming to an end and he was to be sent back to the States. They didn't want to give me up and soon started adoption proceed-ings. There were some difficulties, however, since my mother was still alive and they had to get her permission. They went to see her in Munich at the institu-tion. I don't think she fully comprehended the implication of my being adopted. She had always liked Americans though and immediately bonded with Earl, who joked and made her laugh. He gave her a fifty-cent coin, which she placed into her shoe so no one at the institution would take her treasure.

My brother Dieter, being the oldest, had the final word of consent, as the law now considered him my legal guardian. Both Brigitte and Antje also had to give their signed consent for the adoption.

Earl and Ursula were afraid that knowledge of my father's background and my mother's mental illness would affect my eligibility for a visa to the United States. As a result, the facts surrounding the family I was born into was kept a secret and never discussed.

The thought of going to America was very exciting for me, although I felt sad and a little confused at the thought of leaving my family, wondering if I would ever see them again. I was legally adopted before we left for America in December of 1956.

So it happened that 'the other child', the little girl who was born as Bärbel Ulrike Liebehenschel, was left behind on the shores of Bremerhafen, Germany, on that December in 1956 – abandoned, along with all connection to her biological family for many years to follow. It was thirteen-year-old Barbara Ursula Poune who was heading for America, accompanied by her new parents and 3-year-old brother.

This voyage marked the beginning of a life of secrets and shame, of hidden pictures and concealed identities. My new parents even fabricated an American heritage for me – I was forbidden to acknowledge my family and my father's photo was secreted in the bottom dresser drawer. But my desire to reconnect with my family and to know who my father was could not be so easily swept away. It would be forty years before that photograph of my father was retrieved from its hiding place and proudly displayed in the carved silver frame, now on my dresser, front and center, for anyone to see.

On 16 December 1961 my mother, Gertrud, wrote to my sister Brigitte: 'No one ever mentions Bärbel [Spatzel – little sparrow] anymore, I wonder if she, as the youngest, has a mother or does anyone care?'

The following are excerpts of the last letter I received from my mother. It was in answer to my letter telling her of my daughter's birth. We had not had any contact since I was taken away from her as a young child.

Friday April 24, 1964
My Dear Bärbel-Ulrike Child!
I had given you such a beautiful name, something very beautiful in the German Language. But now I no longer have a Bärbel-Ulrike. Can you imagine in your great youth how that hurts me, that my dear 'Spatzel' lives in a foreign land and what's more, so far over the big pond, as it is said in German?

Of course, naturally I am happy that you are doing well, that you above all are healthy and have a very nice husband. You know dear child, Mutti has an eye for character and he has a good face. Send him my best wishes. When will we see each other again? Thank you for your so tender and affectionate letter. You are still that dear lovable being you once were. But did I read a little loneliness and yearning between the lines … ?

Decent people can also earn a living in Germany. But so many traitors have found their way into the Fatherland [communists and criminals] and because of such people I have been in this Institution for over 13 years and it's no wonder that decent people have to go live in foreign lands. I have always been for the Americans, 'only good that they are here' I have often said. How is your little baby?

Best Wishes!!!

One more thing, I have not given up my sense of humor in here and I have found that an inner compromise helps one to overcome many things. May life continue to go well for you.

How did that come about that you ended up in America? If I had been on the outside it surely wouldn't have come to that.

Always, Your Mutti

Mother may have been mentally ill, but her intellect and wisdom remained – she was well enough to realize that her strength and courage came from within, as it always had throughout her troubled life. She never recovered from her illness, diagnosed as paranoia schizophrenia, and died alone in the institution in 1966.

I often wonder did our father keep a photo of us three girls with him while he was imprisoned? Why were we not mentioned among the photos returned to him?

Was my father, in fact, the war criminal that the Polish tribunal declared him to be? Or did his 'failure' as an SS officer result from some fundamental sense of decency that led him to defy his superiors and, like Oskar Schindler, risk his own safety to alleviate the plight of his prisoners?

Was my father sentenced to death for crimes perpetrated or was it the fact of who he was, an officer who wore the black uniform and death's head insignia of Hitler's SS?

Society has long judged and carried out his sentence but almost sixty years later my generation and family are still haunted by 'the sins of our fathers'. Although our souls have now connected, the handsome vision, wearing the black uniform in that old photograph, will always remain just that ... my Papa ... a stranger from the past.

There are many things I'll never understand or condone about his actions as an SS officer. In the end I must allow these discoveries to speak for themselves.

…Later, you will understand that life can be troublesome and many people who are not bad have to go along a difficult path through life. This is how you must look upon my life, the life of your father. If you ever need me in any way I will help you where I can, as before. . . . If you yearn for me then come to me, my door to my house and heart will always be open to you ... I will never forget you…

Oranienburg, November 9, 1943

Epilogue

The Journey Home

When the opportunity arose to travel back to my homeland in September and October of 1998, I retraced the footsteps of the people from my past. How does one express the tremendous emotions felt at the very source of one's soul? The overwhelming excitement and joy, yet always with that lingering sadness and an unexplained loneliness which a haunting past can hold. As I found myself physically reliving the chapters within my book, I also came to understand that this journey was to help with the closure, that it was now time to ultimately leave the past behind.

Here is my journey taken from the pages of my written diary which was my constant companion during those days in September and October of 1998, as I traveled through Germany, Austria and Poland. In it I shared my daily adventures every evening as I retired, when I found myself alone in my room reflecting over the day's occurrences.

It's Monday September 14, 1998. I've now been in the air for 8 minutes, with 9 hrs 37 min. from our destination, we're presently flying at 8,800 meters altitude and with incredible emotion I am wiping the tears from my eyes hoping the elderly couple sitting next to me won't notice. No, this time I'm not dreaming, I'm headed for Dusseldorf, Germany. After 26 years I am experiencing this real life adventure which will help me to write the final pages of this bittersweet journey … but somehow I am also feeling a void, as I recall the last trip taken in 1972, then with my two small children and their father at my side.

My month-long trip was shared by my sister Antje and her husband Ernst who picked me up from the airport and drove me to their home in Wolfenbüttel, northern Germany. This truly unique historical town dates back to the Renaissance and the original charming framework houses were built in the 1600s and fortunately were spared by the bombs of the Second World War. I found the contrast of the very old in the midst of the new extremely interesting. Their house which is located not far from the town center, has been in the family for over one hundred years. It is located on a corner of a four-way intersection with traffic lights, but little traffic – a very old neighborhood pub is situated across the street and a small used car business on the other side of it. Their own spacious living quarters occupy the entire second story, which has been renovated into a modern and lovely decorated home. The ground floor is leased by various businesses.

Antje is beautiful, looking incredibly younger than her years and more like our father than ever, both she and Ernie were so giving of themselves with so much love, spoiling me and making my visit a most memorable one. This time we shared together was very important for both of us. I want to take this opportunity to thank them both again for everything they have done for me.

Wednesday September 16, 1998: Somewhere I lost a day. The clock on the night table says it's 2:30 am and I'm wide-awake staring at the high ceiling. It's quiet and I'm alone in my lovely room. Two windows covered by lace curtains over-look the deserted main street below, which is illuminated by the changing traffic light. I'm a little confused and very exhausted as a sharp jolt cuts through me ... my God ... I'm really here! My thoughts take me back to my arrival here earlier, Antje showed me Papa's original Journals ... I actually held them in my hands!

Saying a little prayer of thanks I dropped back to sleep. The next few days we visited with family and friends.

September 16, 1998: We stopped to see Dorothea, the daughter of Elizabeth and Michael Lochner with whom Antje and I lived as foster children in Strub/Berchtesgaden, who now lives in Wolfenbüttel. Although I hadn't seen her in almost 50 years I sensed a definite bond, I saw in her that young, angelic and beautiful girl she once was when she burned incense and candles in her room at the old Haus Bergluft. Those memories brought tears. I was thrilled when she gave me the post card I remembered of her as a young girl holding a bouquet of wildflowers, which her father had taken of her so long ago.

We began our 4,000-kilometer tour through Germany, Poland, the Czech Republic and Austria. Ernie was the faithful driver always getting us safely to our destinations, which he mapped out so carefully.

Saturday September 19, 1998: We crossed over what was once the border between East and West Germany. Vacant guard towers still stand, looming eerily over remaining stretches of barbed wire. It seems as though time has stood still here. The narrow cobble stone streets and neglected buildings are obvious remains of the communist influence.

I'm in Oranienburg, the town I was born in. I felt a strange but definite con-nection here, a keen sense of belonging. I had an especially staggering feeling at the old train station, almost as though this part of the country was still at war. (The last time I was here in Oranienburg was in the spring of 1944, before we moved to

Austria with my mother.) It's 10:00pm, I'm in the recently renovated, quaint Hotel Ruperti on the third floor, in a cozy attic room. From my window I can see much of this historic area and I can't help feeling quite emotional that I'm actually here. The original Hotel Tavern was destroyed by British bombers in March 1945, which was then owned by the grandparents of the present landlords. I would imagine that my parents probably frequented the charming old inn in the early 1940s, which was once at this same location, when we lived here only a short distance away, on Adolf Hitler Damm.

We found our old home on what was once Adolf Hitler Damm # 76. There welled up within me so many contradicting emotions! It all seemed more like a dream, to actually see this house in which I was born, where we once had all lived together as a family … this place which had only consisted of imaginary fragments in my mind which I had so longingly pieced together from the faded likeness in the old black and white photographs taken so long ago – today it became an unbelievable reality for me.

The homes on this street, once occupied by people like my family and Chief of Staff of the Wehrmacht, Wilhelm Keitel, are today dedicated as Historical Landmarks. The new owners of what was once # 76 Adolf Hitler Damm, were gracious enough to ask us inside and Antje pointed out the room where I was born. Their request to add a sunroom had been declined in accordance with laws that historical landmarks remain in their original state. They were delighted when Antje showed them some old photos as proof of the existence of the original sunroom built by our parents in 1942. This entire day was an incredible encounter, especially for Antje who had so many memories here. She recalled our brother Dieter sliding down the staircase banister – still there today as it had been 55 years ago – and catching a good sized chunk of his hair on a nail sticking out of the wall … amusing childhood memories! As for me, unfortunately no memories, but because of the stories told to me, I felt my mother and father's strong presence everywhere. Antje also remembered where the bunker was located at one time in the yard. There was of course no evidence now of the war-time bunker in their lovely green garden, bearing an abundance of flowers and trees, but the new owner said that it explained why he is unable to dig into the ground in that area.

We found General Gluecks' old house further down the street. Not far from there was the rather large administration, the 'T' Bldg. where Papa had been Chief of the DI Central Office and where he first met Anneliese almost 60 years ago. This was the same office Bldg. to which Antje would ride with Papa in the back seat of his chauffeur driven car on numerous occasions, usually in the mornings still wearing her nightgown. Everything was closer in distance than I had imagined. The Sachsenhausen Camp was also in this area with its memorials, leaving a penetrating impression. We were stunned however when we inquired about the accuracy of dates on a faded plaque depicting a mass grave for thousands of victims; the years given were 1946–1947. How could this be? It was peacetime and these people were under the so-called protection of our Soviet allies?

September 20, 1998: Rode the train and subway into Berlin, took snapshots of the Brandenburg Gate and the 'Reichstag' Bldg. which was under reconstruction. Walked on the historical street, 'Unter den Linden'.

On to Auschwitz, Poland. I wanted to take a picture of the border guard, not realizing it would cause such suspicion. He treated me like an American spy! Why was I taking photos? I thought he was going to take my camera … interesting. There were many people along the roadside in the wooded areas selling large baskets of mushrooms they had picked in the forest.

Poland and particularly Auschwitz was an experience that I shall never forget. There are indisputable feelings of fear and distrust that are very apparent even today, particularly engrossed in the older generation after years of oppression under communist control. I found a remarkable difference in the younger generation, like the friendly young girl who greeted me on the street with 'Hi!', noticing my sweatshirt bearing an American jeans logo.

Staying at the 'Glob' Hotel, right next to the old Auschwitz train station, in a dreary room with a small bed as hard as a prison cot. This same depot is where Anneliese and her baby were ruthlessly left behind in the cold years ago by the SS Commanders, at the time of the evacuation of the camp. I'm standing alone on my hotel balcony watching the trains and hearing their haunting whistles, this is beyond belief!

September 21, 1998: Today was met with great apprehension as Antje and I went through the Auschwitz Camp this morning. This was to be the final stop in my seven-year search to learn the truth about my father. I arrived full of hope and questions, yet my legs were resisting, rooted to the pavement, as though my body were not ready to experience what my mind already knew. I wondered if my sister, Antje, next to me, sensed my hesitation. I glanced at her, looking for reassurance to go on. She too seemed to be struggling as her eyes met mine. Both of us had so much to say, but a protective silence hung between us. Antje smiled and we proceeded to the entrance.

In my mind I had always imagined the camp in black and white, shrouded in the cold twilight of winter. Warmth and sunlight never reached this perpetually frigid place. Nothing ever grew in the Auschwitz of my mind, and it was always silent. Surely the anguish of its prisoners must be too great to make a sound.

I tried to reconcile these images with what I was experiencing. Warm sunshine and a gentle breeze graced our faces as we walked up the slate path. A lush green lawn spanned out on either side of the path, and poplars and elm trees dotted the grounds. Schoolchildren, wearing colorful clothing and backpacks, rushed past us, talking and laughing. For a moment I felt my body relax. Perhaps this visit wouldn't be so difficult after all.

Yet up ahead, the infamous entrance dispelled any hope of comfort from my mind. *Arbeit Macht Frei* – 'Work Will Set you Free' – was the mocking inscription in the looming wrought-iron gates. Thousands of prisoners had entered these portals to experience hell on earth. No amount of trees or sunshine could soften its grim reality.

Beyond the entrance a group of tourists gathered to listen to a guide. Antje and I glanced at each other. Again silence, but our eyes said it all – we would not be joining the tour. The experience we came here for could not possibly be shared with others. We had to be alone to walk these halls and grounds, to retrace our father's steps, to try to understand what he may have experienced here 54 years earlier. We couldn't be rushed; we needed time to digest everything we saw. This was to be a most private experience and for me the other people around me faded into a distant shadow.

While we waited for the tour to move on, we went into the visitors center. Against a stark white wall in this new building rested an iron sculpture of a naked, emaciated prisoner, his elongated right arm bent behind his back and strung up on a stake, his head hanging down in despair. The prisoner's legs appeared to have sunk into the base, with one leg jutting behind him, as if it had been broken from his body. I felt my heart quicken and averted my eyes as I forced back the powerful emotions that threatened to break through. I had to regain composure if I was to complete what I came here for.

Antje and I were silent, caught up within our own private thoughts as we walked together through the various buildings viewing the exhibitions. Some images remain with me even today, an urn containing a handful of human ashes to commemorate the dead; the Book of Deaths, which listed fictitious causes and times of deaths for prisoners who were gassed; an enormous pile of suitcases with the names of deportees still scrawled on them. A harrowing photo, taken immediately after liberation, showed three emaciated women inmates, their huge sunken eyes staring from faces that were little more than skulls.

Shaken, but still determined, Antje and I walked past orderly rows of red brick barracks, as I had read about in books and as it was mentioned by my father as being 'the best camp'. I distinctly felt him there with me and the sorrow he must have experienced daily in this camp as he struggled with his sense of duty opposed to the compassion he had for the prisoners. Block 11, 'the death block' for severest punishment (from which father had released the incarcerated prisoners when he took over his command), remained as it had been then, with its windows boarded to obscure the executions, hangings and floggings which took place inside. Outside Block 11 is an enclosed courtyard where the 'Black Wall' was located and where prisoners were executed by shootings or hangings. Today people had left flowers and candles at the site. I was relieved to know that our father had also stopped the executions against this wall. The Crematorium which was originally located in the camp Birkenau and destroyed by the retreating SS at the war's end, had been reconstructed here at the Auschwitz I camp as a memorial.

Among the most interesting were the works of art in the exposition entitled 'Artistic output of KL Auschwitz-Birkenau'. These revealing drawings, created by prisoner artists, were accomplished with very primitive tools and materials. They express the rebellion against the inhumanity and also depict their painful existence and the fear with which they lived. Not allowed to take photos inside this building, I scribbled on the back of my pamphlet two of the most moving quotations by these artists:

One does not see what he sees but what he feels (Janina Tolik)

Art in camps co-existed with crime and developed against logic. It came to be a powerful force of resistance against terror, saving prisoners from becoming animals, awakening faith in humanity and durability of mankind's ideals (Grzegorz Timofifjew)

Haunting were these illustrations of the faces of inmates ... but none would be as haunting to me as the faded watercolor painted at Auschwitz in 1944 by the very gifted prisoner artist named Gosior Macknowsky. The wonderful photocopy given to me is of former prisoner Janusz Mlynarski # 355, with whom I had the fortune to become acquainted later on my trip. The portrait is of a handsome young man, gaunt, with a shaven head. This striking masterpiece reveals the reality of his pain through the sorrowful expression on his youthful face – where beyond his large blue sunken eyes lies an emptiness that left a heart-wrenching imprint. This picture moved me beyond words. It is definitely the ultimate artistic expression symbolizing the hopeless lonely existence at the Auschwitz camp – although his very likeness preserved in time, could well represent the tormented soul of every other victim and survivor of any concentration camp. Gosior Macknowsky also painted other portraits after the war, those of Generals Eisenhower and Montgomery. Never before in my lifetime has a portrait left such a profound emotional impression on me.

Despite our mounting sorrow, we had maintained an almost stoic composure so far. It was very important for Antje and I to have come here together ... toward the end of the day we came upon a scene that was too much for any degree of self-control to handle. Walking into another building, we came upon a showcase that displayed the tiny clothes and shoes of infants and children. The tiny hand-knit jackets with their matching knit caps and the delicate shoes – much like those worn by my own children – suddenly brought all the horror home to both of us. We both fell apart, unable to hold back the tears. I was grateful she was with me and we could console each other. People were looking at us with sympathy, they must have thought we were grieving for some lost relative, a victim of the Nazi regime. I remember wondering ... what would they think if they knew who our father had been? Would they still look with compassion if they knew the terrible guilt that consumed us?

An English-speaking lady who had been part of a camp tour was crying and asked me for directions out of the camp. She was not prepared for what she saw...

As Antje and I left the Auschwitz Camp Museum and Archive we realized that aside from the large Informational Plaque which mentioned Hoess's years as Kommandant and the fact he was sentenced to death at the gallows there, there were no exhibits, documentation or information on the other SS people who had been responsible and had run the camp during those years. We both had anticipated some kind of biography on our father.

We left this camp and went on to the neighboring camp of Birkenau less than a mile apart, where our half-brother Hans-Dieter was born in one of the infirmaries. Human transports arrived here at the 'Ramp' daily. It was also where the Gas

Chambers and Crematoriums had been located ... the vast desolate area of this camp was terribly eerie and I could almost hear the hopeless cries ... I looked through the high barbed wire fence across the marshy field where the rows of 300 wooden barracks once stood – it was inconceivable to think that today I could still feel their presence – the lonely desperation and hopelessness. Antje had me pose for a picture in front of the 15-foot-high barbed wire fence and as I stood waiting for her to snap the photo, I thought how at odds with this bleak landscape my bright yellow shirt must look. What incredible despair must have been endured here at this very location over 60 years ago ... something that we who have not experienced this suffering, will never grasp. I will never be able to put into words my innermost feelings, the emotions of compassion and deep sorrow, as I walked through these camps.

No matter how pleasant the weather, how many trees had been planted, how many tourists dressed in bright clothing passed through these grounds, the entire camp even now had the power to oppress, to steal the warmth from one's body. Something evil lingered in the air, hovering over the camp like a restless spirit.

Back to the town center we found my father's former residence on Bahnstrasse where he lived for only a brief time. The Auschwitz Archive personnel had contacted the present owner about our arrival and we were able to look around the yard and take photos. We spoke with the owner whose father had built this home and was then forced to leave by the Nazis after the onset of the war. It was later returned to her family. The 'Siedlungs' houses which were once occupied by father and Anneliese and other high ranking Officers, near the entrance to the camp, were no longer standing.

Today was an extremely emotionally draining day! ... I prepared for bed but had to ring up room # 305 for help ... Ernie quickly came to rescue me from a huge ugly black spider high on my wall! I found this an intensely symbolic ending to my visit through Auschwitz.

September 22, 1998: Yesterday's visit through the camp must have taken its toll. I awoke at 4:00am this morning feeling very ill, it took what little strength I seemed to have left to shower and get myself together as today was to be our meeting with the director of the Auschwitz State Museum and Archive. I had looked forward to this day for months and had not traveled all this way to let an upset stomach stop me. I hoped it wasn't too noticeable but I felt rather weak in the knees as the very charming director Dr. Jerzy Wroblewski greeted us with a hand kiss. I reviewed and requested some more documents and photos of my father. I had previously been in contact with him and he and his staff had been very helpful assisting me in my research. He asked me what type of reader would be interested in my book, when it would be published and which documents I utilized in my writing? I told him not only the positive but that I used *all* of the documents, as the historical story of my father and family was about the truth, but that it is very difficult to convince people of a Nazi Kommandant who actually had some humane qualities. As our young interpreter translated, Dr. Wroblewski smiled, nodding his head with understanding. He voiced his interest in my book for their Archive and asked if he could be of further help. He complied to my request to be able to visit the 'Kommandantur' which had been the Kommandant's office within the camp, this building not open for general public viewing. Miss Barbara Yarosz accompanied us and we walked up the worn solid granite steps which led us to what were once my father's offices. To our disappointment the offices had been changed into guestrooms on the interior. Standing alone adjacent from the Kommandantur, we noticed a large house – strangely it projected an ominous atmosphere – gray and dreary in color, the image even today reflecting its dark and chilling past – we were told it was the former Villa of Rudolph Hoess and family.

The old buildings looked untouched on the outside and I felt as though we really had traveled back into time on this day. One of the staff took photos of Antje and I and we left the Archive with gift copies given us of the 'Pro Memoria', the information Bulletin published by the Auschwitz State Museum and the Memorial Foundation. We also purchased the recommended book *Auschwitz: Nazi Death Camp* also published by the State Museum.

September 23, 1998: We're in beautiful sunny Vienna, Austria, staying at the charming Hotel Mullner in Grinzing. Phoned my son Chris in California to wish him Happy Birthday. I had hoped to connect with Frau Langbein and Sonja Fritz here in Vienna, unfortunately that will not take place. I was still not well when we left Poland, the food and high emotions took their toll and unfortunately I slept through the greater part of the Czech Republic. The heaviness which loomed over us in Poland and the high emotional stress we experienced, seemed to linger predominantly around the camps at Auschwitz – the pressure lifted the moment we were greeted with sunshine as we crossed the border into Austria. Just the thoughts that I was actually here made me feel better. We took the street car and subway into the city center where I lit a candle for peace and all of my loved ones inside the magnificent St. Stephen's Cathedral, then a coach ride to see the historical sights. . . . A wonderful evening walk around the neighboring quaint area of Grinzing with enchanting ivy-covered outdoor wine pubs and beer gardens. I have a special sentiment for Austria and Vienna was an unforgettable encounter!

September 24, 1998: Arrived in my beloved Berchtesgaden and suddenly it seemed as though the years melted away. Papa also came to love this area sometime in the early 1940s, while recuperating from his heart ailment. We're staying in Strub at the old Lochner Haus Bergluft where Antje and I lived as foster children … new owners and a new added guest house is situated where the garden used to be. Still lots of flowers everywhere but I miss the huge Lochner sunflowers. Right next door is the remodeled original home. It all has the same feeling of yesterday especially the wonderful fresh country air. I had a difficult time containing my emotions here … as beautiful things always bring tears … most of these tears were tears of joy for the sheer beauty of this area … but of course also the memories of my childhood.

We're in the second floor apartment and have a wonderful view of the 'Watzmann' mountain and at night, from our balcony, both Antje and I sipped Champaign recalling the times we lived here. We can see the lights on the cable car going up to the 'Jenner' and twinkling lights on the top of the 'Eagles Nest'. From the front of the house on the opposite side we have a view of the 'Witches Head', looking across a beautiful green meadow and farm house where we used to buy fresh milk. As the Strub area, the town itself has changed very little.

I picked wildflowers on the old Soleleitung path where we used to walk near the Haus Bergluft, Antje and I were alone today and it was as though no time had passed ... oh how I adore this area and its many memories. Went to dinner with our dearest childhood friend Puppi – who used to send baskets filled with food up to our balcony when we lived in the two rooms on Hindeburg Allee. Her parents have long passed away and Puppi is now alone, still running the business that belonged to her parents years ago. Today it caters to the many tourists; it too is now a historical landmark. It was wonderful to see her again to share our experiences of the past. I call her my 'Berchtesgadner sister'.

We paid our respects at the old well kept cemetery, looking up the grave sites of the Lochners and the Pfingtles and searched for those other locals we knew with those familiar Bavarian names of the area. It seemed just like it was yesterday when Brigitte, Antje and I stood in front of these same graves which we so often visited when we lived here with our mother. The glass building in which the deceased were laid in state is no longer there.

The original 'Golden Baer' restaurant, still displaying a large gold Bear over the entry, has the most wonderful food and authentic Bavarian atmosphere. After the war they offered 'specials' available with food stamps, sometimes our mother went with us. Wonderful aromas came from the kitchen when we walked by admiring the Golden Bear. The entrance has been changed but I recall my childhood fascination at that time: glancing past their open doors I could see shiny brass walls through a serve-through window where men with mustaches wearing 'Lederhosen' passed their empty amber bottles with a clasp type seal, to someone inside usually wearing an oversized green apron, who would then fill their bottles generously with foamy beer from large casks.

September 26, 1998: Went to the Obersalzberg, found Hitler's Berghof, the ruins of his mountain chalet ... all alone, no tourists in what was once the extensive garage under the house ... walked the whole length and toward the end were small individual sections built of brick, looked like catacombs. I could almost hear the haunting echo of their boots walking around and imagined the large cars parked in their spaces ... what a strange but extraordinary feeling ... I didn't want to leave but I heard Antje faintly calling me from the other end of the old foundation, while I was exploring inside the remains of the catacombs with a great deal of emotion. She and Ernie were becoming concerned as I seemed to have been consumed by the crumbling walls. They found it too uncanny and didn't share my incredible excitement, but were amused about my enthusiasm. Some people might think it was about admiration for Hitler but for me it was the fondness, appreciation and sincere interest for that time in history, all part of my journey and one more physical connection that brought me closer to my father. Situated near the Berghof is the wonderful old 'Platterhof' Hotel built by Hitler, later reconstructed by the Americans as the Hotel General Walker. It had a lonely feeling today, sitting vacant and up for sale. I remembered walking around here as a child when the American Army occupied the buildings and vast grounds. This was a most exhilarating and educational afternoon.

September 27, 1998: Drove to Landshut. This is the town where Heinrich Himmler lived. Visited the Lutheran church and the parish house next door where I lived as a foster child with the family of Minister Paul Krauss. Still living alone at age 87 my foster mother, Friedl Krauss, her hair now white, whom I hadn't seen in 45 years, invited us for coffee and delicious cakes which she had actually baked herself, served at a beautifully set table with special china, flowers and candles. Met Ulrike, the delightful youngest of the daughters who was born after I left to live with the Pounes. I felt very drawn to her and the feeling was mutual as she called me 'her almost sister'. Tante Friedl is a dear lady and seemed so happy to see me, just as I cherished this time with her ... somehow it was very comforting to me ... I could not hold back the tears as we left. Another amazing unbelievable day.

September 28, 1998: Today we went to Bad Reichenhall where my sister Brigitte and I had lived with the family Hutterer and attended the Ballet School. I found the old house after walking around the town which had all been changed into a pedestrian section ... lovely shops and as it had been in the past, still an affluent environment, the area known for its natural health spas. The streets were lined with those huge familiar chestnut trees and I also found the old 'Deserted Mansion' and my 'secret garden' where I used to play when it had been neglected and forgotten. It has been completely renovated, looking like the Villa it must have once been. The fountain is now a pond and the 'wiggly red worms' replaced with Koi fish and water lilies. The tennis courts are still located on the other side of the house where I used to make a few pennies retrieving the balls for the players. I located the building that housed Eva Weigand's Ballet School, recognizing the tall old-fashioned windows. I felt as though Brigitte was there leading me around by the hand as she had done so often then, having to take the place of our mother instead of just being the oldest sister she was.

September 30, 1998: The sun came out and we took the opportunity to take the bus up the steep Rossfeld Strasse which took us to the tunnel area, and finally the brass elevator which was built by Hitler in 1938 reaching the top of the Eagles Nest at 1,837 meters. An incredible view, a beautiful sight. . . . Later met the 'Almabtrieb', the herd of cows with decorated headdresses driven from the higher pastures. . . . Stopped by the Ernst Huber's woodcarving workshop, watched him perform this craft which has been handed down in the family for many generations ... so many beautifully carved angels ... couldn't resist buying a few gifts.

October 1, 1998: Off to Salzburg Austria, which brought back memories of the time my mother took Antje and I on that long desperate trek from Berchtesgaden to the house in St. Gilgen. As we drove through that same countryside, today all those old feelings emerged, remembering how our mother had wrapped her heavy coat around us, the only protection against the fog and cold-damp nights. We took a funicular to the top of the mountain to see the castle, which is the landmark that can be seen for miles around ... walked around the lovely historical city, past the birth house of Mozart ... On to St.Gilgen, which lies on the shores of the Wolfgangsee, to see the home built by our parents in 1942, where we lived with our mother before we were evicted by Rudy after the war in the fall of 1945.

There was no trace of the Railroad tracks that used to run along the lake and no train whistles could be heard, nor the smell of thick black puffs of smoke in the air. As we walked up the lush green wooded path to the house, birds were singing and I was reliving my dreams of coming home. How many nights and days had I dreamed of this! The house was vacant and the shutters on the windows boarded, but the well-kept flower boxes indicated someone had been there recently. As shown in my 56-year-old photos, the rock table was still standing on the terrace and amazingly the original wooden front door had never been replaced. What a beautiful enchanting place ... my heart was pounding with excitement feeling somewhat like an intruder although there is a side of me that will always belong here, if only in spirit ... I had an incredibly sad feeling, bringing into reality that like the people who once lived here, this place was now just part of our memories and gone with them were any claims to this property. It was all lost years ago when Rudy took possession leaving us only with our precious memories. I had really needed to return here to be able to close the chapters of my book and leave the past behind. I wonder ... will I be able to let go? With a tightness in my throat I gathered a few wildflowers and took a small rock from the property. I recalled what was the same fresh but pungent scent of mushrooms in the air after a recent rainfall, it was coming from the woods as we walked back down the path. It had been 53 years since we had played in that forest and somewhere under the thick layers of mulch lies buried a young boy's Nazi uniform ... the boy my mother had nursed back to health after the war.

We stopped and ate along the shore of the lake Wolfgangsee at the famous 'Weissen Roessl' Restaurant but looking across the lake my thoughts were of times so long ago...

October 2, 1998: Leaving Berchtesgaden and also a part of my heart ... heading toward Munich to visit the Dachau Camp where Papa was a POW of the Americans after the war.

Spoke with the Archive Director Barbara Distel about my search for witness testimonies taken here at Dachau, at a hearing, in August 1945. The statements which seemed to have disappeared from father's files. I was told that there was no such documentation here but I would be contacted if anything could be found.

Located the prison section here, where Papa was incarcerated and had written his Journals. The small individual cells had heavy wooden doors and through a peep hole I could see the window which was his only contact with the outside world for the time he was there … the deteriorated condition of this building and the general sense of decay again reinforced a strong feeling of regression and what I had experienced while I had translated his Journals … 'As though he was pulling me into the past draining my emotions and physical strength.'

Arrived at my Brother Dieter's home in Fürth by Nuremberg. I was very excited to see him after 26 years but was also startled how much he looked like our father or that he probably would have looked like him at this age. He's a very quiet person living a great deal within himself and I sensed in him a loneliness that drew me to him. I caught myself staring at him unintentionally, studying him, feeling incredible compassion and wondering what horrible things he was concealing about his time in Russia.

His life consists of a very regimented routine, including his allowance to himself of 8 cigarettes per day which are smoked at certain times by the clock. Although my visit upset his routine he seemed happy to see me … I didn't question him about the past. My sister-in-law Steffie, however, spoke much of her experiences after the war in a Russian Detention Camp outside of Vienna. The conditions suffered in many of these post war camps were very severe. Steffie was separated from her mother and reunited only when she [her mother] begged and agreed to join the work detail that buried hundreds of the dead who were victims of disease, starvation and mistreatment. The women were forced to bathe in front of the drunken soldiers and repeatedly raped. Steffie, at that time a beautiful young girl, escaped their assault by hiding in a shed but was subjected to medical experiments, receiving injections that made her violently ill, her body writhing and convulsing with pain. When they heard a rumor that the whole camp was to be shipped to Siberia, Steffie and her mother took a chance and miraculously escaped through an opening in the barbed wire fence. They made their way through the deep snow until a farmer picked them up in his wagon, taking them away to safety … I never knew she had experienced such harsh times…

October 3, 1998: Still at my brother's … today is my mother's birthday. We went to the cemetery where she is buried and I placed a miniature pink rose bush on her grave, our father's name is also inscribed on this stone, as his remains are somewhere in Poland. Looked up what used to be the American Housing project, where I lived on the third floor with the Pounes when they adopted me. The Americans have left long ago and the apartments are privately occupied. The Nuremberg American school I had attended was replaced by a new school building. The theater was gone and many of the buildings which were in poor condition were now under renovation or demolished. . . . This Journey into the past is beginning to wear on me … Dieter and I both cried when we left Fürth the following day, wondering when we would see each other again, but as for me I also left with feelings of satisfaction knowing he was actually reading my manuscript …

October 10, 1998: Visited with Anita Liebehenschel in Wuppertal [my brother Hans-Dieter's widow], her children and Anneliese my father's second wife. Prior to my visit there had been somewhat of a misunderstanding between family members concerning Papa's Journals, making the visit a rather uncomfortable situation today. Therefore it was unfortunate that I had to avoid the subject of my book or reference to the past with Anneliese. I did show her some of the photos I had taken at Auschwitz and Oranienburg and at that point she had a difficult time hiding her hidden emotions. Tearfully she recalled how that time had been a terrible ordeal for my father and that he would drink to try to forget, although he agreed with her that this was not the answer to his problem.

She asked me for a copy of the photo I took of the 'T-Building' in Oranienburg, home of the Amtsgruppe- D where she and Papa both worked when they met. As she looked over the Auschwitz main camp photos of the crematorium she voiced 'that was never there, these were located at Birkenau!' Anneliese gave me a beautiful gold ring with a green tourmaline stone that had been hers. She said Papa liked to see her wear it many years ago … that made it even more special to me. It turned out to be a pleasant afternoon and a tearful parting while standing under umbrellas in the rain … but … still unanswered questions remaining … if only Anneliese could tell me of the 'little things' about my father, what was he really like? … but unfortunately I don't want to hurt Anneliese by bringing up the painful past … strange … but the truth concerning our family's past still seems a dark sensitive subject, too unpleasant and uneasy for them to openly talk about or face up to after all these years.

Earlier this year the widow of Hermann Langbein (author of *Menschen in Auschwitz*) was kind enough to contact Dr Janusz Mlynarski, a survivor of Auschwitz, who was number 355. He was only 17 when he was sent to this camp on 14 June 1940 and remained until 27 January 1945. We were fortunate enough to meet with this extraordinary human being who emerged from his ordeal not with hatred and self pity but as one who never lost hope or his sense of humor and was willing to share with my sister and me, his experiences of the five years he spent at Auschwitz – and although he didn't know our father personally he recalled for us what was said about him within the camp. Coincidentally his hometown is Posen, Poland, also our father's birthplace. Dr Mlynarski had been a caretaker in the camp hospital and was determined if he survived, that he would continue to serve mankind. Using this to his advantage he later became a respected medical surgeon.

October 11, 1998: We're in the very nice 'Hotel am Wald' in Monheim on the Rhein River recommended by Dr. Janusz Mlynarski. How wonderful this day turned out to be, especially after I had such apprehension about this meeting! Antje and I never expected to be welcomed into his lovely home with such warmth and hospitality. He prepared coffee and Brandy while we listened to his interesting story. I felt an instant connection with this delightful man, who had gone out of his way to do some research of his own. He had written to other survivors he knew and was in contact with and read to us what they had to say about our father the Kommandant. He invited us to dinner at a charming Restaurant and I recorded the conversation with his permission.

Excerpts of Dr. Mlynarski's recorded conversation:
'I survived yellow fever and typhus. The camp hospital needed a caretaker who was immunized – I was naturally immunized therefore I worked in the hospital section for two years, where I saw many things. This determined my desire, if I should survive, to spend my life and future in the medical profession helping people.'

Q: During your stay at Auschwitz did you observe or feel any change when my father took over as Kommandant?

A: Yes, things changed immediately, the standing cells were demolished. Your father released the prisoners from the Bunker. Many said he listened too much to the prisoners. One of them with whom he had contact, unfortunately no longer living, was Hermann Langbein. He was the kind of human being one seldom finds. He wrote very positive things about your father.

    Josef Cyrankiewicz was a man who later became Premier of Poland and he had the luck that your father became Kommandant of the camp. At that time he was incarcerated in the Bunker but then released by your father. As Cyrankiewicz was released I was already caretaker at the hospital when he came to my section. Professor Wladyslaw Fejkiel, who was one of the greatest humanitarians that I know of and an elder in the hospital, said to me: 'This man [Cyrankiewicz] will one day be an important figure, maybe even Minister of his country.'

Q: Fejkiel didn't testify favorably for my father at the trial.

A: Not very highly? I have no explanation for that, but he was a renowned humanitarian, one of the greatest that I know of, that leaves me puzzled … although Fejkiel was very critical and unbelievably cynical … but a very good friend of Langbein and Cyrankiewicz.

Q: But it seems that every camp survivor was left with his or her own impression of what they experienced?

A: I must say however that everyone felt there was a change within the camp … no caps off at roll call – you must understand what that meant to the frail 'Muselmen' who could barely get around … no more beatings …

Q: But you had no personal contact with my father?

A: No, but there was terror and suddenly the air changed for all of us and we were able to breathe … No, no … I must say I cannot understand why your father was convicted.

Q: He was extradited to Krakow, Poland.

A: I must say at that time I followed his trial and I recall that only one was acquitted, I believe that was Dr. Muench. I don't understand that your father did not receive the same verdict as Dr. Muench. When your father was transferred from Auschwitz, we prisoners believed it was because he was too lenient. The rumor around the camp was that he was sent to the east, to get rid of him because he was too soft.

There is a meeting every year on June 14 with the Auschwitz Camp Society in Germany, consisting of survivors from all nations. I belong to this organization in Germany. I was one of 728 prisoners who took part in the first transport from Tarnow on June 14, 1940. Now there are 90 survivors still living from this transport … we gather, they come from all over … but every year there are less … many of them continue to live their lives within the camp. Life has two faces, one can lose everything, but never HOPE and with this opportunity one must continue to never give up on life. There needs to be an orientation of what happened in the world … that it existed, that we existed … for the future … the young people need to know.

I received a letter from Eugeniusz Niedojadto, Prisoner Nr. 213, he writes: 'Received a message from Loisi Langbein that the family of Arthur Liebehenschel is coming from the USA. I was under the command of Bruno Bruehl during the time of 10/1/43 to 5/1/45. I know only from my colleagues that Arthur Liebehenschel was not bad and during his command there was a great alleviation and many spoke good about him.'

I further wrote a letter to Eduard Fish and Garminski of Breslau who were at Auschwitz at that time. Fish said: 'I remember him well, and as you know I was at Auschwitz until the evacuation in 1945. I have read the book 'Menschen in Auschwitz' in Polish, and to tell you the truth, I cannot add much more to what Hermann Langbein wrote about him. We have to remember that the testimonies given in his book did not come from him alone, but from many others … incredible documentation. When Liebehenschel took over, the conditions at Auschwitz distinctly improved. Sometimes it was only little things like not having to remove our caps at roll call. Capos were forbidden to beat prisoners … no more executions at the Black Wall, escapees were not to be executed, etc …'

Q: Why do you think he was convicted?

A: That is a good question but I cannot answer that, or even understand why he was sentenced to death. I can only tell you what I heard about him, since I never had personal contact. But it is very important to know what was said about him at that time … what the general talk was about him … who he was, what he had done and how everything suddenly changed for the better. Every night there was talk of this. A half-year is a short time … what I felt was relief, a different atmosphere. . . . Of course it was concerning the 'selections' but he couldn't stop all the selections and the transports at this time consisted primarily of Jews which ended up being sent to the gas chamber. He could not save everyone. One could say that at this time 'A half Angel' came to us but there is proof and he could only do what he was capable of doing, what more could he do? One had to live in that time, one could not do more … but he did and was able to accomplish a great deal. Another thing … there was the general amnesty from the bunkers; Josef Cyrankiewicz was released from the Bunker … this is evidence. Prisoners were no longer allowed to be placed in the bunker at random. After that, before being incarcerated in the Bunker, everyone had to make an appearance before the Kommandant [your father]. It was the fault of the system not the man … that is how things were in those times … while your father was in command we lived with HOPE, that is an important point. It was proven that in your father's time the death rate was lower, not as many died as previously.

Otto Kusel, Prisoner Nr. 2, escaped the camp in December 1943. He was captured and sent back to Auschwitz. This was in your father's time and he was not executed for his escape. I wrote to him for his birthday and he replied: 'He had a whole different attitude than the others. I found out that his 2nd wife had dealings with Jews and he also had a positive attitude toward Jews.'

I always saw the positive even through the most terrible times of my life. I felt out of human compassion that I wanted to meet with you. I think I too would want to search to find the good about my parents. I was not forced into talking with you and what I have told you are things anyone else in my position would have wanted to explain to your family. Theoretically speaking you can see that for the short time your father was at the Auschwitz concentration camp, suddenly everything changed. Your father was different and I am happy I was able to tell you this from my point of view. … Our hope as Prisoners was awakened … is that not saying a great deal? One can lose everything, but never the hope and your father once again renewed and GAVE US HOPE!'

October 11, 1998 – 10:17 p.m: Alone once again in my room in the 'Hotel am Wald'. CNN News on the TV – good to hear the English language spoken by the American reporters. What a gratifying day! … my mind is so saturated, too much to absorb … all very emotional this meeting today with Dr. Mlynarski. Playing back the tapes hoping they recorded. … Have requested a wake up call for 4:00am to catch my early flight back home to California … having mixed emotions … sad to leave but feeling a twinge of excitement … now I can complete my book…

I hereby want to express my most sincere and profound gratitude to Dr Mlynarski for his kindness and the time given to my family. This meeting has been of major significance, bringing my father another step closer.

It's been exactly a year since Papa came to me in a dream to let me know that he liked who I had grown up to be. Since it was in the month of February I always felt he was remembering my birthday. Curiously, at almost the precise time in February this year, my father appeared in a dream to my sister Antje.

She was back in her childhood in Oranienburg, walking as she had done so often, on the path from our house on Adolf Hitler Damm to the large administrative 'T-Building' where Papa had been chief of the Amtsgruppe D-I of the Inspection. When she reached the building and looked up, she quickly stopped as she saw Papa standing by the entrance. As in my own dream a year ago he was wearing his old worn jacket, looking frail with that same aura of defeat and loneliness. Neither one of them knew what they should do next. Then Papa stretched out his arms toward her and she flew over into his embrace, moved by his familiar affectionate hug. Before suddenly disappearing he said to her: 'Attichen, I am so grateful to you both for what you are doing for me!'

The Journey Continues

When I arrived home a letter was waiting for me. Dr Mlynarski had received this letter from Vienna, dated 7 October 1998, which he was permitted to share with me. It came from Dr Franz Danimann, also a survivor of Auschwitz, who had worked in the office of the prisoner hospital. He studied law after the war and today he is a well-known authority on the Holocaust. As one of the few living survivors he now lectures at various schools sharing with the young people his knowledge and experiences. The truth can only be told and documented by those who are the remaining eyewitnesses to the history of the Holocaust. Dr. Danimann had this to say about my father:

> After thoroughly studying and reviewing the entire complexity, I came to this con-
> clusion. At the accurately conducted Auschwitz Trial in Krakow, it was determined
> that Liebehenschel repeatedly attempted to delay the course of the Extermination
> Machinery and at times the Selections were interrupted until explicit orders came
> from Berlin which Liebehenschel of course had to follow, therefore he was limited,
> unlike Hoess who followed and executed these orders through his own initiative.
> It is my belief that Arthur Liebehenschel's death sentence was probably historically
> and legally a just verdict but because of his diverse and positive initiatives, which
> helped many prisoners, he should have been given amnesty.
>
> Dr. Franz Danimann, October 1998[1]

After I came upon Hermann Langbein's book *Menschen in Auschwitz*, I contacted his family. His widow Loisi answered my two letters that I had written to their son Kurt. She wrote: 'I can sympathize with your position but it is infinitely difficult to write about this. . . . My husband Hermann Langbein dictated from his notes, as I typed his manuscripts at that time. Therefore I have knowledge of many things concerning the camps. I am fully aware of your father's con-duct as opposed to that of Hoess's. He did not really fit into the framework of Himmler's SS.'

She was kind enough to contact other survivors and put me in touch with them. After years of research this was the ultimate reward for me and I was beside myself with excitement.

A letter came completely unexpected from Vienna on Thursday, 16 July 1998 from Sonja Fischmann Fritz. She was a former prisoner at Auschwitz from 1942 until the end of the war, who had been hired as a clerk in my father's office. She shared her memories with me. I telephoned my sister Antje in Germany and read her the letter with great emotion. Sonja Fritz's kind and personal comments about my father were a reassuring validation of his character and compassion. The letter read as follows:

Frau Loisi Langbein, mother of Kurt, sent me your letters, as she believed I would be able to tell you some things about your father. I gather from your writing that you are awaiting an answer. There is not too much that I can tell you, only a few words.

Hermann Langbein and I were at Auschwitz together, from the onset of November 1942. In 1943 I was brought to Vienna for interrogation and three weeks later was returned to Auschwitz for 'Special Custody' until the end of the war. Why 'Special Custody'? For no other offense but that my father was Jewish. The head female guard Mandl, thought as a privilege, I should be sent to the Auschwitz 'Stammlager' as clerk to the Kommandant. Until then prisoners were never allowed to work within the command of the Kommandant's circle. The Kommandant was Arthur Liebehenschel, his adjutant a brutal, vicious man was named Zoller.

Two of us had to take and pass a typing test, from dictation. Your father stood beside me observing me with kind eyes. Zoller immediately concluded that I would be of no use. Your father said, 'She stays'. I managed and kept the 'Bunkerbuch' and prepared documents for the SS.

The front office was your father's room, then came the office of Zoller, beyond there the room occupied by the two Staff Sergeants, Akerman and Herpel. I had to jump to attention whenever an SS man entered the room; this was entirely of indifference to your father.

From the 'Bunkerbuch' I learned that the female guard named Nestroy was arrested. During a house search they found jewelry and unfortunately also my letters she had smuggled to and from Vienna for me. For three days Zoller questioned prisoners to find out the pseudonym until the guard gave him my name. As I was taken to Zoller for interrogation I prepared myself for the most dreadful consequences, the door to your father's office was open.

The threats of beatings, thank God, never occurred. I was returned to the Penal Company at Birkenau to do road construction. Had your father not intervened as witness in my defense, I would not have been spared.

I am happy to be able to tell you that the time your father was Kommandant was a great relief for us. As I heard of his sentence I was very depressed. He did not deserve that, on the contrary, we have him in memory as a very good human being.

Eight days before the liberation of France, my father was taken from a mental clinic in the south of France to the concentration camp Buchenwald from which he never returned. He was only 46 years old.

I am not a good writer but maybe my words can give you some consolation.

I worked within the command, in the office of the Kommandant from January 28, 1944 to May 11, 1944.

Sonja Fritz, July 9, 1998[2]

I discovered additional testimony in Hermann Langbein's book; he wrote: 'Not many former prisoners had the opportunity to get to know Liebehenschel personally during his short six month term of duty as Kommandant but a few had revealing testimony.'

Jenny Spritzer worked in the Political Department as a secretary; she said of the new Kommandant in her book *I was Nr. 10291*:

An enormous relief went through all of our hearts as one day camp Kommandant Hoess was promoted to a higher position in Oranienburg and was replaced with Liebehenschel who was shocked over the conditions at Auschwitz. He immediately brought an end to the death sentences. The punishment by hanging for attempted escapes was terminated. Prisoners were not to be beaten, whether during inter-rogations or at their work places. [She adds that not everyone followed this rule.] While Hoess was seldom seen personally and usually only as he was riding around in his elegant car, Liebehenschel on the other hand inspected the camp in person and observed the prisoners at their outdoor jobs. Sometimes Liebehenschel came into our offices, opening every door and as it would be our custom to jump up, he dismissed this with a gesture of his hand to stay at ease. He among other things even asked me to disclose and describe my job to him. Every Bunker punish-ment imposed by the Political Section was reduced by him into half, as he as the Kommandant had to sign all orders for punishments.[3]

Langbein writes in his book: 'Spritzer's testimony proved how biased and jealous Hoess' character study was of his successor when Hoess wrote: "Liebehenschel spent more time in his office dictating one command and report after another and held hour long conferences while in the meantime the camp fell further into a sinking condition."'

Artur Rablin worked as foreman to the 'Lagerfuehrer' and was able to gain a good general survey of the camp; he said of the Kommandant Liebehenschel: 'He would visit the kitchen and ask, "How does the soup taste?" He wished us not to stand at attention in his presence.'

Rudolf Steiner was once caught as he was pilfering shoes and he was sen-tenced to 10 strikes with a rod on the backside. The sentence was carried out in the Block 11, Liebehenschel was present. Other veteran prisoners advised Steiner to scream loud as Liebehenschel could not bear this. Therefore Steiner shouted as loud as he could after the first blow and the Kommandant actually stopped the flogging before all ten strikes were inflicted.

Dr Erwin Valentin. Still fresh in his memory he had this to say for the record on May 16, 1945: 'Under Liebehenschel our lives changed in the respect that our condition could almost be called tolerable. Liebehenschel had a good attitude especially toward Jews, he prohibited the beating of Jews at their workplaces and relieved those capos and their superiors who had inflicted harm on Jews and he also heard and acted upon their complaints.'

Langbein states: 'This evidence carries weight and importance as Valentin himself wore the Star of David.'[4]

Adolf Eichmann referred to my father's soft policies and the freedom he had given to prisoners with promises to turn the death camp into a normal prison camp; he had this to say about my father the Kommandant: 'Toward the end of his command Liebehenschel's behavior was that of an incorrigible child, ignoring the given camp rules and regulations and running the camp according to his own code of authority.'[5]

After months of unmerciful badgering on my part, the archivists at the National Archives at College Park finally located the long-awaited audiotape of father's Nuremberg testimony. When I heard my father's soft, quiet voice, which sounds remarkably like that of my brother Dieter, I collapsed into tears. Since I had been too young to remember the sound of his voice, my father became real for the first time in my life.

Was my father a man of good conscience who did everything possible, risking his and his family's safety to right a terrible wrong? Perhaps. But the fact remains that hundreds of people were executed under his watch. From all the evidence I have collected, including the personal testimonies of those I have met, I do believe, however, that for the brief time my father was Kommandant, life became better for the camp prisoners, and it seems he did make a difference. The facts remain and must speak for themselves and the readers will draw their own conclusions.

Why did my father remain in the SS once he realized what was expected of him? What were his own convictions about Hitler's Final Solution? Unfortunately I don't have the answers to the many lingering questions. It was only as I regressed deeper into the past, that I began to recognize my father's complexity. Of course I would like to have found that my father was a hero, but at Auschwitz the only heroes were the prisoners themselves. Unlike the black-and-white picture of him, the portrait of my father has taken on many different colors, sometimes clashing. He was by turns courageous and cautious, ruled by his conscience, his integrity and by self-preservation. A loving husband and father to one family and a deserter to another. He was torn by his sense of obedience, duty, and loyalty to the Fatherland on one hand, and his personal struggle and opposition toward the mass killings and desire to help the prisoners under his command, on the other.

Ultimately, Arthur Liebehenschel was a man caught up in a sweep of history – an evil web of circumstances – in which it was impossible to be ordinary. A history professor summed up my father's story this way: 'This is not about making a hero of him but it is a story of a decent man caught in a very bad place who did the best he could under the circumstances.'[6]

Writing this memoir and finally talking openly about my secret past, has helped me to come to terms with my heritage and has made it easier to accept the truth in all its ambiguities, not only for myself, but for my children. Until now, they knew nothing about my father. Like the picture I kept hidden for so many years, I kept the facts of their family history hidden from them. Nothing can change the past or the facts of my father's life. But being able to admit to myself and to others who I am and where I came from, has somewhat lifted the burden of guilt and set me free. I am now determined to pass on this knowledge to my children and granddaughter so that the cycle of secrecy and shame will be broken at last.

This story is for everyone who has struggled to define his or her true identity. It is for every adult who has grown up harboring family secrets or carrying the burden of hidden shame. It is for adopted children seeking answers to these questions of heritage, as well as adoptive parents who feel insecure when their children sense the need to find their roots. I can only speak from my own experience and of my own need to search and write this book — which will never change my deep love and gratitude for Ursula and Earl, for their compassion and generosity — having taken in a girl at my age who would have ended up in an orphanage. Most of all I am grateful that they gave me the opportunity for a life in America.

It is especially for every reader who has yearned for the comforting presence of an emotionally distant or physically absent parent; I hope to provide an important message: You are not alone.

But delving into the past was not only having to deal with my own emotions during the process; often it was the stunning reaction from others, even people close to me. For example, when a friend voiced her frank opinion concerning my father:

> No one, unless a sympathizer with the 1930s to 1940s Nazi movement, will be able to accept or have any patience or believe that anyone who was a Nazi Kommandant at Auschwitz could have had any heroic qualities. The main ideas centered around the idea of the Master Race rejecting Jews as unclean and sub-human, worthy of extinction! Your father chose to be a part of that organization, he wasn't enlisted against his will. He accepted the manifest of Nazism. You will run into a tidal wave of opposition![7]

That certainly awoke me to the harsh reality that my story could be met with great controversy and what I was probably up against — but it never discouraged me or the motivation to write this story. In fact it made me even more determined to find the truth.

Through my research, I have striven to be faithful to the facts I have uncovered. I knew that my account of my father's life had to be scrupulously objective in order to be meaningful. Although his role may have been trivial in comparison to the many powerful figures who reigned during the Third Reich, it was a role significant enough to be found within the pages of history. Some of my discoveries were not necessarily what I wanted to hear.

Not too long after I began my search, this need to find the truth became my ultimate 'Quest'. In the dictionary, 'Quest' is defined as 'an adventurous expedition – a journey of discovery'. Though I feel a great sense of relief with what I've discovered and heard about my father, this Quest has been a bittersweet journey. For me and my family the ending to this story was of course predestined and will remain unresolved, leaving us with many unanswered questions. As so many others like us we are the children of Nazi perpetrators with a past which will always have the power to haunt.

Even now, pieces continue to fall into place one step at a time. I have only recently learned, for instance, that my father met his death at the gallows.

After a frustrating search to find where father's body was interred, I received another letter from Krakow, written in Polish. I placed a call to my friend Dr Mlynarsky and faxed him the letter for translation. Soon I received a return call and listened, as he hesitantly and with apparent empathy, read the translated letter to me. I was suddenly caught up with a great sense of emotion, my voice trembling; I thanked him as I hung up the phone. Alone and quiet in the room, I gazed at the piece of paper in front of me, on which I had scribbled Dr Mlynarsky's words, which read: 'After his death your father's body was turned over to the University of Krakow for medical research.'

After the initial shock I came to realize that it was for a worthy cause and that, in the end, my father had given back something that would truly benefit humanity.

I believe he would have wanted it that way.

Source Notes of Documentation

Quotations and personal letters are from Private Domain.
National Archives, Washington/Nara Unit/College Park, Maryland
Auschwitz Archives, Poland
The Holocaust Archives, Yad Vashem-Jerusalem, Israel
Historical Archive, Munich
Fritz Bauer Holocaust Institut, Frankfurt
Landesjustizverwaltungen, Zentrale Stelle, Ludwigsburg

Chapter One: Party Member # 932766 & Family Man

1. Trial Testimony May 7, 1947, Auschwitz Archives.
2. Nuremberg Interrogation from National Archives microfilm, publication M1019
   [roll 42] dated 18 September and 7 October 1946. Records of the United States of
   Nuremberg War Crimes Trials Interrogations 1946–49.
3. Trial Testimony May 7, 1947, Auschwitz Archives.
4. Nuremberg Interrogation from National Archives microfilm.

Chapter Three: The Last Embrace

1. Roger Mudd, narrator for the History Channel.
2. Father's testimony, Trial Transcripts, Auschwitz Archives.
3. Documents dispatched through Central Office Berlin, Ludwigsburg Archives.
4. Documents signed by my father at WVHA, Die Inspektion der Konzentrations Lager
   1938–1945/documentation by Johannes Tuchel.
5. Nuremberg Interrogation from National Archives microfilm [roll 42].

Chapter Four: Auschwitz

1. Nuremberg Interrogation from National Archives microfilm [roll 42].
2. Excerpts from *Welt Bild* magazine, 23 December 1960.
3. *The Kommandant in Auschwitz* published by Professor Dr Martin Broszat, Director
   of Instituts fur Zeitgeschichte in Munich, 1963.

4. O. Kaduk on statement by Dr Wirths, *Menschen in Auschwitz* by H. Langbein, Europa Verlag GmbH, Munich, 1995.
5. Ludwig Worl in *Auschwitz* by B. Naumann.
6. Quotations from *Menschen in Auschwitz* by H. Langbein.
7. From *Auschwitz Chronicle* by Danuta Czech, Publications International Ltd, Illinois.
8. Dr Wirths in *Menschen in Auschwitz* by H. Langbein.
9. Hoess' Trial Testimony, *Auschwitz Chronicle* by Danuta Czech.
10. Ordinances written by father, Auschwitz Archives, Poland.
11. Baer's meeting and report on my father, from the National Archives Records Group 338 SS Personnel File.
12. Oskar Kieselbach in *Menschen in Auschwitz* by H. Langbein.
13. Conversation with R. Baer, from Records Group 338.
14. Notarized Statement by Anneliese, from Records Group 338.
15. Langbein on Hoess' affair with a prisoner, *Menschen in Auschwitz* by H. Langbein.
16. Anneliese's letter to Himmler, from Records Group 338.
17. Oswald Pohl's letter to Dr Brandt, from Records Group 338.
18. Father's letter to Brigadier General Heider, SS-File Yad Vashem-Israel Archive.
19. Nuremberg Interrogation, 9/18/46 [roll 42].

Chapter Six: One Son Captured, Another Born

1. Document sent from Lublin on 7/18/44, Ludwigsburg Archive.
2. Nuremberg Interrogation, 9/18/46, from National Archives microfilm [roll 42].
3. Father's letter to Brigitte & Dieter, Private Domain.

Chapter Ten: Journals of a Prisoner of War

1. Journal letters, Private Domain.
2. Two letters from father to head of Dachau camp, Dr Dortheimer, Auschwitz Archives, Poland.
3. Extradition, National Archives, 201 records file from IMT Files.
4. Letter from Dr Hans Muench, Private Domain.

Chapter Eleven: The Trial

1. Excerpts of father's statements from Krakow Prison, Auschwitz Archives.
2. Excerpts of testimony from witnesses, from Trial Transcripts, Auschwitz Archives.
3. Quotations by Hofmann from *Menschen in Auschwitz* by H. Langbein, Europa Verlag GmbH, Munich, 1995.
4. Father's testimony from Auschwitz Archive.
5. Trial Summary/Verdict/Sentence, F. Bauer, Holocaust Institute, Frankfurt.
6. Father's last letter, Private Domain.

Epilogue: The Journey Home

1. Recorded conversation with Dr Mlynarski, Private Domain.

Epilogue: The Journey Continues

1. Statement about Father by Dr Franz Danimann, Private Domain.
2. Letter from survivor Sonja Fritz about Father, Private Domain.
3. Quotations by Jenny Spritzer about Father, from her book *Ich war Nr. 10291* (I was Nr. 10291), Darmstädter Blätter, 1980.
4. Prisoners' testimonies about Father from *Menschen in Auschwitz* by H. Langbein, Europa Verlag GmbH, Munich, 1995.
5. Quotation by Adolf Eichmann on Father, *Menschen in Auschwitz* by H. Langbein.
6. Quotation by Professor Robert Barr Smith.
7. Quotation by Jann J. James.

Bibliography

Auschwitz-Birkenau State Museum, *Auschwitz: Nazi Death Camp*, 1996.

Czech, Danuta, *Auschwitz Chronicle*, Publications International Ltd, Lincolnwood, Illinois.

Friedrich, Otto, *The Kingdom of Auschwitz*, Atlantic Monthly Co., 1981.

Garlinsky, Josef, *Fighting Auschwitz*, J. Friedmann, 1975.

Gilbert, Martin, *The Holocaust*, Henry Holt & Co., New York, 1987.

Gutman, Yisrael and Birnbaum, Michael, *Anatomy of the Auschwitz Death Camp*, Indiana University Press, 1994.

Hanisch, Ernst, *Der Obersalzberg*, Berchtesgadner Landesstiftung/Anton Plenk, 1995.

Hitler, Adolf, *Mein Kampf*, Houghton Mifflin Co., Boston, Massachusetts, 1971.

Hoess, Rudolf, *Kommandant of Auschwitz*, Deutscher Taschenbuch Verlag, 1963.

Kessel, Sim, *Hanged in Auschwitz*, Cooper Square Press, USA, 2001.

Langbein, Hermann, *Menschen in Auschwitz*, Europa Verlag GmbH, Munich, 1995.

Lifton, Robert Jay, *The Nazi Doctors*, Basic Books, USA, 1986.

Naumann, Bernd, *Auschwitz*, Pall Mall P., 1966.

Novick, Peter, *The Holocaust in American Life*, Houghton Mifflin Co., New York, 1999.

Payne, Robert, *The Life and Death of Adolf Hitler*, Popular Library/Praeger Publishers, USA, 1973.

Shirer, W.L., *The Rise and Fall of the Third Reich*, Fawcett Publications Inc. Simon & Schuster, Conn., USA, 1959.

Snyder, Louis L., *Hitler's Elite*, Berkley Books, New York, 1990.

Spector, Shmuel, *The Encyclopedia of the Holocaust*, Routledge, 1st edn, 2000.

Speer, Albert, *Inside the Third Reich*, Macmillan Co., Toronto, Canada, 1970.

Toland, John, *Adolf Hitler*, Ballantine Books, New York, 1976.

Tuchel, Johannes, *Die Inspektion Der Konzentrations-Lager 1938–1945*, Brandenburg, Gedenkstaetten, Edn Hentrich, 1994.

Welt Bild Magazine, article by Thomas Gnielka, 1960.

Acknowledgements

I want to take this opportunity to thank my family for their support and also those people whose lives have touched mine throughout the course of my writing. Their expertise, advise and encouragement made a definite difference which so often gave me the needed courage to continue with this relentless labor of love. I want to thank the various historical archives whose files unveiled much of my father's past, such as the Yad Vashem in Israel, the National Archives at College Park, Maryland and the Fritz Bauer Holocaust Institute in Frankfurt for the Trial and Court Summary. I am especially grateful to the Auschwitz State Museum & Archive for their gracious assistance by contributing numerous copies of photos and important documents. I also want to thank Karl Morys who was responsible for the incredible Polish translations.

My son Chris, thank you for your constant support and reassurance. Forgive me for keeping the facts of your ancestry hidden from you … but it has taken me all these years to confront my past.

In ever-loving memory of my daughter Whendy – not a day goes by that you are not in my thoughts. How I wish you were here to share this part of your past with me. Your spirit lives on through your beautiful daughter. Chris and my granddaughter Miranda, I now leave this to you as my living legacy.

In memory of my beloved sister Brigitte without whose audiotapes I could never have attempted this project. I sensed your presence throughout my writing. Also my half-brother Hans-Dieter, who never had an opportunity to discover who his family actually was.

My sister Antje and husband Ernst you two deserve special credit, having contributed so much to the research, but most of all your incredible task of the very tedious German translation of my previous draft. Antje, our shared memories of the past and those of our wonderful trip in 1998, and also the documentary in 2002 is something they cannot take from us – we who are Papa's 'other children'.

Dieter my big brother, I wish you could have been a part of my childhood. You more than any of us had to endure so unfairly, losing your youthful innocence at the hands of those whose unjust retaliations came primarily because you happened to be our father's son. I hope our family's story will answer some of your own children's questions.

Kye, my special nephew, I only wish you could have seen your name in print, and given me the opportunity to thank you again for the laptop computer which was just the beginning, helping to speed up my progress so long ago. I wanted to thank you and Kriste again for the unselfish contribution, which initiated my 1998 trip to Europe. I'll always remember your last words of encouragement to me: 'Don't ever give up.'

I am grateful to Anneliese for sharing those painful memories tucked away for so long. I wish you understood how much your input meant to me. I hope our family's story will enlighten Hans-Dieter's children and grandchildren. Her recent passing sadly closes this chapter in our lives.

My Mom, Ursula, thank you for having chosen me to be your daughter. Our special relationship has endured an often difficult past and as a result it comes with an even greater appreciation of your acceptance and support today.

Marji Tucker, for typing the original rough draft, turning it into my first manuscript … so long ago. Thank you for everything dear friend.

Randy, where would I be without the computer, you helped make it come together with the ease of modern technology.

Jann James, my friend and mentor. I learned much about general writing from you and am very grateful to you for volunteering to edit my original draft (all those commas), also your advice and wisdom. Thank you for once again coming to my rescue by using your writing ingenuity which created a whole new twist to the Prologue and then the final edit and corrections which helped the story to flow more smoothly. But most of all restoring confidence in my ability to write the book in my own voice. Thank you for sharing a most special time in my life. I could not have done it without you.

To the survivors – all of whom have touched a very special place within my heart, those who have long passed on and those remaining who were kind enough to share their memories of the camp and their personal account of my father. A particular thanks to Loisi, the widow of Hermann Langbein, who put me in touch with Sonja Fritz the former Kommandantur office clerk hired by my father. Her letter indicating her memories about my father is of great importance. My sincere gratitude to the delightful survivor # 355, Dr Janusz Mlynarski, and those other survivors who wrote about my father and sent their comments on to you. Your understanding and compassion shown toward my family was more than we ever expected. You reached far beyond the recollections of evil by unselfishly reliving your own agonizing time at the camp during my father's command. You truly touched my soul with your extraordinary spirit and I will always cherish our very special bond.

James D. Dean, wherever you may be today, you were the catalyst and with your encouragement my notes were transformed into a book manuscript. Thank you for your support from the very beginning and believing in my story and my ability to write it in my own voice. For going through all of its many growing pains with me and for giving me the confidence to realize that anything is possible. Through your generosity you turned the long-awaited journey to the past, from a dream into the reality of my 'Journey's End'.

And to my beautiful friend Hazel Court Taylor, whose inspiration, spiritual guidance and relentless assurance that my book would some day be published, helped me to see the light at the end of the often dark tunnel. Always in loving memory.

Chuck Hurewitz, my attorney, I appreciate your counsel and patience.

Others whose contribution I want to acknowledge: Melissa Mueller, my sincere appreciation for your many efforts and your faith on my behalf, and especially the eloquently written Foreword. My Publisher, The History Press. Sophie Bradshaw thank you for your confidence in my story; also Jo Howe and my sincere gratitude to Deputy Editorial Director Simon Hamlet and especially my skilful editor Abigail Wood.

Index